Reformed Virtue
After Barth

COLUMBIA SERIES IN REFORMED THEOLOGY

The Columbia Series in Reformed Theology represents a joint commitment of Columbia Theological Seminary and Westminster John Knox Press to provide theological resources for the church today.

The Reformed tradition has always sought to discern what the living God revealed in Scripture is saying and doing in every new time and situation. Volumes in this series examine significant individuals, events, and issues in the development of this tradition and explore their implications for contemporary Christian faith and life.

This series is addressed to scholars, pastors, and laypersons. The Editorial Board hopes that these volumes will contribute to the continuing reformation of the church.

COLUMBIA SERIES IN REFORMED THEOLOGY

Reformed Virtue After Barth

Developing Moral Virtue Ethics in the Reformed Tradition

KIRK J. NOLAN

WESTMINSTER
JOHN KNOX PRESS
LOUISVILLE · KENTUCKY

First edition
Published by Westminster John Knox Press
Louisville, Kentucky

14 15 16 17 18 19 20 21 22 23—10 9 8 7 6 5 4 3 2 1

Book and cover design by Drew Stevens

Library of Congress Cataloging-in-Publication Data

Nolan, Kirk J.
 Reformed virtue after Barth : developing moral virtue ethics in the reformed tradition / Kirk J. Nolan.—First edition.
    pages cm.—(Columbia series in reformed theology)
 Includes bibliographical references and index.
 ISBN 978-0-664-26020-0 (alk. paper)
 1. Barth, Karl, 1886–1968. 2. Christian ethics. 3. Virtue. 4. Reformed Church—Doctrines.
I. Title.
 BX4827.B3N65 2014
 241′.0442—dc23

2014012630

♾ The paper used in this publication meets the minimum requirements of the American National Standard for Information Sciences—Permanence of Paper for Printed Library Materials, ANSI Z39.48-1992.

Westminster John Knox Press advocates the responsible use of our natural resources. The text paper of this book is made from 30% post-consumer waste.

Most Westminster John Knox Press books are available at special quantity discounts when purchased in bulk by corporations, organizations, and special-interest groups. For more information, please e-mail SpecialSales@wjkbooks.com.

CONTENTS

Preface   vii

Acknowledgments   xi

Abbreviations   xiii

Introduction   1
Should Christians Guided by the Reformed Tradition
    Aspire to Moral Virtue?   1
Approach to the Topic   4
Moral Virtue Ethics in the Wake of Barth   8

1. The Reformed Tradition on Moral Virtue   11
Reformed Virtue before Barth   11
John Calvin and the Presumption of Christian Virtue   12
Virtue in the Westminster Confession   18
Edwardsean Virtue Ethics   24
Reformed Virtue after Barth   32

2. Barth's Objections   37
Karl Barth's Christocentric Anthropology   38
Karl Barth's Rejection of the *Analogia Entis*   46
Karl Barth's Rejection of Habitual Grace   54

3. Objections Overcome   62
William Werpehowski on Karl Barth   62
Evaluating Werpehowski   68
Virtue Ethics without Recourse to Natural Morality   71
Training in Moral Virtue   72

4. The Shape of Reformed Virtue after Barth   83
Characteristics of Reformed Virtue   83
A Comparison of Specific Virtues: Thomistic versus Reformed   90
The Role of the Church in the Formation of Virtue   99
The Role of the State in the Formation of Virtue   101
Conclusion   107

5. Living Out the Reformed Virtues   **109**
Frugality and Social Justice   111
Social Justice Informed by Practical Wisdom   114
Charity as the Grounds for Social Justice   123
Reforming Social Witness   132

Conclusion   **134**
Virtue among the Ruins?   135
From Virtual to Virtuous Communities   140

Notes   145

Bibliography   165

Index   173

PREFACE

When I was a teenager I used to think perfection was within my grasp. That I could think such a thing after several years of churchgoing was in some measure due to teenage naïveté. But it also had to do with a theological misunderstanding resident in my home church, whose summation of the gospel message was reduced to this line, repeated in unison during worship: "You're beautiful. God loves you, and we love you too." Each of these phrases, taken individually, expresses some truth about the gospel message. The way my teenage brain combined them, however, was problematic: You are loved *because* you are beautiful. This misinterpretation fed my youthful optimism in unhealthy ways. And because I had no reason to doubt my moral compass, I believed it.

That estimation changed in the early 1990s when I was working for a reputable consulting firm. I was involved in a project for which I had insufficient experience. My supervising manager knew I wasn't qualified for the job but was determined the client not find out. As we were on our way to a meeting he turned and asked, "What's your story?" I was dumbfounded. My manager was asking me to lie. I should have walked away from the project at this point, but I stayed on. I didn't lie, but I wasn't entirely forthcoming either. It was the first time my moral compass had truly been tested, and I failed.

Once my commitment to that project was over, I left that firm and went to work for a Christian nonprofit organization called Kingdomworks, started by Bart Campolo, in inner-city Philadelphia. On the first night of leadership training, after all of the formal training sessions were over, I joined a small group in an impromptu time of confession. I listened dumbfounded as group members admitted to feeling temptations and committing sins I would be afraid to divulge to my closest friend. What made them strong enough to admit their vulnerabilities? I had come from a community where I was expected to lie to cover any weaknesses I might have into a community where openness was the expected norm. That experience of confession had a transformative effect on me. I realized in a new way what the church was intended to be. How many times had I participated in worship, reading aloud the corporate confession of sin, without realizing at the root that we are a people who make ourselves vulnerable, who identify ourselves as sinners not out of a desire for self-flagellation but out of a yearning to be truthful to God and to each other? Incredible strength comes from the freedom to admit weakness, out of the recognition that we are loved even when we do not live up to the beautiful person God intends us to be.

The church has the potential to be a distinctively virtuous community. Its unique character is derived not from any corner on the sanctity market but instead from its awareness of its sinfulness. This would seem, prima facie, to exclude it from being a community of virtue in the first place. If its members self-identify as sinners, how can they ever hope to be saints? Yet this habit frees the church to pursue a deeper relationship with God and neighbor without the burden of continual self-justification. Virtue is God's gift to us, which we receive only through God's invitation. It is a form of grace, never our sole possession, yet it nonetheless demands our receptive participation.

Readers who do not come from the Reformed tradition may wonder why I situate my account of Christian moral virtue within the Reformed context. Surely there is enough common ground within Christianity to foster such an ethic, and if there isn't, then why not turn to the Roman Catholic tradition, which has espoused moral virtue ethics since at least the time of Thomas Aquinas? My response to the first part of the question is to say that ecumenical ethics too easily papers over important theological differences that exist across denominational lines. To give an adequate theological basis for moral virtue ethics requires making explicit one's theological commitments that undergird the project. I am a Presbyterian pastor and educator. I have learned a great deal from my colleagues who work within the Roman Catholic theological tradition. They have already examined Thomist versions of virtue ethics in great detail, yet the same cannot be said about my Reformed colleagues. This project aims at kindling the interest of the latter while also sustaining a broader conversation about different theological understandings of the Christian life.

Reformed moral virtue has something to contribute to the broader discussion regarding Christian virtue ethics. The first contribution involves the relational dimensions of virtue. The Reformed tradition's emphasis on God's covenantal relationship with humankind requires an account of virtue in which human moral excellence cannot be considered apart from God's initiating influence. One criticism made against virtue ethics in general is that it leans toward egoism. This charge is true where virtue theory focuses too much on the process by which individuals acquire the virtues without touching on how these virtues promote the welfare of communities. Nicholas Wolterstorff, for instance, characterizes the Stoic conception of the virtuous life as follows: "Happiness requires peace of mind. The truly happy life is a life of *apatheia*, as the Stoics called it—a life free of passions, free of negative emotions."[1] It is difficult to see how such a life of virtue would encourage care and concern for others. In contrast, Reformed moral virtue has relationality at its core. God's relationship with us provides not only the framework for virtue but also the pattern for it through the relationship between the divine and human natures in Jesus Christ. That Chalcedonian pattern establishes God's priority and initiative while at the same time protecting the authenticity of human reciprocity. It also places a distinctive spin on the purpose of cultivating virtue, which is to serve God and neighbor rather than to focus on ourselves. The Barmen Declaration states this view eloquently: "As Jesus Christ is God's assurance of the forgiveness of all our sins, so in the same way and with the same seriousness is he also God's mighty claim upon our whole life. Through him befalls us a joyful deliverance from the godless fetters of this world for a free, grateful service to his creatures."[2]

The second contribution is a prophetic one. The Reformed tradition, as its name suggests, emphasizes social and individual reform. Consider the stress placed on confessional documents throughout its history. Creeds and confessions tend to arise out of religious and political turmoil, as careful and constructive responses to crises. Reformed attitudes toward human sinfulness are thus critically realistic. While critical of utopian social programs that promise heaven on earth, they are also hopeful that current social and religious arrangements may be improved. Again, the Barmen Declaration comes to mind. As an ecumenical document, composed primarily by Karl Barth in opposition to those German Christians who embraced Nazism, it forthrightly delineated the mission of the church in distinction from any other mission other powers might seek to impose. While traditional Lutheran understandings of church and state left little room for the church to challenge the state, the Barmen Declaration went further: "We reject the false doctrine, as though the state, over and beyond its special commission, should and could become a single and totalitarian order of human life, thus fulfilling the church's vocation as well."[3] In its criticism of the state, Barmen recognized that the church's function in society went beyond preparation for the life to come and included a commitment to challenge and influence current and future social arrangements.

ACKNOWLEDGMENTS

Justice requires giving to others their due. My debts to others are many. First, gratitude is due to Peter Paris, Nancy Duff, and Mark Taylor, for reading an earlier version of this text when it was in its dissertation form. Dr. Paris deserves special thanks for his willingness to continue to read and comment on this work even after his retirement. Over the last six years he has been not only my advisor but a mentor and friend as well.

Although this book is primarily about Karl Barth and moral virtue in the Reformed tradition, I am indebted to two professors who helped introduce and interpret the works of Thomas Aquinas. George Hunsinger graciously agreed to direct a study of Thomas Aquinas's *Summa Theologiae* with two other graduate students and me. I still consult the summaries we made while plowing through hundreds of pages of dense material. John Bowlin welcomed me as a visitor to his Ph.D. seminar on Thomas Aquinas. His comments on my work helped me focus my engagement with Thomas on those areas where Thomas and Barth parted ways.

My understanding of Karl Barth's work is indebted to many at Princeton Theological Seminary. In direct and indirect ways, Daniel Migliore, George Hunsinger, Bruce McCormack, and Nancy Duff provided helpful insight. While he was still the curator of special collections at Princeton Theological Seminary, Clifford Anderson not only introduced me to specific literature on Barth but also read and commented on chapter 2.

Portions of chapters 3 and 4 were presented at the Annual Conference of the Society of Christian Ethics in 2011. I benefited from the lively discussion that followed and am particularly grateful to Nimi Wariboko for his helpful questions and comments.

Christian Iosso and other members of the Presbyterian Church (U.S.A.)'s Advisory Committee on Social Witness Policy have been helpful throughout this process. My association with Christian goes back to 2006, when he was gracious enough to invite me to a meeting of the committee while it was reviewing recommendations on globalization put forward to the General Assembly. Their contributions were invaluable for the case study found in chapter 5.

I am indebted to Donald McKim and other members of the editorial board of the Columbia Series of Reformed Theology who stimulated me to engage the Reformed tradition more broadly in order to situate Barth's theology and ethics. The overview of Reformed views of moral virtue ethics found in chapter 1 is the fruit of their prodding.

Between numerous work and family commitments, the last four years of writing and revising this work have been an adventure! I would like to thank the students and faculty at Presbyterian College for their support and patience with me during this time. Special thanks go to my student worker, Jessica Carriker, who helped prepare the manuscript in its final stages.

While words cannot express the debt I owe to my wife for her insight, patience, and good humor, suffice it to say that the debt is large. As I began this project, we became new parents and somehow not only survived but thrived through months of sleep deprivation. Now our daughter is seven, and we have two sons, five and three. Tricia, thank you for all the sacrifices you willingly made to help me complete this work.

Finally, I wish to thank my parents for their devotion to education. I am now the third person to receive a doctorate in our family. Thanks go especially to you, Mom, a teacher of teachers, for inspiring me by your example.

ABBREVIATIONS

CD	Karl Barth. *Church Dogmatics*. Edited by G. W. Bromiley and T. F. Torrance. 4 volumes. Edinburgh: T. & T. Clark, 1936–1975.
Hope	Presbyterian Church (U.S.A.). Advisory Committee on Social Witness Policy. *Hope for a Global Future: Toward Just and Sustainable Human Development*. A report adopted by the 208th General Assembly (1996), Presbyterian Church (U.S.A.). Louisville, KY: Office of the General Assembly, Presbyterian Church (U.S.A.), 1996.
Inst.	John Calvin. *Institutes of the Christian Religion*. Edited by John Thomas McNeill. Translated by Ford Lewis Battles. Library of Christian Classics, vols. 20, 21. Philadelphia: Westminster Press, 1960.
ST	Thomas Aquinas. *Summa Theologiae: Latin Text and English Translation, Introductions, Notes, Appendices and Glossaries*. New York: McGraw-Hill, 1964.

INTRODUCTION

SHOULD CHRISTIANS GUIDED BY THE REFORMED TRADITION ASPIRE TO MORAL VIRTUE?

Thirty years ago Stanley Hauerwas's primer on Christian ethics, *The Peaceable Kingdom*, was published. It was not his first writing on virtue ethics, but it nonetheless marked a milestone in that its welcomed reception marked a tidal change in Protestant thinking on moral virtue. Influenced by Bernard Lewis and Alasdair MacIntyre, Hauerwas rejected metaethical approaches to Christian ethics, which attempted to establish universal grounds for moral concepts, and embraced an approach that centered on local communities of character. As Hauerwas understood them, these communities are formed around a shared narrative, a complex of interweaving stories that describe the moral and intellectual excellences to be pursued throughout one's lifetime. They foster virtue in their members through distinctive practices that embody the meaning of their shared narrative. In turn, the health of these communities is strengthened by virtue's embodiment in their members. Christian communities are distinctively shaped by the narratives of the Old and New Testaments, which tell the story of God's dealings with God's people. As Hauerwas notes, "We know who we are only when we can place our selves—locate our stories—within God's story."[1]

Hauerwas's emphasis on narrative had theological implications as well. Christian doctrines, like moral concepts, could not be excised from the stories out of which they were derived in order to universalize them. Understanding the person and work of Jesus Christ, for example, required moving beyond the abstract claims about Jesus' full humanity and divinity made at Chalcedon. Instead, Hauerwas's narrative approach emphasized thick description over parsimonious definition. He argued that it is only by immersing ourselves in the Gospels as well as the overarching biblical narrative that we have any concept of what the words *human* and *divine* even mean. "Theology," Hauerwas wrote, "has no essence, but rather is the imaginative endeavor to explicate the stories of God by showing how one claim illuminates another."[2]

Prior to Hauerwas, Christian virtue ethics had been largely the province of Roman Catholic theologians and ethicists. Drawing on a long tradition

1

dating back to Thomas Aquinas in the thirteenth century, they articulated a two-tier system of virtue. The first tier consisted of those virtues that were available, to some extent, to all human beings. These are often referred to as natural virtues. They include moral virtues such as courage and intellectual virtues such as prudence, which may be acquired through proper training of the intellect and will. Progress in these virtues, while possible, is hampered by the lasting effects of sin. A second tier, known as the theological virtues, is available only to Christians and consists of faith, hope, and love. These virtues are infused in us by God's grace, not by any action or merit on our part. This two-tier system provided Roman Catholics with a vision of the Christian life that was congruent in many ways with life outside the walls of the church. Since God had implanted a natural law in the hearts of all people, it followed that the goals of a diverse society would in many ways intersect with those of Christians.

Since *The Peaceable Kingdom* was published, many ink cartridges have run dry as Protestant thinkers explored the possibilities for virtue in the church. Hauerwas's emphasis on Christian practices, in particular, has spawned a mini-industry of its own. Numerous books have been written about hospitality, prayer, fasting, Sabbath keeping, forgiveness, peacekeeping, discernment, and dying well. Unfortunately, these practices have often been examined in isolation from, rather than in connection to, the virtues they were originally intended to foster. The stampede to practice has unmoored Christian practices from Christian virtue. *Practicing Our Faith*, for instance, covers thirteen different spiritual practices without any mention of virtue. Dorothy Bass notes in her preface the debt this volume owes to the philosopher Alasdair MacIntyre's work on social practices, yet she fails to point out that such work is rooted in a larger concern for virtue.[3]

The reason for this lacuna may be that practices are easier to write about than moral virtues, particularly to popular audiences. Practices such as forgiveness are already central to Christian worship and life. The province of the moral virtues is not so easily situated since their place in the Christian life is not already well-defined. But perhaps another reason may be that discussions about the moral virtues inevitably lead to difficult questions about the possibility of human perfectibility. Even writing about Christian practices can lead one into tricky ground. How, for instance, are these practices to be assessed? What does excellence look like in these areas, and may it be aspired to? Craig Dykstra, writing from a Reformed perspective, notes that while most of the stories we live by are heroic tales in which individuals achieve mastery over their environment, the Christian narrative leads to a different vision of engagement with the world:

> Christian practices are different. And that is because their story is different. While human achievement is valued in the Christian story, it has a

different place and meaning. The human task is not fundamentally mastery. It is rather the right use of gifts graciously bestowed by a loving God for the sake of the good that God intends—*and ultimately assures*. In the Christian story, the fundamental fact is neither a violence that threatens to overwhelm us nor a chaos that threatens to undo us. No. This story's fundamental fact is that the everlasting arms of a gracious and loving God sustain the universe. So our basic task is not mastery and control. It is instead trust and grateful receptivity. Our exemplars are not heroes; they are saints. Our epitome is not excellence; our honor is in faithfulness.[4]

Dykstra illustrates his point by examining the practice of prayer. Prayer opens us up to God's presence in our lives. If we are focusing on mastering prayer as a technique, then the focus is on us, rather than on God, and we miss prayer's purpose. He observes, "The abundance of God's grace relativizes all our excellences."[5] If Christian practices involve God's initiating action and our response, it would seem their efficacy cannot be humanly determined. The purpose, then, of educating folks in these practices is not so much to aim for excellence in their doing them as it is to encourage the importance of the particular ways in which God already acts in our lives, if only we are open to that action.

Dykstra's position is a reflection of the larger, somewhat paradoxical view the Reformed tradition has held regarding the relationship between God and humankind. While the tradition has affirmed the sovereignty of God's action, it has also avowed the importance of human action toward reforming the world. The latter suggests that some form of human advancement is possible in the Christian life; the former casts doubt on the extent to which that advancement is a result of human effort versus the workings of an ever-present, all-powerful God.

Ought Christians guided by the Reformed tradition even aspire to moral virtue? Moral virtue, by most accounts, is a form of human excellence that presumes high-level reasoning, imagination, and willpower. This view of human capacities contrasts with a reading of the biblical narrative that emphasizes God's steadfast love in the face of human sinfulness. Reformed understandings of original sin tend to stress the discontinuity between the human condition prior to the fall and after it. In contrast, the ancient Greek tradition of virtue ethics, especially as expressed by Aristotle, follows from a positive assessment of human capacities. For Aristotle the life of virtue is constituted by a set of excellences of character that are established through practice until they become second nature. Since Aristotle has no account of original sin, there is no need for the gods to intervene in human affairs. In fact, Aristotle presumes that human beings are more like the gods when they are lost in contemplation than when they are engaged in social interaction.

The Roman Catholic tradition also varies from the Reformed tradition's assessment of the human condition, though less dramatically. Roman Catholic dogma affirms the damaging effects of original sin, yet it tends to be more optimistic about postlapsarian human capacity. Thomas Aquinas is thus able to build on both Aristotle's account of virtue and Augustine's account of grace. Like Aristotle, Thomas distinguishes between contemplation and action but manages to incorporate both elements into the well-lived life. Thomas delineates a proximate end that promotes individual and social well-being and an ultimate end that consists in active participation in the beatific vision of God. Whereas in Aristotle's account these two ends appear to be pulling in opposite directions—the political pulling us into social affairs, the contemplative pulling us away—in Thomas's account the two are complementary: the acquired and the infused virtues ultimately work in tandem. This complementarity is possible because of the created order established by God: not only human nature but all of creation is created and ordered for the praise of God. While nonhuman beings participate in this glorification of God unconsciously, human beings are unique in that they do so consciously. The infused virtues, in particular, exemplify the ways in which conscious participation in the life of God is manifest in human life.

Given these different accounts of divine and human agency, Reformed thinkers are right to be cautious about accepting virtue ethics uncritically into the tradition. In its Aristotelian mode, virtue ethics is a perfectionist ethics. Thomas Aquinas's appropriation of Aristotelian virtue ethics adjusts for the impact of original sin on human capacities. Yet his ethics is also perfectionist if one takes into account the work of the Holy Spirit in the lives of Christian believers after they have come to faith. He holds out the possibility of perfection in this life, even though he admits that in actuality the chances of it happening are almost infinitesimal. The differences between Reformed and Roman Catholic understandings of the consequences of original sin indicate that a simple appropriation of Thomas's virtue ethics will not do. Instead, an account of Reformed virtue ethics requires a theological reassessment of virtue's place that necessitates drawing from resources within the tradition as well as outside of it.

APPROACH TO THE TOPIC

The task of assessing virtue's place in the Reformed tradition, as that tradition is understood today, may be approached in different ways. For instance, one could conduct a historical inquiry tracing Reformed views of moral virtue from the sixteenth century up to the present. The purpose of this investigation would be to reveal where the tradition either accepted or rejected virtue ethics and its reasons for doing so. Weighing evidence for and against, one could make a case according to precedent. One could argue, as Richard Muller has done, that the 150-year period of scholastic Protestantism, which was amenable to virtue ethics, has been at least as influential in shaping the Reformed tradition as the fifty-year period of the Reformation that preceded it.[6] One could then trace a trajectory of Reformed moral virtue through time, highlighting figures such as Peter Martyr Vermigli and Francis Turretin and extending beyond the era of Protestant scholasticism to the present.

Another approach would be to zero in on one figure who heralded virtue in his or her theological reflections and then reevaluate those reflections in light of current concerns. Examples of this type of work include two monographs on Jonathan Edwards by Stephen A. Wilson and Elizabeth Agnew Cochran. In *Virtue Reformed* Wilson claims that Reformed concerns about virtue ethics have led scholars of an earlier generation to minimize its importance in Edwards's writings.[7] Cochran's contribution, coming after Wilson, is less defensive and more constructive. She sees Edwards's thoughts on virtue ethics as a needed complement to the dominant Aristotelian/Thomist framework in the field. She also is intentional about demonstrating how Edwards's Reformed commitments shape his virtue ethics in important ways.[8]

A third approach, the one adopted here, is to identify those areas of greatest theological concern in the tradition and seek to address them. The aim of this approach is not to dismiss the various accounts of Reformed virtue ethics offered in the past but rather to broaden the appeal of these accounts as much as possible. It is evident that misgivings about virtue ethics persist in the tradition. Addressing these misgivings head on allows for virtue's full embrace.

The first step in this approach consists of an overview of three accounts of moral virtue from highly influential sources of Reformed thinking: John Calvin, the Westminster Standards, and Jonathan Edwards. Taken together, these accounts suggest a distinctive shape for moral virtue ethics within the tradition. These accounts, however, are not without their difficulties. For example, each account draws a qualitative distinction between those who are elected for salvation and those who are not. True virtue occurs only in the elect, who are privileged to experience regeneration through the Holy Spirit. The notion of true but imperfect pagan virtue, an important concept in Thomistic virtue ethics, is largely rejected here. As a consequence, Thomistic virtue ethics allows for civic virtue while such a concept is suspect according to these Reformed views.[9]

The main reason for the Reformed tradition's skepticism about civic virtue revolves around its understandings of original sin, which renders human beings incapable of fully knowing and doing the will of God. In the work of Karl Barth, the consequences of original sin entail that human beings have no access to God apart from God's revelation. Barth's concerns regarding natural theology, while expressed to a greater or lesser extent within the tradition, have a firm basis within it. There is, for instance, consistent opposition to the use of the *analogia entis* (the basis for much Roman Catholic reflection on natural theology), or analogy of being, to ascertain knowledge of God even in the Protestant scholastic period. For example, Richard Muller observes,

> Where the Thomistic line of thought continues into the Reformation—for example, in the writings of Vermigli, Zanchi, and, to a certain extent, Keckermann—it is modified by a more negative assessment of the powers of reason and by a sense of diastasis between the ways of God and the ways of man that virtually cancels a Thomistic use of the *analogia entis* in theology.[10]

Barth's objections to the *analogia entis*, which will be examined in detail, thus place him squarely within the tradition on this matter. The challenge of addressing Barth's concerns raises the bar substantially in terms of the requirements a Reformed moral virtue ethic would need to meet. However, if these concerns are successfully addressed, the proposed ethics stands a good chance of being accepted as a part of the tradition as a whole.

But Karl Barth's work does more than simply present challenges for the acceptance of moral virtue ethics within the tradition; it also offers remarkable possibilities. While Barth's rejection of natural theology would seem to shut the door completely on the acquisition of pagan virtue, in fact it levels the playing field. This becomes clear when one examines Barth's doctrine of revelation within the context of his teaching on election. Although Barth stops short of endorsing universal salvation, the logic of his understanding of the triune God, who from eternity chooses to be God for us, points in that direction. Against other Reformed accounts, Barth points to a reality in which all humankind is drawn into a relationship with God, where true moral virtue is available to everyone. We will need to investigate whether such virtue is solely eschatological, but as all Christian virtue ethics points to the eschaton as the final end, Barth's view of that end is certainly promising.

Other considerations also come into play regarding the choice of Barth. North American scholarship on Barth's ethics has mushroomed over the last twenty years. From Nigel Biggar's groundbreaking work *The Hastening That Waits*, to Gerald McKenny's recent book *The Analogy of Grace*, interest continues to grow. That interest extends to Roman Catholic scholars, as attested by the 2011 Thomas Aquinas and Karl Barth Conference co-hosted by Princeton Theological Seminary and the Thomistic Institute.[11] Our study seeks to bring together recent Protestant interest in virtue ethics with this growing attention paid to Barth's theological ethics. Engagement with Barth's concerns, addressing the theological underpinnings of Roman Catholic moral virtue ethics of his day, sheds new light on the theological presumptions behind current Protestant and Roman Catholic proposals.

To get a sense of Barth's objections to Christian moral virtue ethics, consider the following statement: "The principle of necessary repetition and renewal, and not a law of stability, is the law of the spiritual growth and continuity of our life."[12] Barth's words here do more than suggest that moral virtue ethics has little place in the Christian life. They present a challenge to the very notion of habitual grace, a notion that has been at the center of Christian virtue ethics since Thomas Aquinas, if not before. Nor are these words idiosyncratic to Barth's theological vision. Barth repeatedly employs the language of divine command when speaking of the relationship between God and us, leading many interpreters to presume that there is little room in Barth's ethics for continuity of character.[13] These interpreters are concerned that Barth's ethics implies if not entails that the Christian life is a series of human responses to God's command, depriving human agency of initiative and stunting any notion of growth in the Christian life.

Since the early 1990s much work has been published on Barth's ethics that sheds a more positive picture of human agency in Barth's thought. These accounts of Barth's ethics have demonstrated that his emphasis on divine command does not obliterate the human as acting agent but rather creates a space for human freedom in response to God's commands. Prominent among these studies is John Webster's book *Barth's Ethics of Reconciliation*.[14] Webster argues that Barth's account of human agency can only be understood within the overall framework of Barth's thinking about the character of God's relationship with humankind. God's covenantal relationship with humanity sets the parameters within which human freedom may operate. True human freedom exists only within the constraints thus established.

Not only has human agency in Barth's ethics been rehabilitated; his theology has also been used as a springboard for virtue ethics. In William Werpehowski's 2007 presidential address to the Society of Christian Ethics, Werpehowski defends Barth against his skeptics by placing the above statement in its proper context. Barth is here elaborating on the role of humility when seeking guidance from God. If we come to God with the presumption that our conversion to God is all but complete, then we come with closed ears. Instead, to be truly guided by the Holy Spirit we must be open to instruction and conversion, again and again. Werpehowski concludes that growth in the Christian life is possible, along Barthian lines, so long as we acknowledge that such growth is marked by "repetition and renewal."[15] Building on Barth's insight, Werpehowski develops his own conception of practical wisdom, which in his schema is one of the chief virtues in the Christian life.

MORAL VIRTUE ETHICS IN THE WAKE OF BARTH

The thesis of this book may be summarized as follows: overcoming the theological obstacles to Reformed moral virtue ethics that Karl Barth raises requires that such ethics be grounded in and shaped by a covenant based in God's free election of humankind. The blueprint for that covenant is the Chalcedonian relationship between Christ's divine and human natures. Such ethics is relational and marked by reform. It is relational in the sense that we as human beings participate in virtue only in response to God's divine commands, which we come to understand more deeply over time. It is marked by reform both in the sense that individual virtue follows a pattern of repetition and renewal rather than gradual growth, and also in the sense that it is committed to social justice, following the command to love neighbor as self.

The title of this book, *Reformed Virtue After Barth,* may thus be interpreted in two different senses. First, it indicates the historical impact that Barth's theology has made on Protestant as well as Roman Catholic thought over the last ninety years. In constructing a Reformed moral virtue ethic for the twenty-first century, Barth's theological concerns simply cannot be ignored. One may refute them, but one must still deal with them. Second, the title also indicates the particular shape of the proposed moral virtue ethics offered here. While Barthians may rightly protest that Barth did not espouse moral virtue ethics in his own work, this book proposes that such an ethic may nonetheless be ventured while remaining faithful to Barth's theological commitments.

Defense of these claims starts by situating Karl Barth's thoughts on virtue within the Reformed tradition. Chapter 1 traces understandings of the Christian life across the first two-and-a-quarter centuries of the tradition, from John Calvin through Jonathan Edwards, including the Westminster Standards in the middle of this period. While presently Edwardsean virtue has the greatest presence in modern scholarship, a broader overview of the tradition's approach to moral virtue is necessary to identify the distinctive shape of Reformed moral virtue before Barth. The end of this chapter will identify the ways in which Barth's theology challenges these three models and requires a reconsideration of moral virtue after Barth.

In chapter 2 I address three major hurdles Karl Barth's theology raises for Reformed moral virtue ethics. I show that Barth's theological reservations not only challenge the framework within which virtue ethics has been typically cast but that they are also Reformed in character. As such, they cannot be dismissed as beyond the pale of the tradition. Chapter 3 presents a way around these hurdles. The focus turns to an evaluation of William Werpehowski's claim that Barth's is a type of virtue ethics. I will argue that certain features of Werpehowski's argument need to be altered, yet his account largely provides the basis for the Reformed moral virtue ethics I propose.

Chapter 4 begins the major constructive work of the book. Based on Barth's suspicions regarding natural theology, a case is made for moral virtue ethics that highlights the role of God's revelation to us. This is but one of the ways that Reformed ethics is distinctive. In all, five defining characteristics are derived from the analysis of chapters 2 and 3. Thomistic virtues are then compared alongside of their Reformed counterparts. The final section of this chapter examines the roles that the church and state play in the formation of virtue in our account. Following Barth's insights, an argument is made that both the church and the state play important roles in the covenant God establishes with humanity through divine election. God's command is the impetus for virtue, whether individuals recognize it as God's command or not.

Chapter 5 supplements the model of virtue ethics presented in chapter 4 by demonstrating how a Reformed body may incorporate a virtue ethics framework into its social-justice demands. The case study involves the social witness policy on just and sustainable development of the Presbyterian Church (U.S.A.).[16] As stated in the social policy of the PC(USA), an ethic of frugality is integral to the satisfaction of the church's commitments to sufficiency, sustainability, and eco-justice. This ethic requires an account of habits and practices of individuals and congregations that fits well with a virtue ethic. Yet a framework for developing such behavior is never explicitly articulated in the church's documentation.

What emerges from these five chapters, I trust, is not merely a model of moral virtue that satisfies Reformed and Barthian concerns. While that is a substantive achievement in itself, my hope is that these chapters will also advance broader discussions regarding virtue. Reformed moral virtue ethics has much to offer. As highlighted in chapters 4 and 5, it provides a compelling account of the Christian life that engages the world through the lens of God's reconciling love made known in Jesus Christ. It resolves concerns leveled against virtue ethics in general over the last thirty years: concerns about how to ground accounts of the purpose and meaning of human life, concerns about justice, and concerns about overly restrictive traditionalism. Furthermore, as pointed out in chapter 3, it resolves criticisms that derive from Christian circles over the agent-centered char-acter of virtue ethics. All of these criticisms are met by rooting Reformed moral virtue ethics in God's command and our faithful response, and by extending the circle of that command beyond the life of the church to include God's dealings with all of creation. It is time, now, to discover what such ethics looks like.

1

THE REFORMED TRADITION
ON MORAL VIRTUE

Historically, virtue has taken different forms. For the apostle Paul humility was a virtue; for Aristotle it was a vice. Even when cultures share the same virtue, the expression of that virtue may look very different. In Homer's *Iliad*, Greek warriors exhibit courage in battle. Their willingness to place themselves in physical danger is necessary for the welfare of their cities in the face of foreign threat. Courage takes a different form in Jane Austen's *Pride and Prejudice*, in which it revolves around marriage. Given Elizabeth Bennet's rather diminished family circumstances, her original refusal of Mr. Darcy's proposal on moral grounds is just as courageous as Hector's stand against Achilles outside the walls of Troy.

However they are expressed, virtues shape public norms as well as private values. Austen's depiction of Elizabeth's choice enriched the English understanding of the institution of marriage in the face of pressures to reduce it to an economic exchange. Homer's depiction of courage on both sides of the Trojan war set an example of sacrificial heroism that helped advance Greek thinking beyond its own parochial interests. Thus while conceptions of virtue vary, in every formulation there is a close link between individual virtue and the flourishing of communities. The end of moral virtue is not simply individual well-being but also the well-being of the *polis*, or society. This makes reflecting on the *kind* of virtues a society pursues doubly important.

REFORMED VIRTUE BEFORE BARTH

What does Reformed moral virtue ethics look like? What shape does it have? The question remains an open one even though the Reformed tradition, dating back at least as far as John Calvin, is almost five hundred years old. While there have been periods in which Reformed conceptions of virtue were articulated, the impact of those periods goes largely unnoticed in today's Reformed churches.[1] The current lack of attention to virtue in the tradition is particularly noticeable given the fact that an account of virtue may be found in the works of some of its most prominent figures.

Two such figures are John Calvin and Jonathan Edwards. Calvin, whose theology has proven enormously influential within the tradition,

presumes an audience for whom virtue is an integral part of the Christian life. That he never published a special treatise on ethics, such as
Melanchthon did, owes more to his agreement with his contemporaries
on matters of virtue than it does to any lack of interest on his part. Writing two hundred years later on the other side of the Atlantic Ocean,
Jonathan Edwards did expound on the differences between true and
false virtue in the Christian life and so valued virtue that he incorpo-
rated it into his reflections on Christ's work of atonement. This chapter
will examine Calvin's and Edwards's theologies and ethics to shed light
on their particular expressions of moral virtue ethics found within the
tradition.

In addition, the Westminster Confession will be examined with the
same purpose in mind. This confession and the catechisms that accompanied it were written in the middle of the seventeenth century and had a
profound influence on American Presbyterian churches. In fact, they were
considered the sole confessional standard from the early eighteenth until
the middle of the twentieth century.

Taken together, the Westminster Confession and the works of Calvin
and Edwards represent major streams of Reformed thought that continue
to influence the church today. Each will be considered in chronological
order. Points of continuity and difference between them will be examined in order to demonstrate, in microcosm, the variety of expressions
that make up Reformed understandings of the Christian faith. At the end
of the chapter, these expressions will be analyzed from the perspective of
today's theological concerns, particularly those raised by the work of Karl
Barth. These concerns challenge the underpinnings of the Reformed moral
virtue ethics that preceded Barth.

JOHN CALVIN AND THE PRESUMPTION OF CHRISTIAN VIRTUE

A quick look at the opening chapters of John Calvin's 1559 *Institutes* suggests that human virtue has little place in his theological schema. For Calvin human preoccupation with moral excellence gets in the way of the
proper knowledge of God and of ourselves. He observes that people tend
to see themselves in the best possible light because they compare themselves to others around them rather than to God. The comparison ends up
clouding their judgment, for "an eye to which nothing is shone but black
objects judges something dirty white or even rather darkly mottled to be
whiteness itself."[2] Calvin argues that proper self-knowledge thus requires
acquaintance with God's perfections: beside God's justice, human justice
pales; next to God's wisdom, that which passes for human wisdom looks
shortsighted.

Yet Calvin's rhetoric points to another goal beyond that of humbling human pride. He hopes to bring his readers to a joyful faith in which they recognize God's goodwill toward them. Like other rhetors before him, Calvin aims to move his audience to action, not merely to give their assent to the truth of his words. By coaxing them toward faith, he also hopes to draw them into a different kind of virtuous life from the versions offered by the pagan philosophers.[3] These philosophers summon their listeners to self-examination through an investigation into the natural order. They observe that human beings are, of all animals, uniquely qualified to grasp that order through reason. Calvin sets the scope of investigation more broadly to include investigation of the creator of that natural order. While he is notorious for his comments on human depravity, ironically, those comments are meant to goad his readers into "sound virtue," which is to be found in God's righteousness alone.[4]

Even though virtue is important to Calvin, he offers no defense of the Christian life of virtue because he is never pushed to do so. His interlocutors tended to agree with him on this matter and challenged his views on other connected matters, such as free will, justification, and regeneration. Thus while Calvin offers no extensive theory of virtue, one nonetheless emerges through the claims he makes in these other related areas. For instance, at the beginning of his discussion of the Christian life in book 3 of the *Institutes*, Calvin notes that the early church doctors could, without mincing words, expound on a single virtue at length. For the sake of brevity, Calvin prefers to direct readers to the sermons of these early church fathers rather than to repeat them.[5] Yet in the matter of free will, as we will soon see, Calvin does not rest content to lean on these same individuals. He finds their explanations regarding free will to be unreliable. Since the life of virtue requires a good will, it follows that their account of virtue would at the very least warrant more investigation. That Calvin fails to take up this issue is not the result of a lack of interest in virtue but rather due to the fact that his detractors forced him to think more carefully about free will, whereas his understanding of virtue during his time was not an issue of contention.

In 1543 Calvin wrote a defense of his views of free will and predestination in response to Albert Pighius, a Dutch Roman Catholic theologian. In *The Bondage and Liberation of the Will*, Calvin carved out his own position in distinction from that of Luther and from Roman Catholic dogma. Pighius asserted that Calvin misrepresented Augustine's views on free will. Although Calvin's position was largely derived from his reading of Scripture, he felt compelled to refute Pighius's claims directly and thus presented a defense of his reading of Augustine on free will.

To set the context, one needs to understand how influential Augustine's work on free will was from the Middle Ages through the sixteenth century. Medieval conceptions of grace were strongly influenced by a distinction Augustine makes, but does not systematize, between operative and cooperative grace. In *On Grace and Free Will*, Augustine argues against the Pelagians, who claimed that grace must be in some way merited; otherwise God's choice to damn some to eternal hell appears arbitrary. Augustine asserts instead that God's work in us is twofold: God *operates* in a bad will to turn it to good, and God *cooperates* with a good will to enable it to perform good acts.[6] Augustine's assertion, on the one hand, that the will is free, and on the other, that God moves the will, left the need for later interpreters to explain how this could be so.

Pighius interprets Augustine's comments to mean that the will is free to choose either good or evil prior to God's intervention, a position that is clearly in contradiction with Augustine's. Calvin's refutation of Pighius on this error is straightforward. However, his task of clarifying Augustine's views on cooperation proves more challenging. Medieval scholastics like Thomas Aquinas describe the operation of grace on the sinner in terms of infusion. Calvin rejects such language as synergistic. If this is what Augustine means by cooperative grace, then Calvin's views diverge from Augustine's. However, Calvin maintains that Augustine has a different conception of divine-human interaction in the sinner when the will is turned toward God. He contends that Augustine's position may be understood using an organic metaphor. Calvin writes,

> Then [we learn] what it means for him to act with us: this is obviously when, by the continuous supply of his aid, he assists, increases, and strengthens that power which he has granted us, both for the completion of each particular work and for final perseverance through life. Or if you like to maintain that fine image of Paul's, it is when he invigorates by his own heavenly warmth the olives which have already been made fertile and waters them with dew, so that they may bear fruit. . . . What is there in that which we can claim for ourselves? But after we have begun to be guided by the Spirit of holiness, we are now olives which are green and lively, drawing their vigour from their good root. Of our own accord, then, we are now disposed towards bearing fruit. But is that our own doing or may we boast of it even in the smallest measure? [No,] it is entirely derived from the root. Moreover, the root itself is [ours] not by nature but by grace; and even it is still not sufficient, unless God supplies from Heaven continual power for life.[7]

Calvin clarifies how Paul's metaphor both upholds humankind's complete dependence on God while also maintaining the integrity of human willing. The nature of the ungrafted wild olive does not change with the grafting, yet the nourishment for which it is entirely dependent comes from outside itself. The same may be said for the sinner, who, through God's act of justification and God's regenerative power, produces the fruit of repentance through his own free will. Here the relationship between God and human beings is not synergistic, since the integrity of their human nature remains intact.[8]

Calvin's defense of his views on free will also rests, rather interestingly, on Aristotelian categories. Calvin argues that God's turning of the will does not create a new will but rather a new habit within the will. Calvin's reference to habit relies on an Aristotelian distinction between substance and accident. According to Aristotle, the substance of a thing consists of those characteristics that make it distinct from other kinds of things. That thing may or may not have certain accidental features as well, but those features are not essential. Human beings have free will; it is one of the faculties that makes them what they are. Whether or not human beings use that free will for evil is an accidental feature. If it were substantial, then God's action would divinize the sinner rather than keep his or her human nature intact.

Yet Augustine's description of the change in human nature from bad willing to good suggests a critical difference between the two. Claiming this as an accidental difference does not appear to go far enough. Calvin's use of the term *habit* helps satisfy this concern as well. Through habituation the substance of human beings is modified significantly without changing it altogether. The change is a difference in degree rather than in kind. Calvin concludes, "The will remains in man just as it was originally implanted in him, and so the change takes place in the habit, not in the substance. By a renewal of such a kind I say that the heart is made different."[9]

Calvin's discussion of free will in book 2 of the 1559 *Institutes* extends his analysis beyond Augustine's work but remains indebted to it. He explores the effects of the fall and contrasts the views of the ancient philosophers with his own. For instance, according to Cicero virtue is a human achievement, "but virtue no one ever imputed to a god's bounty. And doubtless with good reason; for our virtue is a just ground for others' praise and a right reason for our own pride, and this would not be so if the gift of virtue came to us from a god and not from ourselves."[10] Calvin finds surprising congruence between Cicero's views and those of the early church leaders. He argues that they too easily accept the views of the pagan philosophers for two reasons. One is apologetic. They seek to avoid being jeered at by their contemporaries who embrace pagan thought. Thus, in order to make Christian doctrine more respectable, these early church leaders often repeat pagan notions of free will. The second reason relates to a worry regarding human sloth. They fear that presenting the case for the bondage of the will might lead many to despair and inaction.[11] Neither are good reasons to accept an understanding of the will that comes from sources that do not recognize the fall in the first place. The result, according to Calvin, is that most thinkers in the first five centuries of the church's existence fail to articulate the devastating consequences of sin on human willing.[12]

Even the church fathers, however, admit virtue is beyond the grasp of human beings apart from the work of the Spirit. Calvin notes, "They have had this end in view—to teach man utterly to forsake confidence in his own virtue and to hold that all his strength rests in God alone."[13] Calvin's rejection of pagan virtue mirrors one church father in particular: Augustine. Augustine called the virtues the pagans aspired to "glittering vices" inspired by pride rather than true nobility. These so-called virtues bear the outward appearance of something solid and real, but this appearance is deceiving, for the individuals who exhibit them are motivated by a desire to be accepted by others.[14] True virtue must be inspired by the greatest good, which is God. Yet in order to know that good and to desire it, one must first be drawn by God.

Not only do Calvin's views lead him to reject pagan virtue; they also cast a decisive spin on his understanding of Christian virtue. Consider Calvin's commitment to the Reformation claim that justification is by faith alone in contrast with Thomas Aquinas's claim that justification is by faith working through love. Thomas asserts that there are four movements in the justification of the unrighteous: the infusion of grace, the movement of free choice toward God by faith, the movement of free choice away from sin, and the forgiveness of sin.[15] His account of justification does not distinguish justification from regeneration. For Thomas the concept of justification includes the work of the Holy Spirit in us to make us just. That work depends in part on a proper ordering of our loves. If justified sinners turn from God to pursue a lesser good, they commit mortal sin, and the effects of God's justifying grace are nullified. For this reason Thomas attributes merit to human perseverance in the joint work of cooperative grace.[16]

Calvin, in contrast, does distinguish between the concepts of justification and regeneration, though he is careful to maintain that they both stem from the one atoning work of Christ. Regarding justification, Calvin claims faith as the essential virtue, not love. He defends his views in his commentary on 1 Corinthians 13. Paul ends his paean to love by asserting that of the three—faith, hope, and love—love is the greatest. Calvin notes that in two senses this is true. Faith provides benefits to the believer while love benefits others. Love also continues when human beings meet God face-to-face whereas hope and faith become unnecessary at that point. However, because it is by faith that we receive Christ's righteousness, it is faith that makes justification efficacious, not love.[17]

Calvin's emphasis on faith extends to regeneration as well. Faith is the means by which sinners receive the grace of God that constitutes their regeneration. Without it, lives of virtue would be impossible. Calvin attributes no merit to human beings when they maintain their faith in God through difficult circumstances. Faith's continuance is not the result of human love working in cooperation with God but rather the result of the nurture of the Holy Spirit alone. Calvin writes in the *Institutes*, "It is the Lord's doing that the will conceives the love of what is right, is zealously inclined toward it, is aroused and moved to pursue it. Then it is the Lord's doing that the choice, zeal, and effort do not falter, but proceed even to accomplishment; lastly, that man goes forward in these things with constancy, and perseveres to the very end."[18]

Finally, another reason that Calvin presumes virtue in the Christian life but does not expound a general treatise on moral virtue has to do with his commitment to one virtue in particular: humility. Throughout the *Institutes* Calvin hails humility as an essential virtue in the practice of the Christian religion. From his opening words regarding humankind's true condition to his last words of caution regarding loyalty to earthly rulers in book 4, Calvin hammers home the message that God alone is to be worshiped. He warns against preoccupation over progress in moral virtue and repeatedly uses rhetoric to beat that temptation out of his listeners. Citing Augustine, he exclaims, "You must remain unarmed, you must have no help in yourself. The weaker you are in yourself, the more readily the Lord will receive you."[19] Humility is the mark of our regeneration, "the true turning of our life to God, a turning that arises from a pure and earnest fear of him."[20] The end result of our coming to humility is not self-paralysis but freedom for witness. Calvin writes,

> Ever since the Holy Spirit dedicated us as temples to God, we must take care that God's glory shine through us, and must not commit anything to defile ourselves with the filthiness of sin [1 Cor. 3:16; 6:19; 2 Cor. 6:16]. Ever since both our souls and bodies were destined for heavenly incorruption and an unfading crown [1 Peter 5:4], we ought to strive manfully to keep them pure and uncorrupted until the Day of the Lord [1 Thess. 5:23; cf Phil. 1:10]. These, I say, are the most auspicious foundations upon which to establish one's life. One would look in vain for the like of these among the philosophers, who, in their commendation of virtue, never rise above the natural dignity of man.[21]

Humility also gives rise to other virtues. Calvin picks up this theme in his commentary on Romans. Since our justification is by faith and not by works, we have a peace that makes perseverance in the midst of suffering possible. Commenting on Rom. 5:3–5, Calvin notes that it is through humility that we may, while facing trials, be able to turn to God in patience rather than hardness of heart. Humility also gives rise to hope, which, by calling to mind the ways in which God's grace has provided help in the past, projects an expectation of God's deliverance into the future.[22]

Calvin's moral virtue ethic rests in the shadow of a larger purpose, which is to glorify God. The Christian life, made possible by the continual regeneration of the Holy Spirit, is marked by slow advances in virtue. Due to God's justifying grace, Christians now have a new habit of willing that aims toward God's will rather than away from it. Christians cooperate with the Holy Spirit in the life of virtue in a manner that is constitutive of their own willing and acting, yet its sole source is divine. The virtue of faith makes regeneration possible, and the virtue of humility keeps the sinner focused on the grace of God rather than on the sinner's own advances in the Christian life.

VIRTUE IN THE WESTMINSTER CONFESSION

From time to time Reformed churches have felt the need to write a confession that expresses their understanding of the Christian faith for a new age. This felt need presupposes that the original creeds and confessions of the church are not static expressions of faith but contextual documents that, no matter how eloquent, stand in need of supplementation. The Reformed attitude toward the confessions is that they are provisional and local but important nonetheless. As human words, they do not have the same status as Scripture and may thus be superseded at a later time. They are also local expressions, reflecting the norms of a particular place and time. While certain Reformed bodies have sometimes decided to hew to one particular confession, there has been no consensus on one universal confessional standard. This makes identifying the unifying characteristics of Reformed churches trickier than, say, those of Lutheran churches, which identify the Augsburg Confession as their primary confessional document.

Despite their provisional nature, the confessions are nonetheless important. The work of even the most influential theologians reflects the thought of one mind, whereas the confessions usually reflect the collaboration of many. Typically confessions are developed under the guidance of the church during a time of conflict. While written in a polemical context, they tend to be more irenic than the polemics of the early embattled Reformers. Reformed confessions emphasize an ecumenical spirit over a strictly denominational stance. They are directed toward practical matters of the church and avoid esoteric discussions surrounding the essence of God. The sixteenth-century Reformers, with their emphasis on *sola scriptura*, saw in confessions and catechisms an important pedagogical tool. Even as they recognized Scripture to be of central importance in worship and Christian life, they also realized that without proper training it would be difficult for lay readers to understand its meaning. As Calvin noted,

"Observe well, it is not said that God has left the Scriptures for everyone to read, but has appointed a government that there may be persons to teach."[23]

The Westminster Confession is in some ways representative of the influence confessions have had in Reformed churches, and in other ways it is unique. Completed in the middle of the seventeenth century, almost ninety years after Calvin finished his work on the *Institutes*, the document was composed by a group of men (and they were all men) selected by the English parliament in the midst of the English Reformation. These individuals held different views on church governance, from independent, to Presbyterian, to Episcopalian, to Erastian.[24] Members of the Scottish state church had a voice in the deliberations but no voting power. The work of the Westminster Assembly took five years to complete, and the documents they produced had a Calvinist thrust. This influence is not surprising given Calvin's impact on English thought over the preceding century: between 1548 and 1600 no other writer had as many works published in England.[25] The Westminster Standards supported a system of church governance that was more Presbyterian than the previous Anglican polity. Yet for all of the work that was put into this confession and the two catechisms that accompanied it, the end result was the collapse of Presbyterianism in England when Cromwell led his successful rebellion against the king. The primary influence of the Westminster Standards would spread from Scotland, not England.

The Westminster Confession, like those Reformed confessions before it, placed a high priority on the practical application of the faith within the church. Like other Reformed confessions, it was written during a time of controversy but in an ecumenical manner that attempted to capture the essentials of the Christian faith rather than pick a fight. The confession is the result of an unusually high level of collaboration between church and state compared to other Reformed confessions, yet this type of collaboration was nothing new. For example, in the sixteenth century Frederick III, the elector of the city of Heidelberg and the area surrounding it, was very involved in the production of the Heidelberg Catechism, from its commission through its completion.[26] What really sets the Westminster Standards apart is their lasting and powerful influence on Presbyterian churches in the United States. Starting with the Adopting Act of 1729, the Westminster Confession and its accompanying catechisms were *the* confessional standard of American Presbyterian churches up until the twentieth century. During this era all ministers were required to recognize the authority of the Westminster Confession and catechisms "in all essential and necessary articles."[27]

What is the position of the Westminster Confession on whether the life of virtue is possible in those who are not regenerate and in those who are in the midst of regeneration? Second, to what extent is this life of virtue encouraged and emphasized, if it all? Answering the first question requires examining the confession's position on good works. The Westminster Confession does not necessarily reject the idea of good works in the unregenerate, yet it finds such works utterly lacking regarding faith in Christ, which is requisite to enter the kingdom of heaven:

> Works done by unregenerate men, although for the matter of them they may be things which God commands, and in themselves praiseworthy and useful, and although the neglect of such things is sinful and displeasing unto God; yet, because they proceed not from a heart purified by faith; nor are done in a right manner, according to his Word; nor to a right end, the glory of God; they come short of what God requires, and do not make any man meet to receive the grace of God.[28]

Could it be that these acts, while not salvific in and of themselves, are the fruit of imperfect virtue? Thomas Aquinas uses the term "imperfect virtue" to refer to moral excellences that result from right reasoning regarding those ends that human reason may attain, not divinely revealed ones. The works cited above are considered from a different standpoint. They are referenced in relation to the true end God seeks, which is only attainable through revelation. That these works happen to correspond to that true end is purely accidental and thus not representative of a virtuous act.

While not quite in the same boat as the unregenerate, those enjoying the fruits of the Holy Spirit are certainly not participating in the life of completely perfect virtue either:

> The persons of believers being accepted through Christ, their good works also are accepted in him, not as though they were in this life wholly unblamable and unreprovable in God's sight; but that he, looking upon them in his Son, is pleased to accept and reward that which is sincere, although accompanied with many weaknesses and imperfections.[29]

The process of sanctification is likened to a war between the flesh and the Spirit that is "continual and irreconcilable."[30] Yet the Westminster Confession nonetheless emphasizes the work of the Holy Spirit in human sanctification in ways that other confessions do not. Willem van Vlastuin, in his comparison between the Heidelberg and the Westminster Confessions, concludes that the Heidelberg Confession emphasizes mortification, or the putting to death of our sinful self, over vivification, the regeneration of the image of God and the experience of new life in us. This weighting is fitting for an audience that was predominantly Lutheran. The majority of the catechism's questions are found in section 2, "Of Man's Redemption," which, though it mentions sanctification, emphasizes our repentance in light of the justification of Christ. In contrast, the Westminster Confession stresses the new life available through the Holy Spirit. Vlastuin points out that Westminster's depiction of the state of our soul is more sanguine than Heidelberg's. While Heidelberg stresses our sinful nature, Westminster speaks of "pollutions." Vlastuin notes, "There is a difference between a nature which tends to sin or a (healthy) nature with pollution. The Westminster acknowledges indwelling sin, but it functions in the scheme of the *regeneratio* (regeneration)."[31]

The confession's portrayal of regeneration is not, however, without flaw. A comparison with Calvin's understanding of regeneration is illustrative here. As T. F. Torrance points out, the Westminster Confession places union with Christ last in its *ordo salutis* whereas Calvin places it first.[32] Torrance notes that Westminster's ordering is indicative of medieval conceptions of grace's slow operation, in contrast to that of the Reformers. Torrance concludes that this view of grace, combined with a seventeenth-century federalist theology that translated covenant into constitution, led to a legalistic conception of regeneration.

First, Westminster emphasizes the legal dimensions of Christ's role in our justification. It frames the relationship between God and human beings within the context of a covenant of works that human beings have failed to fulfill. Christ's death on the cross restores that covenant through substitutionary atonement. In essence, Christ takes our place and bears our punishment. Once the Son assuages the Father's wrath, God can look on us with favor and love. In Calvin's conception of the *ordo salutis*, God's love toward us anticipates our justification rather than awaits it. By placing union with Christ at the beginning of the *ordo salutis*, Calvin emphasizes God's desire to be in relationship even before we have been justified.

Westminster's conception of regeneration is an outgrowth of its overall understanding of God's relationship with humankind. Chapter 21 highlights the role of the law in shaping the behavior of the regenerate: "It is likewise of use to the regenerate, to restrain their corruptions, in that it forbids sin, and the threatenings of it serve to show what even their sins deserve, and what afflictions in this life they may expect for them, although freed from the curse thereof threatened in the law."[33] Contrast this with Calvin's description of the third use of the law, which enlivens believers who already long to obey God. Reflecting on the great love the writer of Psalm 119 has for the law, Calvin writes, "For what would be less lovable than the law if, with importuning and threatening alone, it troubled souls through fear, and distressed them through fright?"[34] While the words of the Westminster divines echo Calvin's third use of the law, they have sucked the life out of that use by stressing law's threatening nature, rather than the sweetness of the grace that dispenses it in pleasing form. Regeneration under this conception, then, is motivated more by fear than by love.[35]

The consequences for a conception of moral virtue are as follows. Within the context of covenantal theology, the law takes a central place. Morality is construed in terms of obeying laws, which place restrictions on allowable behavior. This can lead to a rather limited conception of morality that focuses on those actions that are permissible or, in contrast, those that are prohibited. Virtue ethics, in contrast, works within a much more expansive field of human action. It involves any human action that involves choice. Law, in this conception, is for the promotion of virtue (moral excellence in pursuing human and divine goods) rather than in the prevention of vice. The covenantal theology of Westminster follows the more restrictive conception of law than the more expansive one.

Karl Barth's 1923 lectures on the Reformed confessions also point out flaws in Westminster's account of regeneration. Barth's concerns relate to the confession's overemphasis on what happens in the human subject and its neglect of God's initiating action. Westminster's opening paragraph on sanctification points out that those who are regenerated are "more and more quickened and strengthened, in all saving graces, to the practice of true holiness."[36] Since the title of the chapter reads, "Of Sanctification," Barth raises the question of whether sanctification is here confused with holiness. Behind Barth's question is a distinction between the work of God and the effects of that work on us. Barth asks further, "It is clear that there is growth in 'holiness,' but is there in 'sanctification' through the Holy Spirit?" Barth views sanctification from an eschatological perspective, as a whole and completed work, while Westminster views the subject from within a human framework in which progress in the Christian life occurs over time. The result in Westminster is an emphasis on quantitative changes rather than a qualitative transformation. Barth finds the whole treatment of regeneration centers on what happens to us as human beings rather than on the exchange that takes place between God and human beings. He thus asserts, "This means that the original unity in which the original Reformed dogma defined repentance and sanctification as human question and divine answer is no longer understood here."[37]

Yet Westminster's conception of grace's operation as a slow, gradual process in us is mirrored in Calvin's writings as well. Calvin writes, "This restoration does not take place in one moment or one day or one year; but through continual and sometimes even slow advances God wipes out in his elect the corruptions of the flesh, cleanses them of guilt, consecrates them to himself as temples renewing all their minds to true purity that they may practice repentance throughout their lives and know that this warfare will end only at death."[38] The process is never complete in this life. As Calvin puts it colorfully: "There remains in the regenerate man a smoldering cinder of evil."[39] Both views appear more conducive to moral virtue ethics in comparison to Karl Barth's, at least at first glance.[40] Moral virtue ethics presupposes a period of growth in which the moral virtues are instilled in us through training. Growth in the virtues may be measured quantitatively in a manner akin to the process of growth in sanctification found in Calvin's and Westminster's accounts of regeneration.

While there is very little basis for pagan virtue in the Westminster Standards, whatever exists is based on their conception of natural law. Here is where Barth is particularly critical. He notes with concern Westminster's use of natural law to justify Sabbath observance in a civil context. The confession states, "As it is of the law of nature that, in general, a due proportion of time be set apart for the worship of God; so, in his Word, by a positive, moral, and perpetual commandment, binding all men in all ages, he hath particularly appointed one day in seven for a Sabbath, to be kept holy unto him."[41] While this appeal to natural law allows followers of Westminster to apply Sabbath restrictions to the general public as well as to the churched, the appeal stretches the notion of natural law. Is the Sabbath commandment perceptible to human reason, or is it revealed by God? This concern of Barth's crops up again when he looks at the second question of the Larger Catechism: "How doth it appear that there is a God?" The catechism's answer is that "the very light of nature in man, and the works of God, declare plainly that there is a God; but his word and spirit only, do sufficiently and effectually reveal him unto men for their salvation."[42] Barth's main opposition to this statement comes not from its appeal to natural law (this commentary was written in the early 1920s before he rejected its usage). Rather, it is the stale conception of God that follows from this natural law. In reference to the distinction Westminster makes between a primary cause (which is divine and necessary) and a secondary cause (which is contingent or natural), Barth writes,

> The God of revelation is the creator, the pure origin, not the "first cause" [*prima causa*] of the world. In the Westminster Confession, the safeguards against this dangerous use of analogy are still present. But the moment could come in which this analogy would gain a terribly independent significance, and the skilled apologist could then dare to make God plausible to the erudite among religion's despisers by using the name "Universal."[43]

One can almost hear the haunting ghost of Schleiermacher howling in Barth's ears!

The next chapter will demonstrate that Barth's concerns regarding God's revelation to us lead him to reject an *analogia entis*, or analogy of being, that allows human beings to perceive something about God's being and will for humankind based on a common point of reference between God's existence and human existence. Once Barth has thought through the theological consequences of this analogy of being and its implications regarding God's revelation toward us, he will reject natural theology as an unreliable basis for a Trinitarian understanding of God. This will have significant consequences for the type of moral virtue that may be developed based on Barthian theological commitments. Such a discussion, though, requires more attention than can be given here.

EDWARDSEAN VIRTUE ETHICS

The reception of Jonathan Edwards's work has often been selective. The Edwards one reads is often dependent on where one stands on particular theological and ethical issues. Even during his lifetime, Edwards was a controversial figure. Edwards's *Some Thoughts Concerning the Present Revival of Religion*, published in early 1743 in the midst of division over the excesses of the First Great Awakening, came across to many of his contemporaries as overly optimistic.[44] In the middle third of the nineteenth century, the Princeton school appropriated Edwards as a stalwart of doctrinal orthodoxy in their opposition to developments in New England that challenged traditional Calvinist assumptions about God.[45] While the Princeton school embraced Edwards's views on the bondage of the will and the sovereignty of God, it was uneasy about his involvement in the First Great Awakening.[46] Yet around the same time Charles Finney's embrace of religious revival, published as *Lectures on Revivals of Religion*, drew directly from Edwardsean sources.[47] H. Richard and Richard R. Niebuhr reinterpreted Edwards's reflections on the religious affections in the twentieth century as a challenge to nineteenth-century optimism regarding a common moral sense.[48] In doing so, they also departed from Edwards's doctrinal orthodoxy by rejecting his doctrine of original sin. Perry Miller's biography of Jonathan Edwards in the middle of the twentieth century sought to broaden Edwards's appeal by distancing him from his theological context.[49] And, in the latter half of the twentieth century, Roland Delattre's monograph sparked interest in Edwards's aesthetics and its connection to his ethical vision.[50]

Recent interest in Edwards's virtue ethics reflects this trend of reading Edwards selectively.[51] It mirrors the broader interest in virtue ethics that has grown over the last forty years. In the years prior to this era the role of virtue in Edwards's thought was often minimized or ignored. Stephen L. Wilson, for example, points out how the influential work of Conrad Cherry and Roland Delattre in the 1960s fails to do Edwardsean virtue ethics justice.[52]

The latest turn is fortuitous, as the work of Jonathan Edwards is an excellent place to look for a carefully articulated Reformed moral virtue ethic. Because of the interconnections between his theology, aesthetics, and ethics, Edwards offers a comprehensive vision of how Reformed theological commitments, which initially seem to make human moral excellence impossible, offer the grounds for moral virtue.

Edwards's most explicit and systematic treatment of virtue ethics is found in *The Nature of True Virtue*, written late in his life while he was a missionary to the Mahican Indians in Stockbridge, Massachusetts. True virtue, Edwards claims, consists in a benevolent disposition, or goodwill, toward all being.[53] A person may exhibit a benevolent disposition toward others without possessing true virtue, for much of what passes for virtue, argues Edwards, is actually self-love in disguise. The mark of false virtue is a love limited to a certain group of beings: one's family, those things considered to be beautiful, and so forth. The motive behind such benevolence may be due to instinct or to attraction, but it always has its limits. True virtue, on the other hand, extends benevolence to being itself. Its motivating ground is not based in any individual qualities of existent things, save their existence, but rather in being in general. It is this commitment to being in general that thus motivates us to love others in their individual existence.[54]

Not surprisingly, God, the Being of beings, is the proper object of true virtue. God's greatness consists not only in bestowing life on all creation but also in God's moral goodness. Thus true virtue is properly a characteristic of God's being, who as the source of all things living is kindly disposed toward them. Even more to the point, only God is uniquely qualified to love being in general, as the only supreme and infinite Being.[55]

While *The Nature of True Virtue* depicts virtue as singular, a broader investigation of Edwardsean virtue reveals a breadth of virtues. This is particularly evident in Edwards's Christology, where Edwards moves beyond a standard doctrine of atonement that focuses on Christ's sacrifice on the cross to include Christ's virtuous acts in his work of redemption. Christ dies to satisfy the penalty for our sinfulness; he goes one step further in securing our salvation through the merit of his virtue.[56] He also serves as exemplar for us. His human life displays for us the contours of the Christian life of virtue in a way that is much more comprehensible than exposure to God's overwhelming glory. Christians see in Christ glimpses of what they could be, and thus their desire for salvation is spurred on by his life.

Aesthetic considerations also come into play in the pursuit of virtue. Edwards's *Religious Affections* highlights the importance of motivation for drawing individuals into what he refers to as "true religion." The essence of true religion is love, which can be seen by looking at the two greatest commandments, to love God and to love neighbor.[57] The passion required to love with all of one's heart, soul, and mind does not come from purely rational argumentation. Instead, Edwards contends, it must be the result of an aesthetic experience of God. One is so moved by the sacrifice that Christ makes on the cross that one is drawn to love God completely. Edwards writes,

> If the great things of religion are rightly understood, they will affect the heart. The reason why men are not affected by such infinitely great, important, glorious, and wonderful things, as they often hear and read of, in the Word of God, is undoubtedly because they are blind; if they were not so, it would be impossible, and utterly inconsistent with human nature, that their hearts should be otherwise, than strongly impressed, and greatly moved by such things.[58]

The analogy to blindness is not accidental. Grasping the beauty of God is akin to grasping the beauty of Niagara Falls. It does not require the kind of studied appreciation that, say, leads one to admire the work of abstract expressionists such as Jackson Pollock. Unless one is blind, when one stands at the edge of the falls, one is automatically overwhelmed by their tremendous power and beauty.

Such love is measured not necessarily by the strength of one's outward display of affections but rather by the habitual nature of such love. Edwards notes,

> The degree of religion is rather to be judged of by the fixedness and strength of the habit that is exercised in affection, whereby holy affection is habitual, than by the degree of the present exercise: and the strength of that habit is not always in proportion to outward effects and manifestations, or indeed inward effects, in the hurry and vehemence, and sudden changes of the course of the thoughts of the mind.[59]

Edwards's emphasis on habit in the Christian life is important for an account of Reformed moral virtue ethics, yet it is hard to reconcile with Reformed understandings of *sola fide* and *sola gratia* in distinction from those of Roman Catholicism. Just as the sixteenth-century Reformers emphasized the sovereignty of God in their understanding of justification by faith alone, they also emphasized that sovereignty in their descriptions of regeneration, or sanctification. According to these thinkers, the efficacy of our sanctification as well as our justification depends on God alone. But if this is true, then it is not clear how virtue rests in us rather than in God. Roman Catholic notions of cooperative grace avoided this issue but raised anxieties about semi-Pelagianism. As seen earlier, Calvin resorts to an organic metaphor to avoid these problematic conceptions of cooperation while also maintaining the integrity of human acts. Yet that metaphor is itself problematic because it reduces the relationship between God and us to a nutritive level. A proper Chalcedonian understanding of that relationship requires redefining the relationship to engage human faculties at every level, just as the human and divine natures meet in the one person of Christ. What is Edwards's solution to the problem?

Elizabeth Cochran addresses the issue in *Receptive Human Virtues* by distinguishing between Edwardsean and Aristotelian accounts of virtue. She notes, "Whereas Aristotelian [moral] virtues are excellences proper to human nature, Edwardsean true virtue is an excellence most proper to God."[60] Second, for Aristotle repeated practice leads to habit formation. For Edwards, in contrast, while virtue is exhibited as a settled disposition, that disposition is not formed through repeated practice but is a gift of the Holy Spirit.[61] Such differences highlight the sovereignty of God and the primacy of grace in the acquisition of virtue, drawing Edwards's account closer to Reformed commitments.

It is, however, these very commitments that complicate the role of human agency in the acquisition and growth of virtue. Edwards asserts that God is not only the primary cause of our initial reception of grace but also the primary cause of our continuance in virtue. Our role in virtue is secondary and receptive, thus the title of Cochran's book. What is surprising is that this receptivity is active in the sense that our love becomes conjoined to God's love. Our will is moved by God's love so that we willingly choose to do that which is virtuous. The virtuous act represented to us is now viewed as a good worth pursuing. Therefore, our participation in virtue is active, not passive. Our conversion leaves us with a spiritual sense and divine taste. We see things from God's view and thus approve of them accordingly.[62]

A comparison with Thomas Aquinas's conception of grace is instructive. For Thomas human nature must be open to grace, or the effects of grace would destroy human nature. In that respect the two thinkers are agreed. However, where Edwards emphasizes human receptivity, Thomas uses a stronger term: *cooperation*. Cooperation could consist solely in one partner's listening and obeying another partner's requests, or it could consist in a much more active, leading role. Thomas means by cooperation the movement of the will away from sin and toward God.[63] This movement is effected not by changing human nature but by restoring order to already existing human faculties. Edwards also describes this double movement but is more chastened in his views of how extensive such transformation really is in practice. There is less at stake here for Edwards than there is for Thomas. Since Edwards distinguishes between justification and sanctification, and since his account of the virtues depends on sanctification, it is not necessary that it be complete in this life. Thomas, writing in an earlier time, does not have this conceptual distinction to draw from. Justification must be effective, or our salvation is in peril. Our wills must be directed toward God and away from sin. Should we fall into mortal sin, only repentance and restoration through the offices of the church will save us. For Edwards, in contrast, our salvation does not depend on our moral virtue but solely on Christ's redemptive work.

Another area of distinction between the two is that Edwards claims, unlike Thomas, that grace creates in us a new spiritual sense that wasn't present in even an incipient form previously. Edwards writes,

> The Spirit of God is given to the true saints to dwell in them, as his proper lasting abode; and to influence their hearts, as a principle of new nature, or as a divine supernatural spring of life and action. The Scriptures represent the Holy Spirit, not only as moving, and occasionally influencing the saints, but as dwelling in them as his temple, his proper abode, and everlasting dwelling place (1 Cor. 3:16; 2 Cor. 6:16; John 14:16–17). And he is represented as being there so united to the faculties of the soul, that he becomes there a principle or spring of new nature and life.[64]

This passage from *Religious Affections* distinguishes the work of the Holy Spirit in the true saints from that of other human beings. While the Holy Spirit influences all people, in some that influence is temporary, and in others it is permanent. When saints are converted, it is not that the Holy Spirit is at work in them for the first time but rather that for the first time the Holy Spirit establishes an active principle within them. God's Spirit acts like a spring, continuously nourishing the human soul and disclosing to it God's beauty. Such nourishment is transformative.[65] Edwards's metaphor of a spring bears striking resemblance to Calvin's image of the grafted wild olive. Importantly, though, Edwards adds an aesthetic dimension to his example. Our minds are captured by God's beauty and thus moved toward love. Calvin's image stops at nourishment whereas Edwards's example comes closer to a Chalcedonian description of divine and human life together.

Edwards contrasts the work of the Holy Spirit in the saints with those who are not. He writes,

> From these things it is evident, that those gracious influences which the saints are subjects of, and the effects of God's Spirit which they experience, are entirely above nature, altogether of a different kind from anything that men find within themselves by nature, or only in the exercise of natural principles; and are things which no improvement of those qualifications, or principles that are natural, no advancing or exalting them to higher degrees, and no kind of composition of them, will ever bring men to; because they not only differ from what is natural, and from everything that natural men experience, in degree and circumstances; but also in kind; and are of a nature vastly more excellent. And this is what I mean by supernatural, when I say, that gracious affections are from those influences that are supernatural.
>
> From hence it follows, that in those gracious exercises and affections which are wrought in the minds of the saints, through the saving influ-

ences of the Spirit of God, there is a new inward perception or sensation of their minds, entirely different in its nature and kind, from anything that ever their minds were the subjects of before they were sanctified.[66]

Scholars of Edwards are divided as to whether this new sensation constitutes a sixth sense or if it is a new source of inspiration that wells up within us from the Holy Spirit.[67] Is human nature added onto, or does the presence of the Holy Spirit put us in touch with spiritual matters through our existing five senses, imagination, and understanding? In either case, the sharp distinction between those who receive saving grace and those who do not is startling. It raises questions about the possibility of pagan virtue in Edwards's ethics, which requires another look at *The Nature of True Virtue*.

Edwards actually attributes to non-Christians a rather robust common morality on which pagan virtue may rest. Ethicist Paul Ramsey identifies four sources of this common morality in his introduction to this treatise: (1) our sense of the secondary beauty in moral dispositions and relations, (2) self-love extended by association of ideas, (3) natural conscience, and (4) instinctual affections such as pity and familial affection.[68] While God's primary beauty must be revealed to us in order for us to recognize it, everyone has access to a second level of beauty found in moral behavior. Ramsey links this to Edwards's doctrine of creation. God has so established in creation a moral sense in human beings that they delight in its use.[69] Regarding self-love, Edwards notes that our tendency to self-love may be trained to extend beyond ourselves to others around us. Edwards sees in self-love an opportunity. Because we have to work with others in order to satisfy our self-interests, we learn by necessity how to recognize the self-interests of others and in that recognition possess the potential to move beyond our own self-centered perspective.[70] Regarding conscience, Edwards defines it as "a disposition in man to be uneasy in a consciousness of being inconsistent with himself and, as it were, against himself in his own actions."[71] Ramsey reflects that Edwardsean conscience differs from Francis Hutcheson's "moral sense" because it constitutes a relationship between oneself and one's consciousness that suffers when disagreement occurs. As Ramsey describes it, "It is golden rule morality writ small in the self's consciousness *to* self."[72] Finally, Edwards recognizes the special bonds of love that exist in familial relationships and in feelings of pity for those who suffer.

From this description of common morality, one may derive an account of imperfect pagan virtue in Edwards. Its content may be sketched from four moral virtues: courage, justice, temperance, and practical wisdom. Familial affection may lead us into courage in defense of our own communities; the extension of self-love may lead to just dealings with others;

our natural conscience may lead us into temperance; and our appreciation for moral beauty may inspire practical wisdom in us. Such expressions are, of course, not of the same quality as found in true virtue, which leaves out self-concern, yet they are remarkably close in their expression. They constitute, to borrow a phrase from Paul Ramsey, "a rather splendid thing."[73]

But is such an account closer to Thomas Aquinas's, for whom civic virtue is a distinct reality, or is it closer to Augustine's, who considers pagan virtue a "glittering vice"? Aquinas, like Edwards, recognizes a common morality that remains after the fall. When considering the question "Can man will and do good without grace?" Aquinas examines two contradictory answers: (1) Aristotle's claim that the intellect's good is truth and the intellect can know truth by itself, and (2) Augustine's claim that "without grace, men do no good whatsoever, either by thinking, or by willing and loving, or by acting."[74] Aquinas's position is a modification of both these proposals. Closer to Aristotle, Aquinas affirms that sin has not completely destroyed our ability to act to the benefit of our nature. For example, we still have the capacity to build houses, cultivate the land, and so on. But contra Aristotle, human beings cannot know the truth without divine assistance. Even more confounding, the effects of sin are even stronger in terms of corrupting our desires for the good.[75] However, Aquinas's position does not agree with Augustine's either since he recognizes the possibility of true but imperfect virtue, a position that Augustine denies.[76] In this respect, Edwards's view of pagan virtue is closer to Augustine's, and for the same reasons. While such virtue has the semblance of true virtue from the outside, it is riddled with sinful pride. Thus both Augustine and Edwards are agreed that such virtue is not merely imperfect but altogether false.

Thomas's views on pagan virtue also reflect a sharper distinction between the operations of the will and intellect than that found in Edwards. Some modern interpretations of the will conceive of it as a well-greased wheel that moves in a variety of directions based on the movement of some external force (e.g., reason). In Thomas's conception the will is more like the wheels on an ornery grocery cart that have a bent or inclination all their own. The will, he says, has an appetite for goodness. Rightly ordered, it hungers for the beatific vision.[77] However, determinations regarding the good are not the province of the will but of the intellect. The function of the intellect is to present to the will those objects or actions considered to be good within a particular context. The function of the will is to will these goods since they are presented as goods for which the will hungers. The will is thus "a moved mover."[78] According to Thomas, after original sin the will is ruled more and more by the passions, which resist the rule of reason in the intellect.

In Edwards's account, the affections themselves have an intellectual dimension. A dynamic relationship exists between the affections and the other faculty of the soul, the understanding. These affections are both swayed by and sway the understanding. Without understanding, it is impossible for the affections to be aroused. On the other hand, the understanding grasps truths through experiences that inevitably contain an affective dimension.[79] Edwards thus sees the religious affections, rather than the intellect, as the sole key to the Christian life. It is through these affections that God's beauty is both ascertained and desired. Such affections may only be aroused by God's revelation, making true pagan virtue, and by extension true civic virtue, impossible.

Mention has already been made of the role Edwards ascribes to the Holy Spirit in instilling a new spiritual sense in the Christian believer. An account of his Reformed moral virtue ethic would not be complete without addressing the following question: Was Jonathan Edwards too optimistic about these spiritual effects of regeneration in Christians? The question is important to consider, for it relates directly to Edwards's expectation that moral virtue is the result of spiritual regeneration.

Near the end of his tenure in Northampton, Edwards changed a long-standing policy regarding church membership. A century earlier, it was the custom among New England Puritans to examine prospective members, who would come before a church council, state their faith, and submit to examination. Only those who did so were eligible to have their infant children baptized. When fewer and fewer prospective members came forward, the practice was reconsidered. In 1662, New England pastors signed a halfway covenant that granted baptized members who had not sought full membership greater standing. These individuals were still not considered full members of the church—they had no voting rights, for example—but they were allowed to have their children baptized.[80] In Northampton, Jonathan Edwards's grandfather, Solomon Stoddard, went even further. He allowed all baptized members full membership so long as they exemplified certain minimal moral standards as determined by the leaders of the church.[81] This policy was well received in Northampton and stood for over forty years until Edwards challenged it in the 1740s.

Initially, when Edwards took over pastoral responsibilities for the church in Northampton, he continued to abide by the policies established by Stoddard. Eventually, though, Edwards pushed to reintroduce the old Puritan practice of examination before the church council. His motivation for doing so was the result of a shift he perceived in the seriousness of his parishioners toward their faith. He felt the enthusiasm caused by the Great Awakening had died down. One indication of this letdown involved a controversy in which Edwards found a group of young men in their twenties who after examining a medical manual started heckling young female parishioners about their anatomy. His attempts to discipline them were seen as heavy-handed, particularly since some of the young men were from prominent families in the congregation. He, on the other hand, felt the congregation's moral laxity in this matter disconcerting. Thus, when Edwards moved to deny baptism to the children of those who were not full members, he met with stiff resistance. As a result of this and other related controversies, Edwards was asked to leave the church, a huge blow for such a publicly revered figure.

It is difficult to judge fairly Edwards's actions from a twenty-first-century perspective, far removed from eighteenth-century Puritanism. Yet if we are to embrace his understanding of the religious affections as expressed through moral virtue, we need to be aware also of the attendant dangers of such an understanding. Edwards's emphasis on settled dispositions of character in the Christian life places a substantial burden on human communities to discern the work of the Spirit within particular congregants. Is such a discernment process possible, and even if it is, is it in the best interests of the church to pursue? One can easily see how, even in a willing congregation, the process would devolve from earnest discernment into a form of legalism. Edwards required that congregants not only produce statements of faith but also demonstrate the process by which they came to faith and the evidence for the transformation of their character. Under such a system congregants would no doubt feel pressure to tailor their accounts to reflect the predilections of the church council rather than their own sincere beliefs.

Very few Reformed churches would embrace the requirement that moral virtue be a condition for full church membership. The membership rolls would dwindle quickly! In this decision Edwards showed a lack of pastoral wisdom as well as impatience with his congregation. Thus, Edwards's final years at Northampton stand as a cautionary tale in regard to misplaced expectations for spiritual regeneration. The Reformed view of moral virtue must always keep in mind the hampering effect of sin in regard to progress in the Christian life, for the effect that sin has on both congregants and their leaders.

REFORMED VIRTUE AFTER BARTH

Whether or not one agrees with Karl Barth's theology, it is difficult to argue that it has not had a profound effect on the course of twentieth-century theology, both Protestant and Roman Catholic. Barth's commentary on Romans, first published in 1919, created a huge theological stir in Germany, the focal point of world history over the preceding five years. His critique of Protestant liberalism, which had fueled German nationalism in the lead-up to World War I, proved just as apt in the years that followed. As translation of his work reached the United States, it helped spawn a theological movement known as neo-orthodoxy, which had profound effects on American Protestantism at a time when mainline Protestantism had deep cultural influence.

Barth's trenchant criticism of Christianity's domestication of God is just as relevant in today's era of declining church membership as it was almost one hundred years ago. In the context of the church's struggle to be more culturally relevant, his words of warning serve as a reminder that the church's primary task is to witness to the God made known in Jesus Christ. In this task the church has a powerful ally, the Holy Spirit. And, in any event, God's plan of salvation does not depend on the church's success in recruiting new members. That work has already been accomplished in Jesus Christ. Barth's words remind the church that it has one Lord who is ruler over all history. This fact frees the church to joyful witness rather than anxious surrender to other powers.

Barth's reflections on God's transcendence echo the thoughts of Reformers past, yet they also challenge some of their presumptions. Barth spent decades and wrote thousands of pages for the sole purpose of redescribing God's dealings with humankind. Over the last three decades American scholars have begun to appreciate in an even deeper way the ethical implications of Barth's theology. What at first appears to be a condemnation of human arrogance turns out after in-depth study to be a profound reflection on the integrity of human action in the context of God's self-initiating love.

What light do Barth's reflections shed on the three accounts of Reformed moral virtue delineated in this chapter? First, Barth's understanding of the Chalcedonian relationship between the divine and human natures of Christ has something important to say about God's dealings with all of humankind. Where Calvin and Edwards express those dealings, they often employ images from nature, such as the Pauline image of engrafting or the Neoplatonic image of light illuminating the soul. They do so for various reasons. Calvin, in order to distinguish his own position on the Lord's Supper from Zwingli's, indicates that our union with Christ is substantial, not merely commemorative.[82] Edwards uses images from nature both as a typology of God's grace as well as an explanation for why God brought creation into being.[83] Barth, on the other hand, is relentlessly christological. His approach also serves a rhetorical purpose. Barth wishes to train his audiences away from understanding God through nature and point them instead to the Word of God as the sole source of revelation. Christ, as that Word of God and as the one attested to in Scripture, is ultimately the source of all there is to know about God.

Barth's christological approach does not negate the moral virtue ethics of Calvin and Edwards, but it does require a redescription of it, and with good reason. If taken in isolation, the use of natural metaphors to describe God's dealings with us, for example, will leave out important dimensions of human and divine relatedness. Calvin's plant analogy fails to explain how God's regenerative work in us engages our higher faculties of willing and knowing. Natural metaphors also fail to do justice to God's reason and intention. Light illuminates, but it has no intelligence; it is not responsive to its environment and shines unaware of its effects on surrounding objects.

In contrast, Christ presents a concrete example of God's relationship with a particular human being. When Christ displays the virtues, he reveals how human nature remains human at the same time as he reveals what obedience to God's will looks like. Calvin and Edwards are, of course, christocentric thinkers. To Edwards's credit, his doctrine of the atonement spells out the ways that Christ's virtue is central to an understanding of the Christian life, but if one takes Edwards's work as a whole, Barth's relentless focus on Christ challenges the central role that Edwards's doctrine of creation plays. It raises the following questions: To what extent does that doctrine shape Edwards's Christology, and to what extent does his Christology shape his views on creation? In Barth's work, the answer to those questions is clear.

All three examples of moral virtue ethics examined in this chapter presuppose that at least some human beings will reject Christ's work of atonement and suffer the consequences of eternal damnation. Barth's theology challenges that assumption. While Barth is careful to assert God's sovereignty regarding God's choice to elect or damn sinners, his characterization of God as the electing God points in the direction of universal salvation. Barth's thinking about the humanity of God has profound implications. God chooses from eternity to be not only for human beings but to become human (and remain human beyond his earthly existence)! How can Barth maintain the integrity of human willing and suggest at the same time that all human beings may come to worship the God they naturally rebel against? He does so by indicating that God's infinite patience will outlast human resistance. God does not coerce us to worship but waits in eager anticipation for the turning of our hearts.

The implications for pagan virtue are profound. Calvin, Westminster, and Edwards all agree that true virtue is impossible in the unregenerate. Barth's doctrine of election points to an eschatological reality in which all will become virtuous! Barth's detractors point to his rejection of natural theology as an indication that Barth has no account of common morality. Yet in doing so they neglect to consider how Barth's doctrine of revelation is framed by his doctrine of election. The latter indicates that God is actively at work in the life of every individual to reveal Godself to her or him. The reason Barth rejects natural theology is not that it fails to reveal something about God; rather, Barth realizes that the god revealed through nature is a mere idol next to the real, transcendent God. Yet the God made known in Jesus Christ does not leave us in the dark. Instead, we are relentlessly pursued by God until our vicious wills turn and accept God's gracious offer in faith. Barth's doctrine of revelation thus does not negate the possibility of Reformed moral virtue ethics; instead, it establishes a new basis for such ethics in God's revelation to us rather than in our natural capacities to ascertain and will the good.

Finally, Barth's theology challenges the Constantinianism resident in the thought of Calvin, Westminster, and Edwards. While all three recognize the dangers of the state to intervene in the affairs of the church, they all also presume church-state relations in which the church is the dominant force in society. This context simply does not exist today. Certain events in the church's history also demonstrate that such an arrangement often brings out the worst in the church where it does occur, as evidenced by the role the Dutch Reformed Church in South Africa played in perpetuating the racial injustices of apartheid. Barth was keenly aware of the dangers of church-state collaboration, and he challenged the church to think in a post-Constantinian manner about its ordained role in the world. He also sought, like the earlier Reformers, to transform the world for Christ.

Barth's ecclesiology has important implications for the expression of Reformed moral virtue ethics in today's churches. Unlike Westminster, which attempted to employ the power of the state to impose Sabbath-day restrictions on the general populace, Barth's view of the church's role as witness is much more humble. Barth nonetheless depicts Christ at the center of the state's area of influence. The church's role is simply to point out the place of Christ, not to coerce all to recognize that place. Barth's ecclesiology also challenges the ways in which Calvin and Edwards sought to impose moral and spiritual requirements on the citizens of their societies through the offices of the church. The power of the Word of God comes not from the authority of the pastor who preaches it but from the Holy Spirit who brings that word to life in those who hear it. Communities of virtue have to arise from the bottom up rather than top down. Congregants, inspired by the fruits of the Spirit, ought themselves seek to initiate these communities through a living out of the narrative that has come to have central importance in their lives.

Thus, Barth's theology has the potential to make powerful contributions to Reformed moral virtue ethics in today's churches. It provides an exhaustive explanation of how God engages human beings through a sustained reflection on Christ as the meeting place of that engagement. It delineates an account of revelation that does not negate common morality but rather reorients us as to the proper source of that morality. It offers an expansive doctrine of election that points to the eschatological regeneration of all people. And it provides a post-Constantinian ecclesiology that recognizes the changing role of the church from cultural hegemon to countercultural witness. Describing the kind of virtue ethics that emerges from Barth's thought is the main work of this book. But first, we must turn to Barth's objections to the theology that determined moral virtue ethics before Barth.

2

BARTH'S OBJECTIONS

"Is it possible to have virtue ethics in Barth's theology?" The question was posed at the joint Thomas Aquinas–Karl Barth conference, cohosted by the Thomas Aquinas Institute and the Karl Barth Society in the summer of 2011. The presenter, John Bowlin, deflected the question to me. Even though I had just the previous year finished a dissertation on this very topic, I did not have a quick answer. Perhaps due to an undiagnosed case of postdissertation stress disorder, I had forgotten the elevator-ride version of my thesis. Rather than risk a long and rambling answer that would detract from the presenter, I gave a brief, cryptic answer that could have been boiled down to this: "Yes, but . . ." Yes, it is possible to have virtue ethics that conform to Barth's theology, but such ethics has to meet some steep obstacles. In fact, the answer appears at first glance to be "No," given that Barth has significant reservations about the theological assumptions behind the standard Aristotelian/Thomistic accounts of virtue ethics.

Not only do these reservations run deep, but they also follow from his commitment to the Reformed tradition's emphasis on God's sovereignty, human sinfulness, and the christocentric nature of justifying grace. Trying to circumvent these reservations by appeal to other parts of the tradition, then, will not do. Instead, these concerns must be faced head on. This is the task of the current chapter. Barth's theological reservations provide a strong test for the suitability of virtue ethics in the Reformed tradition. If one is able to address these reservations directly, then a well-built case may be made for accepting virtue ethics into the tradition. If they cannot, then one needs to call into question versions of virtue ethics that already circulate in Reformed circles.

The features of Barth's work highlighted here are by no means exhaustive, but each reveals important ways in which his theology challenges, for Reformed reasons, the framework within which virtue ethics has traditionally operated. These features are as follows: his christocentric anthropology, his rejection of the *analogia entis*, and his rejection of habitual grace. The first feature provides the framework by which the other two are understood. His rejection of the idea that there is an innate human capacity for relationship with God (the *analogia entis*, or analogy of being) would lead to hopelessness if it were not for God's initiative in Christ to be God for us. God initiates contact despite our inability to understand who God is or to initiate a relationship from our side. Similarly, Barth's rejection of habitual grace is based on an understanding of the relationship between the human and divine natures of Jesus Christ. The human nature of Christ does not experience grace habitually, as if it had control over the divine nature of Christ. Rather, that human nature receives grace freely from God. The relationship between the human and divine natures of Christ sets the pattern for how we experience grace. If we possessed grace as a habit within us, then we would also have some control over how God dispenses grace, according to Barth. This conclusion follows directly from his observations about the way grace functions in Christ's human nature.

KARL BARTH'S CHRISTOCENTRIC ANTHROPOLOGY

Karl Barth claims that the defining features of our relationship with God through Jesus Christ are also the determinative characteristics of what makes us human beings. Thus his anthropology is christocentric in the sense that any true description of what makes human beings human must have Christ at the center. Human beings derive their identity exclusively through their relationship with God in Jesus Christ. Whether we know it or not, we are beings in relation to God, a relationship that is most fully expressed in the relationship between God and human in Jesus Christ. This christocentric anthropology, and in general the emphasis on God's side of the God-human relationship in Barth's theology, has been criticized by some and ignored by others because of a perceived deficiency in Barth's account of human agency and a lack of attention to ethical concerns.[1] If these charges are true, and if such deficiencies in Barth are symptomatic of Reformed thought in general, then they represent an enormous hurdle for the development of Reformed moral virtue ethics.

Deficiencies in Barth's Christocentric Anthropology?

This section will show that the charges that Barth's christocentric anthropology is deficient are not true. To see that this is the case, the historical reasons behind Barth's early decision to reject an anthropological starting point for his theology will be investigated. While this change in Barth's theology during and immediately after World War I temporarily shifted his attention away from human agency in favor of God's sovereignty, a study of Barth's mature anthropology reveals that human agency is central to his conception of the relationship between God and humankind. Thus, throughout his life Barth continued to have a deep concern and appreciation for the freedom of human agents.

Sheila Davaney's concerns serve as a good measure of the misgivings scholars have regarding Barth's anthropology. She argues that throughout his *Church Dogmatics* Barth's account of divine and human interaction fails to provide a place for human responsibility and integrity. Moreover, Davaney concludes that this failure is not a mere oversight or underdeveloped aspect of Barth's theology but is rooted instead in fundamental presuppositions that Barth held. Davaney writes,

> In the last analysis a conception of relationship which is built on the premise that one of the participants is a self-completed, totally self-sufficient being and the possessor of all-determining power will inevitably raise questions concerning the status of the other participants. It will always prove difficult if not impossible, to move from a notion of self-sufficient, self-completed, self-positing being to that of creative and fulfilling relationship in which the integrity of all participants is safeguarded.[2]

Barth's turn to theocentrism and his description of God as complete in Godself led him into a corner from which it became difficult if not impossible to extricate human freedom and responsibility. So argues Davaney.

If Davaney is correct, then Barth's position raises an insurmountable hurdle for a virtue ethic. Without human freedom and responsibility, such an ethic, or any ethic, would be jeopardized. In addition, the implications of Davaney's criticisms would also ripple over to the work of many Reformed thinkers who also emphasize God's sovereignty. It turns out that Davaney's critique is only partially correct, and it is relevant only if we examine Barth's early work in isolation. If we analyze Barth's initial rejection of an anthropological starting point for his theology, we find that he deemphasizes human action in order to turn his concentration toward God's activity. Because Barth is so critical of the prevailing anthropocentric method of doing theology, he has a tendency to reduce the human response to God's commands to a whisper.

However, three points must be made here in Barth's defense. First, when looking at what Barth wrote toward the end of World War I and shortly afterward, we must consider carefully the historical context. Barth's concerns about the hubris of human knowing are well-founded considering the devastation that war caused and the complicity of German theologians in supporting that war. Second, by emphasizing the thundering presence of God, Barth is by no means removing or reducing human agency. Here the meteorological metaphor breaks down. In a violent thunderstorm we are reminded of how powerless we really are in the face of powerful acts of nature. Barth, too, would affirm that human beings cannot stand up to the power of God if God so chooses to use God's power against us. But Barth also affirms that God does not use God's power in this way. God's power is constrained by God's love. And that brings us to the third point, which is that Barth's christocentrism, developed over many years, demonstrates that the fullness of human agency is found in Jesus Christ, whose relationship with God is perfect yet whose human agency is not overpowered but instead fully realized.

Barth's recognition of the problematic theology and ethics of his mentors is vividly portrayed in his recollection of the events leading up to World War I:

> One day in early August 1914 stands out in my personal memory as a black day. Ninety-three German intellectuals impressed public opinion by their proclamation in support of the war policy of Wilhelm II and his counselors. Among these intellectuals I discovered to my horror almost all of my theological teachers whom I had greatly venerated. In despair over what this indicated about the signs of the time I suddenly realized that I could not any longer follow either their ethics and dogmatics or their understanding of the Bible and of history. For me at least, 19th-century theology no longer held any future.[3]

The theology that Barth came to reject was individualistic and idealistic.[4] Both these dimensions are evident in the work of Wilhelm Herrmann, who was a formative influence on Barth during Barth's student years at Marburg. Herrmann and his colleagues were embroiled in a dispute about how an individual can come to know anything about God's existence and action in the world. The question held particular attraction due to the idealism of Kant, whose *Critique of Pure Reason* placed the noumenal realm outside the scope of scientific investigation. This meant that whatever access we have to the events of history, we cannot glean from these phenomena any conclusions about whether or not God exists or is involved in any way in history.[5]

Herrmann argued that we do have such knowledge, but it is miraculous and not derivable by scientific observation. However, because Herrmann was also committed to God's action in human history, he had to account for that action while at the same time arguing that it was not perceivable to the senses. He did so by distinguishing between historical facts and natural facts. He took natural facts to be processes that are perceivable by the senses. History, according to Herrmann, was different from natural facts because it included a spiritual reality that has the capability to make history but cannot be gleaned from the natural facts of history.[6] Such a view of history meant that God can act in the world and that knowledge of such action is made possible by God's Spirit even though it is not detectable through our senses like natural facts are.

Herrmann's position had important implications for his Christology. Our faith in God is grounded in the historical Jesus. However, what

Herrmann means by this historical Jesus is not the one that is open to the kind of historical-critical research then making its way in Germany but the inner life of that Jesus. According to Herrmann, the decisive moment for Christian believers is not captured in the historical crucifixion, death, and resurrection of Jesus Christ. Rather it is the moment in which God's Spirit touches an individual believer so that Christ becomes real to them. This account neglects the objective significance of Christ's life, death, and resurrection apart from our perception of these events. It also minimizes the relevance of the church's collective witness to those events. It is idealistic because it is based on an idea of who God is rather than on a concrete narrative such as that found in the Bible. As Bruce McCormack writes, "He posited God as the answer to the existential and ethical problem of how one can be truthful while believing in the existence of one's self. The effect of this move was to reduce 'God' to an Idea, postulated in order to account for a particular human experience."[7]

It is important to note that Barth's move away from his predecessors' thought was influenced by Reformed as well as political concerns. Barth's turn from Herrmannian individualism began after he accepted a call to be a pastor in Safenwil. It took the form of an embrace of socialism that was inspired in part by Calvin's understanding of the kingdom of God as well as by his reading of Werner Sombarth's book *Sozialismus Bewegung*. He was motivated by the fact that for Calvin the kingdom of God was not solely an eschatological reality but also an ever-present one in this life.[8]

Another significant development in Barth's thought took place in 1915 after a meeting with Christoph Blumhardt. A year after this meeting Barth wrote in admiration,

> Blumhardt always begins right away with God's presence, might, and purpose: he starts out from God; he does not begin by climbing upwards to him by means of contemplation and deliberation. God is the end, and because we already know Him as the beginning, we may await His consummating acts.[9]

McCormack notes that shortly after his meeting with Blumhardt, Barth had a new theological starting point. Barth's focus was no longer on the kingdom of God but on Jesus Christ, who challenges and calls into question all human endeavors. This was to have decisive consequences for Barth's ethics. As McCormack observes, "The central question of ethics, 'What should we do?'—had become exceedingly problematic, as Barth now saw all human ethical striving as law, that is, as constructed on the grounds of the old world that is passing away."[10] This new starting point marked a clear and decisive break from the liberalism that shaped Barth's thought during his student days. No longer was Barth thinking in idealistic terms about the problem of the knowledge of God. The problem was now turned on its head so that it was human action and knowing that were suspect while God's presence and action proved to be the reliable anchors.

Ironically, Barth's turn to theocentrism was thus provoked by a deep concern for ethics and human agency. We see this in the fact that it was Barth's involvement in socialism, motivated by his concern for the material well-being of others, that began the changes in his theology. And it was partly due to his frustration with the political activities of the socialists that led him to reject a political theology that was so tied to human agency.

Barth's visit with Blumhardt took place at a time when he was struggling to choose between two leaders in the religious socialist movement: Herrmann Kutter and Leonhard Ragaz. While Kutter doubted that any political movement could be Christianized, Ragaz was more optimistic. At the heart of their quarrel was a disagreement about whether or not the religious socialist movement could with confidence claim to be advancing the kingdom of God. Ragaz claimed that it could, but Kutter demurred. During Barth's early involvement with the movement he was more inclined to follow Ragaz.[11] However, struggles within the movement left him doubting. Sometime shortly after his meeting with Christoph Blumhardt he sided with Kutter's view that no one political movement could be directly associated with the advance of the kingdom of God; this political decision was precipitated by a more theocentric shift in his theology.[12] Barth became convinced that to do theology correctly one needed to center one's inquiry into who God is on God's own self-revelation rather than on the human subject's experience of that revelation.

But was Barth's correction actually an overcorrection? Is it possible that in seeing the obvious theological errors in his peers, he reacted too strongly and thus undervalued the contribution human beings make to divine-human history? Davaney does appear to have a point when we consider what Barth writes in his commentary on Romans: "The history of the church is a secular history written under the title, 'How the ring was—lost.'"[13] Does not the church participate at some level with God in the writing of history? Do its members only fall short of God's will, or do they perhaps also in their faithfulness reflect the reign of God on earth as in heaven?

Davaney's critique turns on a misrepresentation of God's omnipotence as well as a misrepresentation of human agency in Barth's account. It is true that Barth's formulation of the divine-human relationship reflects commitments to the sovereignty of God and the devastating effects of sin typical of the Reformed tradition. In addition, Barth's objective soteriology ensures that salvation is purely the work of God in Jesus Christ rather than a shared work. However, Barth's christocentric anthropology, as expressed throughout *Church Dogmatics*, is a tale of God's humbling as much as it is a tale of God's sovereignty.

Interestingly, Barth accepts with qualifications Thomas's formulation that "grace does not destroy but perfects nature."[14] At one point in his *Church Dogmatics* Barth embraces the axiom but turns the original meaning on its head. For Thomas, the axiom affirms human receptivity to grace. For Barth, it affirms God's willingness to participate in the wretchedness of humanity after the fall. Barth writes,

> What our God has created he will also uphold, and sooner or later control by His grace. He will control it—but not in such a way that grace means the catastrophic destruction of nature. It means radical judgment upon nature. It means its radical transformation and renewal. But it does not mean its violent end.
>
> In this sense we must admit the truth of that maxim of Thomas Aquinas which is so often put to dangerous use and in the first instance was no doubt dangerously meant: *gratia non tollit (non-destruit) sed (praesupponit et) perficit naturam.* God deals with His creature in such a way as to share his wretchedness. This is the meaning of His mercy. In this way it is more powerful than if it had to kill and slay in order to arrive at its goal. It is so powerful that it can wait, allowing us to continue.[15]

Barth asserts that God's grace is defined as much by God's condescension—by God's becoming human and suffering death on the cross—as by the triumph of the resurrection.[16] God's grace is thus completely bound to the person of Christ. It is in Christ, in Christ's work inseparable from Christ's person, that grace comes to us. That invitation is the keystone to the relationship between God and us. It comes hand delivered, with much cost to the carrier. God's invitation is thus not a summons to imprisonment but a call to responsibility.

Human agency is in fact a critical part of Barth's theological program. The logic of the covenantal relationship between God and human beings demands that human beings be real partners, not simply actors reciting lines given to them by the divine playwright. Barth's divine command ethics is a summons to responsibility that stretches us beyond our comfort zone because it requires us to reexamine our presuppositions about who God is. Just as Jesus confronted the Pharisees regarding their too-rigid understanding of the Sabbath, God calls us to follow the living Christ, even when that following calls into question widely accepted interpretations of the divine law. At each step in our journeying with God, we are in a constant state of alertness to see what new turns the steadfast love of the Lord has in store for us. Thus God's commands do not stifle our agency but instead call forth our true humanity.

How, then, are we to interpret the requirements that the divine command places on us? Consider the argument made in John Webster's landmark book *Barth's Ethics of Reconciliation*. Webster's thesis is that Barth does have a coherent account of human agency, but that account can only be understood within the overall framework of Barth's thinking. That framework highlights a theological description of the God-human relation. Webster notes that in Barth's understanding of human agency we can only act within the limits that God has placed on us. But these limits are not barriers so much as they are "the form within which and as which the human moral agent may exist, and outside which it is not meaningful to speak of good human contact at all."[17]

The key to Barth's conception of human agency, Webster argues, is his ethics of reconciliation. This is the ethics found in *CD* IV/4, which Barth never finished. Webster notes that for Barth the basis of reconciliation is God's presence with us. In order for this presence to be a true presence, mutuality between God and human beings must exist. If God's presence obliterated human agency, then God would not truly be with *us*. Webster writes, "'Immanuel' cannot be construed as a statement having God for its exclusive logical subject, for the God who is 'with us' is 'the God who does not work and act without his people.'"[18] As Webster points out here, Barth's covenantal understanding of the relationship between God and us ensures that human agency is real. If it weren't, it would make no sense for God to enter into a covenant with individuals who had no freedom to act. While Barth's emphasis on God's initiating action may appear to threaten our freedom, it instead points to the basis and security of that freedom. It also distinguishes between what we take for freedom and what actually constitutes freedom. Barth writes,

> He has the freedom to be this man who is justified before God, sanctified for him, and called by him. He only has this freedom—everything else called freedom is unfreedom—but he really has it. . . . Whoever he may be, he has it in all circumstances, and in every conceivable condition and situation in which he may find himself. As man he is always and everywhere to be addressed in terms of it. He may and can be this man, and as he makes use of this freedom, he is this man. He does not have this freedom of himself, however; he has it only as God's gift.[19]

Here we see that Barth's theology is very much concerned with the freedom of the human agent. That freedom has a distinctive character since it is linked to our election made known in Christ. Barth affirms, however, that the reality of such freedom does not depend on our awareness of its point of origin. We are free in Christ, whether we know it or not. Such freedom is much more radical in many ways than one that is dependent on our human situation, since the grounds for that kind of freedom are contingent.

Barth's account of human freedom has deep roots in the Reformed tradition. John Calvin has a similar understanding of how human action is circumscribed by God's sovereign plan for creation. Here too is an emphasis on human freedom only in relation to God, with the recognition that within that relationship a true freedom exists. Calvin emphasizes that on our own we remain in bondage to sin. However, by God's grace, and through the justification that is ours thanks to Christ, Christians are free in three respects: we are free from the judgment of the law; we are free to obey God's will; and we are free in "things of themselves indifferent."[20] Each of these freedoms presupposes a comprehensive human agency that responds to God's grace in confidence. In regard to the first two freedoms, Calvin highlights the fact that while we are no longer slaves to the law, as if our justification depended on it, we are now free to willingly obey God's will.[21] Regarding the third, our freedom in "things of themselves indifferent" means that in relation to those things that are not constitutive of the Christian life our conscience is free to act as we see fit. So whether or not we decide to become teetotalers or vegetarians, our conscience is our guide. Like Barth, Calvin's understanding of freedom underscores its relational dimensions: we are free only in relationship to the God who created us and redeemed us.

Implications for Virtue Ethics

Although Davaney's concerns about Barth's account of human agency have some merit if one looks at Barth's work selectively, particularly in the period when *Epistle to the Romans* was written, they fall flat when looking at Barth's subsequent work. Therefore, one hurdle for a Reformed moral virtue ethics has been successfully navigated. It remains to be seen what such an ethic would look like in terms of its material content. But at least conceptually there is room for it within Barth's ethics and within Reformed ethics from the standpoint of anthropology. In the next chapter attention will be given to William Werpehowski's attempts to show how Barth's ethics constitute a virtue ethic. There we will see in more detail what the contours of a Reformed virtue ethic might look like. But before we do, we need to consider two other potential hurdles: Barth's rejection of the *analogia entis* and his rejection of habitual grace. Both of these moves on Barth's part challenge the traditional conception of virtue ethics found in the Roman Catholic tradition. Then, through an investigation of Werpehowski's account, the issue of whether virtue ethics can be reformulated along Reformed lines will be considered.

In his rejection of the analogy of being (*analogia entis*) between Creator and creature, Barth is concerned that at the heart of the Thomistic notion of cooperation is a conception of the *analogia entis* that dangerously minimizes the distinction between the two. Rather than postulating a human nature that is "pure," the *analogia entis* postulates a nature similar to God's, one already touched by grace at its creation. Barth's objective soteriology protects against this kind of conceptual interdependence since the operation of God's grace on humankind does not require some conception of analogy (at the level of being) between God and us.

If Barth is right about the *analogia entis,* then moral virtue ethics is imperiled. Thomas Aquinas and other Christian virtue ethicists affirm that human beings have the capacity for virtue based on the *imago Dei.* However, Barth argues that any access to those capacities has been severed as a consequence of original sin. Instead, God must initiate contact, and only through that contact may we know and do the right thing. For Thomas, grace heals the wounds caused by original sin, and through the restoration of will and mind, grace also enables our capacity to love God. For Barth, it is difficult to see how grace changes us other than by raising our awareness of God's presence. However, as we will see later, it is this very awareness that opens the door for virtue.

KARL BARTH'S REJECTION OF THE *ANALOGIA ENTIS*

Much ink has been spilled in scholarly circles regarding Barth's rejection of natural theology, usually centering around his public disagreement in the 1930s with Emil Brunner when Barth issued his famous "Nein!" to Brunner's suggestion that natural theology has a place in Reformed thought.[22] Their disagreement has thus been taken as an intermural dispute between two prominent, twentieth-century Reformed thinkers. However, Barth's rejection of natural theology took place earlier, in the 1920s, and his dialogue partner was a Roman Catholic thinker. By the time Barth engaged Brunner on the issue he had already made up his mind.

Barth's turn to theocentrism in the first and second editions of his commentary on Romans caused uproar and criticism not only within his own evangelical circle but also from a Roman Catholic scholar, Erich Przywara. The disagreement that resulted from Barth and Przywara's discussions reveals the reasons that Barth rejected natural theology throughout his career. While his disagreement with Przywara has not gotten the press it deserves, two recent Ph.D. dissertations have brought the encounter to light in greater depth. Amy Marga's dissertation, "Partners in the Gospel: Karl Barth and Roman Catholicism, 1922–1932," includes mention of the student protocols for Barth's seminar on Thomas Aquinas at which Przywara appeared. Keith Johnson's dissertation, "*Analogia Entis*: A Reconsideration of the Debate between Karl Barth and Roman Catholicism, 1914–1964," describes the debate in great detail and evaluates Barth's position on the *analogia entis* throughout the rest of his life. The discussion that follows is indebted to both.[23]

This section will support the following theses: (1) Barth rejects Przywara's conception of the *analogia entis* precisely because of the emphasis Przywara places on the continuity between God's being and creaturely being; (2) Przywara's account of such continuity depends on Thomas Aquinas's, thus reflecting an important basis for Roman Catholic virtue ethics for centuries; and (3) Barth's rejection of Przywara's position is fundamentally the result of a central doctrine of the Reformation: justification by grace through faith alone and Luther's corollary that we are *simul iustus et peccator*, simultaneously justified and sinner.

Why are these theses significant in relation to the overall proposal for moral virtue ethics in a Barthian theological framework? Each presents problems for such a proposed ethic. In regard to the first, it is much easier to have a virtue ethic in which the effects of sin on the *imago Dei* are debilitating but not catastrophic. This leaves room for a description of the *imago Dei* in which there are continuities between Creator and the created in such a way that moral excellence is possible. Barth's rejection of such a view of the fall and his embrace of the Reformed emphasis on the devastating consequences of sin pose significant challenges for virtue ethics. His position claims that after the fall our likeness to God is shattered and we no longer possess an innate capacity to emulate God or even to know anything about God. God's grace then comes to us as a disruptive force, upsetting our settled habits, rather than as a perfecting force that adds supernatural virtue to natural.

Second, the Roman Catholic tradition of virtue ethics owes a huge debt to Thomas Aquinas and his formulation. But not only does Barth reject the use of a doctrine of creation as a foundation for doing theology; he specifically rejects Thomas's approach, particularly where Thomas presents human nature as already graced before justification. Thomas's work relies on substance metaphysics, a philosophical presupposition that who we are is defined by what we are. A change in our substance, brought about by grace, thus changes how we act. Barth rejects this philosophical view in favor of actualism. He argues that we are defined primarily by what we do. For Barth, unlike for Thomas, grace changes us at the level of our actions, not at the level of our being.

Third, Barth's rejection on firm Reformed grounds means that we cannot simply write off Barth's objections as being in some way unrepresentative of the tradition in order to reach a Reformed virtue ethic. Rather, these concerns must be addressed head on to see if there is a way forward for such an ethic or if Barth has permanently closed off such a possibility.

Erich Przywara's Challenge

In 1923 Erich Przywara published a short article titled "Gott in uns oder über uns?" in the journal *Stimmen der Zeit* that claimed Barth's theology had a significant weakness. Przywara argued that Barth's description of God in his commentary on Romans placed so much emphasis on the transcendence of God that it left no room for God's immanence. If Przywara was right, then there was no way to account for the incarnation in Barth's theology. In order for the incarnation to take place, the Son of God needed to be united with human nature. Przywara argued that if God were so unlike a creature in the created order, then this would prove impossible. He put forward his own conception, the concept of the *analogia entis*, as the distillation of the Catholic answer to this question. Przywara contended that there is an analogy of being between God and creature. Just as an analogy between two terms points out both similarity and dissimilarity, the *analogia entis* demonstrates that God is both above us and with us, transcendent and immanent.[24] Przywara argued that while the exact term "*analogia entis*" was a new one, it was based on the thought of Augustine, Aquinas, and other significant theologians of the Roman Catholic Church.

Przywara's article led Barth to rethink his theology and doctrine of the incarnation, a rethinking that took several years to fully develop. During this time of germination, Barth was teaching at Münster, a predominantly Catholic city. Przywara had recently published *Religionsphilosophie katholischer Theologie*, which Barth and his students read and reflected on. They discerned that Przywara's starting point, human consciousness, was faulty because it did not take into sufficient account human sinfulness. While Przywara did note the influence of sin on individuals, he saw sin as a disease within a creature rather than a decisive break between creature and Creator. In order to understand why Przywara came to this conclusion, it is helpful to turn to Thomas Aquinas, from whom he derived it.

Thomas had argued that a creature's form consisted in those characteristics that distinguish it from members of other species.[25] Such characteristics are taken as a given; that is, they are presupposed to inhere in the species itself. These characteristics may be posed of the species as a whole regardless of whether individual instances of the species actually exist. For instance, outside of the make-believe world of *My Little Pony*, there are no individual instances of a unicorn. Yet one may nonetheless say that unicorns are distinguished from horses in that all unicorns have one horn on their heads. Even something as big as the universe need not necessarily exist, because for Thomas the universe is created by God out of nothing. It follows that the existence of a particular creature is not a given but a gift from the Creator. And while existence is a contingent attribute of all creaturely beings, God is the kind of being that must exist, by definition. Since necessary being is what defines God as God, it is logically impossible to posit a hypothetical instance of God that is not also actually an existent God. Conceptually we may speak of a dead horse, but it is a contradiction in terms to speak of a dead God.[26]

Nonetheless, despite this radical difference between God and us, Przywara argued that Creator and creature are connected as well as distinct
from each other. The creature is the analogy of deity in that the creature
possesses a unity of essence and existence, but differs from God in the
sense that the creature's existence is not a necessary existence that flows
from the creature's form. God's unity is found in an identity in which existence follows directly from God's essence. Creaturely unity is one of tension, since creatures derive their existence not from their own essence but
as a gift from God. They are always in the process of becoming, of receiving existence from God. Przywara thus states, in good Thomistic fashion,
that God's act of creation is continuous. Our likeness to God means that we
are, according to Przywara, always "open upwards," incomplete in ourselves and yet open to God in God's completeness and dependent on it.[27]

Przywara argues that human beings not only seek the transcendent but
also to a certain extent have access to experiences of the transcendent. His
argument is based on the *analogia entis*: because of our constant receptivity to God's gift of existence, we are made in such a way that the natural
world becomes a window for us to know God. All creatures are drawn to
God as the source of life. Human beings aware of this state of dependence,
whether confessing Christians or not, have at least the natural knowledge
of their reliance on an uncreated being. On the basis of this claim, Przywara comes to the conclusion that natural revelation and supernatural
revelation are congruous.[28]

It follows that Przywara holds the conception that sin is a disease
within a creature rather than a decisive break between creature and Creator. This conviction allows him to start his investigation of the relationship between humans and God with human consciousness rather than
with a description of who God is based on God's revelation in Jesus Christ
(Barth's method). According to Przywara, while sin damages our ability
to know God, we are not completely cut off from God. We are healed
through the offices of the church, which restore a proper understanding
of who God is to us.[29] Here he follows Thomas Aquinas's notion of how
grace does not destroy our nature but works to support and perfect it.
Since our natural orientation toward God is already "open upwards," the
repair that needs to take place after we sin involves a course correction to
realign us with our proper nature, rather than a radical break or departure
from it.

Barth, aligned with the Reformed tradition, holds a quite different
understanding of sin and grace that leads his doctrine of creation in an
opposing direction. According to Przywara's presentation, it is just as
valid to begin with a doctrine of creation to understand God's revelation
to us as it is to begin with a doctrine of incarnation; this view is evident
in his choice to start his theological inquiry with human consciousness.

Przywara argues that our knowledge of our contingency, of which we become aware through our relationship with God, becomes a prelude to the incarnation. It gives us access to an understanding of God in an analogous manner to what the incarnation does for us.[30] Barth, on the other hand, sees sin as a decisive break between Creator and creation. We cannot attain knowledge of God through the created order; it has to come to us from God. Barth's doctrine of revelation thus emphasizes God's initiating action in relation to human beings. This means that human consciousness is not a valid starting point for Barth, and he is skeptical of any theology that presupposes that our being is so continuous with God's being that we can derive some knowledge of God out of our own capacities.

But what of the *imago Dei*? If we are made in the image of God, do we not have some access to God through our created capacities? Barth rejects such a possibility and highlights the discontinuity between Creator and creature such that there is irreversibility in the relationship. This means that, contrary to Przywara, we cannot come to knowledge of God through any created likeness to God. For Barth the *imago Dei* is not something that we possess apart from God but rather is the continual work of the Holy Spirit.[31] He writes that the *imago Dei* "is a process of revelation, which, in the strictest sense, is first coming to us and to come, moment by moment, if, as we should, we have taken seriously what is meant by the *Deity* of the *Creator* Spirit."[32] For Barth the crux of the matter has to do with grace, which is an ongoing reality, not a completed fact embedded in our being. During his lecture series on the Holy Spirit in 1929, Barth comments, "It [grace] is never at all a quality of ours, inborn in us, such as would enable us to know of it in advance. Every other interpretation signifies, covertly or overtly, in the premises or conclusions, another interpretation of the Holy Spirit than as the creative power of our own spirit."[33] For Barth, grace is solely the work of the Holy Spirit that interrupts our hostility to grace rather than an event that calls forth our cooperation. Grace confronts our desire to justify ourselves by our works, forcing us to turn to God for our justification. To claim that we cooperate in this event is to challenge the radical sinfulness to which we are subject.

Barth on Disruptive Grace

What is the basis of Barth's rejection of Przywara's position? Przywara claims that there is congruity between revelation and reason. In fact, he argues that revelation supports and perfects reason in the same way that grace supports and perfects our nature. Barth's understanding emphasizes the opposition between revelation and reason and closes off the possibility that human reason is empowered to discover who God is and what God is doing in the world. The difference between their two interpretations is evident in their different understandings of the doctrine of creation. Przywara, in line with Aquinas, sees a discontinuity between Creator and creation but not outright opposition, whereas Barth, in line with the Reformers, argues that as a result of the fall, in our sinful condition we stand in opposition to and separate from God.[34] The gulf between God and us can only be bridged by God, and therefore revelation needs to be moment by moment. Whereas Przywara's position allows him to postulate that we have certain inherent capabilities to know God, Barth writes off this possibility.

Barth's position follows from the actualism inherent in his covenantal ontology.[35] He claims that who we are is determined by our relationship with God in Jesus Christ. Our being is thus determined by God's covenant with us. This claim, coupled with his insistence that revelation is unidirectional, from God to us, leads Barth to emphasize individual moments of revelation rather than continuity in the Christian life. If revelation occurs moment by moment as Barth insists, then our relationship with God does not depend on some unchanging set of capabilities that allows us to know God but on moments in time in which we hear God's command and respond accordingly. Hence Barth's account of the relationship between God and human beings places much more emphasis on the discontinuous elements in the relationship rather than the continuous.

To understand how Barth is different from Aquinas here, something needs to be said about Thomas's substance ontology. Thomas derives his conception of being largely from Aristotle. Aristotle's *Metaphysics* treats the nature of being, which Aristotle ties to the concept of *ousia*, or substance. Everything that is said to have being is related in one of three ways to substance: it is itself a substance; it is a property of some substance; or it creates/destroys some substance.[36] Thomas, in his commentary on this passage, largely agrees with Aristotle. He disagrees, however, on the relationship between existence and essence (being). While Aristotle believed the existence of the world is a given, Thomas's reading of Scripture led him to the conclusion that God did in fact create a world where there was no world. That meant that existence was not a necessary predicate of essence. The created order was a contingent order, which owed its first cause to God.[37] Despite this contingency, Thomas could still write about the incorruptibility of the human soul. Human beings are composite beings whose bodies are made up of multiple parts but whose souls are of a simple spiritual substance that is incorruptible. While our bodies are subject to decay after death, our souls are not.

Thomas's substance ontology explains continuity of character in the Christian life in a way that is more problematic to explain in Barth's actualistic understanding. In Thomas's conception, such continuity is linked to our souls, which abide over time and in fact are eternal. Because Barth's ontology emphasizes discrete moments of revelation and our responses to them without reference to our character, it is less clear where our lives derive their continuity. As a result, some ethicists (e.g., James Gustafson) have argued that there is little room for continuity of character in Barth's theology. Since continuity of character is an important part of a virtue ethic, Barth's actualism is a potential barrier to a virtue ethic developed within his theological constraints.

The Basis of Barth's Rejection: Justification by Grace through Faith

One way to get around the hurdles raised by Barth is to claim that in some way his theology is an aberration from the Reformed view. We could then ignore them and move on with our proposal for Reformed moral virtue ethics on the grounds that there are other theologians within the tradition whose work is more conducive. However, Barth's concerns lie squarely within the tradition since his objections are based on a central doctrine of the Reformation: justification by grace through faith alone.

Barth's views on grace are in fact faithful to one of the central tenets of the Reformed tradition, first expressed by Martin Luther: we are simultaneously justified and sinners, *simul iustus et peccator*. For Aquinas, this dictum is complete nonsense. Either we are justified, in a state of grace, or we are in a state of mortal sin. Thomas's position is a direct consequence of how he perceives justification: as a movement whose origin is a state of sin and whose end is God. Thus Thomas writes,

> The justification of the unrighteous is a movement in which the human mind is moved by God from the state of sin to the state of justice. Therefore the human mind must be related to both initial and end-term in its movement of free choice, just like a body moved locally by some mover with regard to the two terms of its movement.[38]

Mortal sin committed after the moment of justification reverses the direction of the movement so that the initial term is God and the end is a state of sin.

On the other hand, for Barth the two have to coexist; that is, God's grace has a *both-and* quality to it.[39] The sin of the sinner remains and is at war with the new self that has been redeemed in Christ. Barth argues that our state after sin is one of misery (*status corruptionis*). Even in the life of the sanctified man who participates in Christian freedom, this is true. The presence of sin and the presence of Christ do not, however, coexist on the same plane. There is no doubt in this struggle that Christ is Victor, Savior, and Lord. The completion of this victory, however, is realized only eschatologically. Sanctification is not a change in our nature; it is not even a change in our nature that is made possible by grace. It is instead an identification with Christ that is renewed again and again.

Barth's commitment to Luther's dictum may also be seen in his conception of the *analogia fidei* as an alternative to the *analogia entis*. Here his emphasis on faith is in line with Luther's doctrine of justification by faith alone. For Barth there is an analogy between human beings and God, but that likeness is only possible through God's self-revelation, which is given to us moment by moment. He is very clear to deny any natural point of contact (*Anknüpfungspunkt*) through which we have access to God. Any contact between God and us is initiated on God's side through God's grace in Jesus Christ. Barth is not asserting that our human agency is compromised by God's grace. Rather, he is claiming that we now have the possibility to hear God, a possibility that previously was closed off due to sin. This new correspondence between God and us does not change our constant need for God's grace; we remain, according to Luther's dictum, *simul iustus et peccator*. Yet we are aware of God's grace in a way that we were not before.[40]

Challenges for Moral Virtue Ethics

The challenges for moral virtue ethics within a Barthian theological framework are considerable. Such ethics focuses on practices and habits that shape an individual over time. The virtue ethics of Thomas Aquinas is built on a robust doctrine of creation in which human goodness survives after the fall (albeit in a weakened state). The challenge for Reformed moral virtue ethics is to affirm, on one hand, the depth of human sinfulness and, on the other, the sovereignty of God's grace so that human virtue is still possible. The tricky part of this equation is to describe the human response to God's commands in ways that recognize their continuous character.

The second challenge arises due to the differences in Thomas's doctrine of justification and that of the Reformation encapsulated by Luther's dictum that we are *simul iustus et peccator*. How is it possible to have virtue and sin exist side by side? Either virtue drives out sin, or sin drives out virtue. In Thomas's conception of justification, justifying grace drives out sin. We still have the capacity to sin, but when we commit a mortal sin, we lose the habitual grace that keeps us in a justified state, and we require the church's offices to return us to a justified state. In Luther's and Barth's understanding of justification, God's act of justification contains an eschatological promise that we will indeed stand before God justified, but that act does not result in a fully justified state here and now. Nor does the Reformation distinction between justification and sanctification, which was not a part of Thomas's terminology, settle the difference between the two accounts. In Barth's understanding, our sanctification is not the process by which we gradually become holier and holier as we acquire the virtues of faith, hope, and love through the infusion of God's grace. Instead, for Barth our sanctification consists in increased awareness of our relation to and our identity in Christ. The ramifications for virtue ethics become clearer through an examination of Barth's doctrine of incarnation, to which we now turn.

KARL BARTH'S REJECTION OF HABITUAL GRACE

Barth's emphasis on the disruptive nature of grace has already been mentioned in the context of discussions about the differences between Thomas's conception of grace and Barth's. But why does Barth emphasize the disruptive nature of grace? Part of the answer to this question arises out of Barth's historical context and his rejection of the liberal theology evidenced in the work of Herrmann and others who anchored knowledge of God in human experience. As noted at the beginning of the chapter, Barth rejected this view by embracing a theocentric approach in which God's revelation radically challenges our presumptions rather than our human presumptions dictating our knowledge of God.

But Barth's position is more than a negation of the prevailing theological trends of his time. On the positive side, Barth's commitment to the disruptive nature of grace follows from his Christology, particularly as it is expressed in his doctrine of incarnation in volume 4 of *Church Dogmatics*. A treatment of this doctrine is relevant for our purposes because it not only clarifies Barth's view of grace; it also forms the centerpiece of Barth's christocentric anthropology and informs his views on the relationship between nature and grace. The mystery of the incarnation is the mystery of how God remains God and the human nature assumed by Christ remains human. How is it that God's all-powerful being does not in fact overwhelm Christ's humanity? How does the union in one person of God and a particular human nature come to be?

Barth's Doctrine of Incarnation in *CD* IV/2, §64, 2

While all of *CD* IV deals with the doctrine of reconciliation, the second part offers an account of sanctification that addresses possibilities for a virtue ethic. The selection of the particular section under review is a propos because in it Barth offers his reasons for concern in relation to habitual grace, and habitual grace is a key concept in Thomas Aquinas's account of virtue ethics. Even more important, this section, as Barth notes, forms "the decisive center" of his Christology.[41]

The section under investigation is found in paragraph 64, "The Home-coming of the Son of Man." Barth is looking at the incarnation in the context of (1) our election in God, (2) the historical event of the incarnation, and (3) the resurrection and ascension of Jesus. The central section on the historical event of the incarnation is the focus of our investigation here. The inquiry will be directed toward addressing the concerns about habitual grace raised by Barth. With these concerns at the forefront, the challenge that Barth's doctrine of incarnation presents for a Reformed virtue ethics will become clearer.

The Grounds for Habitual Grace and Why Barth Rejects Them

At the heart of Barth's doctrine of incarnation is an event-driven approach to the union of the Word of God with the human nature of Christ. Because Barth's focus is on the covenantal relationship between God and humanity, he rejects a description of Christ's being behind or apart from who he is revealed to be in history. Barth argues that the traditional conception of this union, from the Chalcedonian formula through the Middle Ages to the scholastic Lutheran and Reformed reformulations of it, is too static.[42] These formulations and reformulations do not capture the dynamic character of the incarnation found in the biblical narrative. They bifurcate the humiliation and the exultation of the Son of God by separating the history of his humbling, which encompasses his incarnation to his death, from the history of his glorification, which encompasses his resurrection, his ascension, and his rule at the right hand of God. Barth instead describes the incarnation in terms of the downward and upward movements always occurring together. God's decision to be God for us means that the Son of God cannot be considered apart from the incarnation. Therefore, the humiliation of God is not a transitory affair, from which God has recovered postresurrection. God does not "escape" being a human, but rather God's electing decision to be God with us means that the identity of the Son of God is inextricably linked with one particular human nature. The consequences of that union spread beyond that one particular human nature, and thus the upward movement affects humanity as a whole.

One of Barth's concerns about traditional conceptions of the incarnation is that they suggest that the humanity of Jesus Christ, and by extension all of humanity, is divinized in the union. Considered from the perspective of nature, divinization is problematic because our human nature, which should retain human properties, takes on divine attributes (divinized flesh). Considered from the perspective of grace, divinization is problematic because grace, which only properly belongs to God, becomes the possession of the human (created grace). Habitual grace involves divinization, and, in Barth's estimation, it blurs the lines between nature and grace, creature and Creator.

In order to keep these lines of distinction clear, Barth's doctrine of incarnation establishes a pattern of divine and human interaction such that the divine nature is always the one that takes the initiative and the human always responds. This pattern is embedded in Barth's anhypostatic/enhypostatic Christology.[43] Christ's human nature is anhypostatic in the sense that it has no existence outside of the union with the eternally existing Logos. Yet within that union Christ's human nature does exist and is complete (the enhypostatic affirmation). This understanding of the union precludes the possibility that Christ's humanity in any way initiates or directs the relation. Instead, Christ's humanity is dependent on Christ's divinity for its very existence, so it is the Son of God in his divinity who determines and orders Christ's humanity.

With this understanding of Barth's Christology in view, it is easier to see why Barth rejects depictions of habitual grace in which grace takes human form through the possession of certain habits. Barth is critical of Lutherans and Reformed dogmaticians in the late sixteenth and early seventeenth centuries who embraced the concept of habitual grace. Both used terminology borrowed from medieval scholasticism, particularly in their use of *gratia habitualis,* imparted to Christ's human nature through infusion. Barth objects: "*Habitus* comes from *habere,* and therefore denotes possession. But grace is divine giving and human receiving. It can be 'had' only in the course of this history."[44] For Barth if there is a *habitus* in the human essence of Jesus Christ, then the actual history, the events of the incarnation, become warped. Perhaps at the point of conception or sometime during Jesus' development into adulthood, Jesus' human nature possesses God's grace in the form of a certain habitual disposition. But this idea goes against the anhypostatic/enhypostatic logic of the incarnation because it means that Christ's human nature is no longer in need of the grace that comes to it through the divine.

From Barth's Christology it follows that human agency and human nature must conform to the pattern found in the relationship between the two natures in the one person of Jesus Christ. If even Jesus' humanity does not possess God's grace, then certainly we do not either. If Jesus' humanity relates to God as one who receives from one who gives, then certainly we do too.

Barth views accounts of habitual grace, particularly those coming out of Roman Catholicism, as pernicious. From his perspective they divide up grace so that a piece belongs to God and another piece belongs to us, as if grace were like the Eucharist broken and distributed, consumed and then assimilated into our bodies, becoming a part of us.[45] The Lutheran and older Reformed dogmaticians held to a more acceptable version of grace, but it was still, according to Barth, tainted with medieval scholasticism. To understand the weakness of their positions and Barth's specifically Reformed reasons for rejecting them, it is helpful to turn to Barth's treatment of the disagreements between Reformed and Lutheran dogmaticians that began in the sixteenth century regarding the relationship between the human and divine natures of Jesus Christ.

Barth examines the disputes in terms of two doctrines: the *unio hypostatica* (hypostatic union) and the *communio naturarum* (communion of natures). The *unio hypostatica* is the precondition for the *communio naturarum*. First comes the affirmation that Jesus Christ is one person both human and divine; then in terms of that union a consideration may be made of the communion of natures. Reformed dogmaticians therefore placed emphasis on the *unio hypostatica* in their treatment of the two doctrines. In contrast, Lutheran theology focused on the *communio naturarum*, and specifically on the *communicatio idiomatum*, or communication of attributes between the divine and human natures.

This emphasis in Lutheran thinking follows from Luther's position on the Eucharist, in which Christ's human body and blood are truly in, with, and under the elements of bread and wine. Luther's doctrine of ubiquity allows for this to happen in the Eucharist as it is celebrated in different places at the same time, something that would not be possible of a human body without the intervention of the divine. Lutheran theologians thus needed to explain how it could be possible, and they did so by mining the *communio naturarum* to explain how the divine nature in Christ penetrates into the human.

Lutheran and Reformed theologians had different interpretations of the Chalcedonian formula, "without confusion, without change, without division, without separation."[46] Reformed dogmaticians emphasized the first two descriptors. What was paramount for them was God's sovereignty in the incarnation. They were careful to ensure that the Son of God took the initiating action and was always directing the divine-human relationship. They tended to emphasize the distinction between the divine and human natures in Christ. Lutherans, on the other hand, emphasized the latter two descriptors. They claimed that Christ had conquered the division and separation between God and humankind that had taken place due to human sin. Christ's victory consisted not only in his resurrection but also in his incarnation. They emphasized that God is made known directly through the humanity of Christ.[47] This view was rejected by Reformed theologians at the time because it divinized the humanity of Christ and made that humanity something different from our humanity, thus jeopardizing Christ's role as our mediator. Barth sides with the Reformed theologians here.

The Lutheran position has an advantage in that it clearly answers the question of what makes the humanity of Jesus Christ unique. Something happens in Jesus that does not happen in us. Jesus is the incarnate Word of God, and we are not. That uniqueness is not as clearly spelled out in the Reformed position described above. Therefore, Barth has to explain on his own terms how humanity's relation to God is different than Jesus Christ's. As we will see, this description has specific implications for Barth's understanding of sanctification. It also has important consequences for virtue ethics, since a Christian virtue ethics presupposes that what enables us to be excellent is the sanctifying and hallowing work of God in our lives.

Before turning to the uniqueness of the relationship that Christ's humanity has to his divinity, it must be said that the humanity of Christ is also *our* humanity. Barth describes the effects of the incarnation as the exultation not only of Jesus' particular human nature but of all human nature: "Jesus of Nazareth was and is a man as we are—our Brother. But he was and is our firstborn brother."[48]

Barth's concept of "exultation" does not include a divinization of human nature as it is elevated. Rather, the emphasis is placed on the character of the hypostatic union. The acting subject in this relationship is the Son of God. The starting point is not some abstract "divine essence" or "human essence" derivable from Greek philosophical concepts. Instead, the origin is scriptural. The Son of God, revealed in Scripture, has determined to be with humanity, and that decision has implications for the Son as well as for the human essence in Christ.[49] Barth here maintains the anhypostatic/enhypostatic distinctions of later Reformed thought: that Jesus' human nature does not exist apart from his divine nature (anhypostatic) but also that in the presence of Jesus' divine nature, his human nature really is fully and truly human and is not compromised by that nature (enhypostatic).

The issue at stake regards the human essence of Jesus Christ in the union with the Word. Is there in any way a change in Jesus' human nature in the hypostatic union, and if not, how is Jesus different from other human beings? Barth takes up again the Lutheran understanding of the *communicatio idiomatum* as well as the Reformers' reluctance to address the issue. In this Lutheran understanding the divine nature is present to the human nature in such a way that the human nature is not altered but nonetheless has access to the divine. This means that the human nature of Jesus Christ has access to God's omnipotence, omniscience, and omnipresence.[50] Barth argues that this explanation opens the door to the divinization not only of Christ's human nature but human nature in general.[51] If this is the case, then we may now do away with our dependence on Christ for our salvation. The anthropology that results does not require any intrinsic dependence on Christ other than as the initiator of our own perfection. Once Christ opens the door to divinization, we may trample through without looking to him for our salvation. Barth acerbically concludes that the "apotheosized flesh of Jesus Christ, omnipotent, omnipresent and omniscient," far from deserving our worship, is merely an empty shell waiting for us to occupy for ourselves the divinity found there.[52]

In what way then is Christ's human nature distinctive? In the quotes above it is clear that Barth excludes the possibility of a change in Christ's human nature because of his union with the divine. If that were the case, his nature would be set apart from that of other human beings. Instead, Barth uses the language of determination. The human nature of Jesus Christ is determined by the grace of God in a way that is unique among all human beings.[53]

How does Barth characterize this determination? Very carefully! First, he is cautious to say that we cannot abstract from anything outside of the biblical witness to explain what is going on in the human nature of Jesus Christ. All analogies fail here. Second, he affirms what we already know. There really is a union of the divine and the human in Jesus, and this union is determined on the side of the divine. This relationship is asymmetric in that control rests with God. That does not mean, though, that God is unaffected by the relationship. In fact Barth goes so far as to say that the Lutherans would have been better off to consider the possibility of a *genus tapeinoticum* (a humbling of the divine nature of Christ in its union with the human) rather than place so much emphasis on the *genus majestaticum*. Third, this human essence, "is an essence which exists in and with God, and is adopted and controlled and sanctified and ruled by him."[54] Without becoming divine, it nonetheless is more deeply involved in relationship with the divine essence than any other human being. Exaltation for Barth thus entails no habitual grace or a change in human nature but instead a properly ordered relationship in which the human essence of Christ is perfectly in tune with God.

In contrast to the Lutheran dogmaticians of the late sixteenth and early seventeenth centuries, Barth argues that it is enough to distinguish the human nature of Christ in this way and go no further. Postulating godlike properties of this human nature in the Eucharist is unnecessary. Christ's uniqueness is found in his absolute obedience to God. He is, "from the very outset, determined by the grace of God. This is the qualitatively different determination of his human essence, and of His alone as that of the One who as the Son of Man is also and primarily the Son of God."[55]

By describing Christ's uniqueness in this way, Barth protects the humanity of Jesus and also establishes his credentials as our mediator. If Jesus Christ were something different from us, he could not be our savior. But because the Son of God took on human essence, stained by Adam's sin, he also elevated it through his relationship with God.

The idea that we can own God's grace is rejected by Barth because it misconstrues the character of the relationship between God and us. Grace is not something we can own; it is God's possession and God's to grant as God sees fit. Thus we cannot look to any other source for grace but God. Looking elsewhere is what Barth refers to as a "side glance," a grave error in our theological thinking. Barth also rejects any concept of synergy between the Holy Spirit and our spirit, because it denies our freedom to respond to God's call. When the Holy Spirit influences us to act in certain ways, our freedom is undermined. Barth's own conception of divine and human interaction denies that there can be habitual grace. Yet he also promotes a robust doctrine of sanctification and vocation due to his Chalcedonian formulation of these doctrines.

The Chalcedonian Pattern

This Chalcedonian formulation is carefully elucidated by George Hunsinger,[56] whose insight begins with his claim that the circle is the root metaphor of *Church Dogmatics*.[57] This metaphor is evident where Barth describes the union between Christ and the Christian in volume 4, part 3. This union is so complete that, in Hunsinger's paraphrase of Barth, "both may be said to exist 'eccentrically'—centered, that is, on one another respectively. The Christian places herself or himself at Christ's disposal just as Christ has placed himself at the disposal of the Christian. The Christian comes to live from 'the center of [Christ's] intention and action,' and Christ takes up his abode in the Christian's 'innermost being or heart.' "[58] While such a description of the relationship focuses on its horizontal dimensions, there are important vertical dimensions as well.

Hunsinger interprets Barth's understanding of divine and human interaction through the lens of the Chalcedonian formula that has the following attributes: asymmetry, intimacy, and integrity. Asymmetry is found where Barth speaks of God's leading and humanity's following, in God's ruling and humanity's being ruled, and in God's transcendence and humanity's humble state. The characteristic of intimacy is noticeable when "we hear of divine actions coinciding with human actions (and vice versa)," and integrity, finally, is in evidence when we hear of the two "coexisting and coinhering without any confusion or mixture" and "without the transformation of the one into the other."[59] Hunsinger asserts that Barth's treatment of the relationship between divine and human agency consistently follows this scheme throughout *Church Dogmatics*.

Taking Hunsinger's lead, we need to read Barth carefully so as not to overemphasize one aspect of his thought. For example, it would be easy to look at portions of *Church Dogmatics* that highlight asymmetry, say those on the divine command, and miss the tension in Barth's dogmatics by understating those portions that highlight the integrity of the relationship between the two (as does Davaney). On the other hand, it is possible to do the reverse and highlight those portions that suggest growth in the human life apart from God without considering Barth's Chalcedonian asymmetry. This latter temptation must be particularly kept in mind when sketching out an account of moral virtue ethics using Barth's theology as a basis.

Reformed Virtue Ethics in Light of the Chalcedonian Pattern

How, then, can there be a virtue ethic that follows this Chalcedonian pattern? Virtue presupposes some excellence. That excellence is, from the standpoint of an observer, something that the actor initiates on his or her own. But it need not be the case that the excellence is solely attributable to the actor. Barth's affirmation of human freedom found in the human response to God's sovereign grace allows for a rich understanding of sanctification that involves excellence in the Christian life. Therefore, his theology does not close down the possibility of moral virtue ethics. It does, however, raise some questions about how to articulate that ethic such that the focus remains on God in Christ and not humanity as such. Taking a lead from Barth, a Chalcedonian virtue ethic would focus on the pattern of command and response embedded in the relationship between God and us, with the model of the circle with the christocentric center being a guiding metaphor for the process of sanctification.

How would such a focus be maintained? One answer to the question comes from William Werpehowski, a scholar whose engagement with Karl Barth's work spans decades. An investigation into his argument for a Barthian virtue ethics proves a good starting point for addressing the concerns raised in this chapter.

3

OBJECTIONS OVERCOME

The last chapter considered three features of Karl Barth's theology that present challenges for a Reformed virtue ethic: (1) an account of human agency that focuses on God's command, (2) a rejection of natural theology, and (3) a rejection of habitual grace. The first challenge has been successfully navigated. Concerns that God's sovereignty overwhelms human freedom have been met by demonstrating that for Barth God's commands circumscribe but in no way undermine human freedom. Overcoming the other two obstacles requires further investigation. Fortunately, a template has been laid out by the work of ethicist William Werpehowski, who has already investigated related concerns regarding Barth's theology. Werpehowski's work will provide an important first step toward the construction of a moral virtue ethics along the lines of Barth's theological framework. To complete the project, however, will require making modifications to Werpehowski's proposal along the lines of the Chalcedonian pattern of divine-human interaction highlighted at the end of the last chapter.

WILLIAM WERPEHOWSKI ON KARL BARTH

Since the early 1980s William Werpehowski has consistently argued that Barth's ethics may be interpreted as virtue ethics. Werpehowski demonstrates this congruity by highlighting three aspects of Christian virtue ethics that may be found in Barth's work: a description of human being that includes continuity of character, attention to biblical narrative, and practical wisdom. Three different essays from Werpehowski will be reviewed, each of which highlights one of these aspects.

Continuity of Character in Barth

In a 1981 essay, "Command and History in the Ethics of Karl Barth," Werpehowski responds to two ethicists, James Gustafson and Stanley Hauerwas, who argue that Barth's ethic of divine command has serious deficiencies.[1] Gustafson argues that Barth's ethics of command, under the sway of existentialism, emphasizes discrete moments of choice to the extent that it minimizes the "perduring order of moral life and the continuities of human experience."[2] Gustafson criticizes Barth's occasionalism here, stating that Barth's focus on the moment of command and the subsequent passive response of the agent undermines any account of continuity in the Christian moral life. It also minimizes the need for the agent to come up with reasons for action, since those reasons are already given in God's command.

Stanley Hauerwas criticizes Barth for not adequately explaining how Christian moral experience deepens through time. Such deepening requires continuity as our character is shaped in response to God's own determination of who we are. Hauerwas notes that Barth is not antithetical to this description of the Christian life, but in his work it is not fully developed. Hauerwas writes, "By describing the Christian life primarily in terms of command and decision, Barth cannot fully account for the kind of growth and deepening that he thinks is essential to the Christian's existence."[3]

Werpehowski observes that what these two criticisms share is a concern that Barth's ethics do not provide room for consistent human self-determination across time. Both Gustafson and Hauerwas worry that "the Barthian self is unable to express itself as shaped through a *history*. This history, as such, would provide an explanation of the changes that take place in and through the actions of a continuous subject."[4] Against this criticism Werpehowski argues that such history is in fact an important element in Barth's divine command ethics.

Werpehowski notes that *reformation* is the key concept for understanding how Barth combines an emphasis on command and response with an attention to history.[5] He supports this thesis by examining a text from *Church Dogmatics* II/2:

> The principle of necessary repetition and renewal, and not a law of stability, is the law of the spiritual growth and continuity of our life. It is when we observe this law that we practice perseverance (ὑπομονή) in the biblical meaning of the term, a perseverance corresponding to the steadfastness of God Himself, which does not signify the suspension, but the continuing and indestructible possession and use of His freedom.[6]

For Barth our history is determined in Christ's history. We are re-formed by that history again and again in the events of our own lives. The mechanism for that re-formation is God's command and our response. Barth argues that we need to have complete openness to God's command.[7] Such openness suggests that our previous history with God is inconsequential and that continuity in the Christian life holds little place for Barth. But, as Werpehowski argues, this is not the case. He argues that for Barth hearing the command of God does not require removing past decisions entirely from consideration. It does, though, require epistemological humility in relation to those decisions. A statement from Barth, which he cites, cements the point: "It is not the effacement but the questioning of all our previous answers which takes place when we begin to put seriously the What? of the ethical question."[8]

Therefore, the reason that Barth emphasizes the need for openness to God's command is to protect the sovereignty and freedom of that command from any domestication of it on our part. Our readiness to obey God's command does not exempt us from reasoning carefully about our future actions. We still need to recognize God's command as *God's* command. We cannot, as Werpehowski notes, reduce this process to a set of utilitarian or deontological rules. We will need to discern the "What?" of God's command by combining an in-depth understanding of Scripture with a proper understanding of the relevant contextual factors. Barth's commands therefore have an important horizontal as well as vertical dimension, since they are always embedded in our current situation and take into account our age, vocation, and other life circumstances. It is this horizontal dimension that provides continuity both in terms of our relations with others and our ongoing history of relationship with God. God is calling us to do something new now. However, that new thing is possible only because of the history of events leading up to the current moment.[9]

So far Werpehowski has addressed concerns about the place of history in Barth's divine command ethics. He has also explained how reason plays a role in the acts of assessing and responding to God's commands (another concern of Gustafson's). What remains to be dealt with is Hauerwas's concern about the growth or "deepening" of the Christian life. Werpehowski does so by noting that for Barth such growth is possible only as it reflects repetition and renewal. Growth is not, as Hauerwas's criticism suggests, only a gradual process of building on past experiences. Rather, growth also requires fundamentally testing one's preconceived notions. For Barth, it is this willingness to relinquish our prior conceptions of God and ourselves that is necessary for growth in the Christian life. Werpehowski writes, "There is growth (a deepening of the self's determination through the testing of one's current posture against one's central orientation and loyalty) in that in the new ethical event one has the opportunity to apprehend more deeply who God is and what he has done."[10] Werpehowski emphasizes that for Barth this growth can only be understood in terms of our relationship with God. It is not something intrinsic to us but rather reflects the maturity that takes place over time in that relationship.

Narrative in Barth

Narratives hold an important place in virtue ethics because they help to shape an ongoing discourse about the good life. They provide concrete examples of lives we would do well to emulate, and they situate these lives within a broader social context. They also provide an explanation of how current social practices developed and thus offer a basis on which we can evaluate those practices.

In his 1986 essay "Narrative and Ethics in Barth," Werpehowski seeks to demonstrate how Barth uses narrative in the development of his theological ethics.[11] The theological space within which these ethics operate is defined by God's relationship with creation. This relationship is characterized by two types of freedom: freedom *from* us and freedom *for* us. Werpehowski demonstrates how Barth goes about establishing each of these types of freedom using biblical narrative.

Christ's freedom *from* us is demonstrated in the biblical narratives that speak of Jesus' challenge regarding Sabbath law, his parables that confront economic inequalities, and his recognition of political authority as ultimately limited. Christ's freedom from us allows us also to look at the institutions of our day with a critical eye. As Christ's disciples we are challenged to witness to the "radically new thing Jesus brings."[12] This freedom to stand in judgment of our world is not rooted in our own freedom and independence but rather in our obedience to Christ and to his own example. In the same way that Christ stands as judge over the economic and political spheres, Christ stands as judge over us.

However, Barth's thinking here is dialectical, and the picture of Christ's freedom in relation to us would be faulty if we stopped at this point. As Werpehowski indicates, the other half of the dialectic has to do with Christ's freedom *for* us. Christ stands with us as well as above us. For Barth God's command has both an indicative and an imperative dimension. While the imperative dimension convicts us, the indicative reminds us that we are already in covenant with God.

Both these dimensions are fleshed out by biblical narrative, particularly that found in the exodus story. This narrative provides the essential context within which divine commands are interpreted. Barth insists that even the Ten Commandments cannot be understood without telling the story of the relationship between God and God's people. These commands are a part of the covenant that God has already made with the Israelites.[13] In relation to our own life circumstances, interpreting God's commands requires familiarity with God's covenantal dealings with Moses, Aaron, and Miriam in the Old Testament, and Peter, James, and Mary Magdalene in the New. While we recognize that our obedience will look different from theirs, nonetheless our stories are woven together. As Werpehowski observes, Barth's vision of the obedience of the disciple is therefore made richer and more complex by Barth's use of the biblical narrative to describe it in detail.

In his concluding remarks, Werpehowski claims that Barth's ethics are an ethics of virtue. He bases this claim on the fact that Barth is concerned

about history, namely, God's history of graciousness to us in Jesus Christ.[14]
Building on the observations he made in the previous essay on Barth's
ethic of divine command, Werpehowski notes,

> Barth's biblical interpretation concerning moral questions can be seen to
> impart a sense of these moral skills and perspectives. One may come to
> learn of penitence when contrasting the narrative expressions in Judas
> and Jesus; one may learn something more of the joy one is permitted to
> live by in its contrast with the fear of Saul or the reserve of Judas. That
> we may learn these things and come to be a person grateful and faithful
> to God is finally made possible by the gift of God's self-manifestation
> and the faithfulness God displays across the course of our lives.[15]

But Werpehowski is also careful to attest to the other side of the dialectic in Barth's thinking on this matter. The life of discipleship is not a gentle
progression. As he writes, "On the contrary, the disciple for Barth lives
simul iustus et peccator; therefore, he or she is always only 'falling out with
oneself.'"[16] God's commands in our own lives remind us that like those in
the biblical narratives, we remain sinners in need of God's grace.[17]

The narratives we hear about ourselves and others are not ethically
neutral. People in positions of power may abuse that power by framing a
sequence of events in such a way as to promote their own narrow interests. Therefore, it takes a person of practical wisdom to discern the right
use of narrative. Werpehowski explores what this looks like in the third
essay under investigation, to which we now turn.

Practical Wisdom and Barth

In his 2007 presidential address to the Society of Christian Ethics, Werpehowski lays out his understanding of practical wisdom in three theses.[18] While Barth is not the main subject of this address, his ethics are
engaged both implicitly and explicitly throughout. Werpehowski's speech
aims to provide an avenue for rapprochement between Roman Catholics
and Protestants regarding disagreements over how ethics should proceed.
There is a tension in his thought that tries to bring together approaches that
emphasize natural law and virtue with those that emphasize divine command and grace. He here warns that an overemphasis on either approach
to the detriment of the other leads to problems.

Werpehowski states his first thesis as follows: "Acts of practical wisdom, as acts in keeping with the reality of things, are grounded in and
communicate God's decisive action in Jesus Christ in his presence and his
power."[19] We cannot thus derive guidance regarding how we ought to
act in practical matters from our observations of the created world alone.
Reality is grounded in God as made known in the acts of Jesus Christ.

Therefore, the virtuous life and the cultivation of practical wisdom depend on an acquaintance with our Creator and Redeemer. As Werpehowski notes, that concreteness is an essential feature of an adequate grasp of this reality. God is made known in the thick description of the biblical narrative regarding Israel and Christ, which is ordered by the foci of creation, redemption, and consummation.[20] While Christians understand their life purposes in terms of this narrative, Werpehowski is not advocating they separate themselves into isolated communities. God's revelation comes to us outside of the Christian community as well as within it.

Werpehowski's second thesis relates to Luther's *simul iustus et peccator*. As he notes, such a doctrine does not at first glance appear to allow for the development of moral wisdom. Yet despite its sobering diagnosis of the human condition, this doctrine holds within it seeds of hope because it testifies to the fact that we remain within the circle of God's love even in our sinfulness. The Christian life is thus marked not by our own growing self-awareness but by a growing awareness of God's love. Werpehowski writes,

> The awareness is instead of the love of God, some turning to God, and, with both, some healing and peace in the turning, as well as a sort of fearless vulnerability or vulnerable fearlessness. There is also an increasing comprehension of the power of sin that grace opposes. . . . All this indicates that we may live as selves outside ourselves and in Christ in response to the need of our neighbors, whose needs we share as the needy beings we are. Such is the moral meaning of the *simul justus et peccator*.[21]

This account of transformation in the Christian moral life avoids the dangers of self-justification to which such accounts may, by the nature of their subject, be susceptible. Werpehowski uses the tension in Luther's doctrine as a hermeneutical rule for Christian moral wisdom—as we live out our lives in faithfulness to the Christ who has saved us, we are reminded again and again of the reality that we still stand in need of saving.

Werpehowski's third thesis is drawn directly from a statement that Barth makes in his *Church Dogmatics* about the Christian life.[22] This thesis is that "the integrity and growth in the moral life that Christian practical wisdom affords consist in an ongoing practice of repentance, renewal, and perseverance."[23] Here Werpehowski reiterates the points he makes in "Command and History." Barth's ethics of divine command has been criticized for reducing accounts of human and divine agency to the "episodic and voluntarist." Such an interpretation falters on close inspection. Barth is here addressing the need for humility; his intent is to remind us that we are not to be so complacent about the moral course we have taken as to assume that we are already on the right path. Instead we ought continually to repent of those things that we have done wrong and seek the goodness of God's grace in instruction and guidance.

Where does moral continuity exist in such an account? For Werpehowski it consists in an ongoing experience of conversion that involves a growing readiness to ask for and seek God's instruction. In Barth's schema we are not the sole proprietors of our own practical wisdom but instead humble seekers in search of concrete guidance. Seeing the world rightly requires avoiding certain traps. On the one side lies the trap of arrogant self-assertion; on the other lies that of self-neglect brought on by despair.[24] Such a vision of practical wisdom treats sin as a reality but not as the final reality within which we live. It requires modesty regarding the source of what is good in us, as well as a hopeful orientation regarding the future that is able to withstand the disappointments and hardships that arise from our own failings, the failings of others, and circumstances beyond our control.

EVALUATING WERPEHOWSKI

William Werpehowski's position on Barth's theology and ethics may be judged according to the obstacles discussed in the previous chapter: Barth's christocentrism, his rejection of the *analogia entis*, and his rejection of habitual grace found in the doctrine of the incarnation. Does Werpehowski's reading of Barth remain faithful to these dimensions of Barth's thought, and by extension, does it comply with the Reformed tradition? In some respects it does, and in one important respect it does not.

Werpehowski's account is faithful to Barth's understanding of human agency. His reading is more perceptive than those that argue Barth's account is merely episodic and voluntarist. The history of Barth interpretation on this issue supports Werpehowski's claim, much of it done ten or more years after his essay.[25] While the subsequent work of John Webster in particular has done much to flesh out the ways in which Barth's work affirms both God's sovereignty and the integrity of human agency, Werpehowski's unique contribution is his description of the ways in which history and command are linked in Barth's ethics. He does so while maintaining an emphasis on the christocentrism of history that is faithful to Barth.

Regarding Barth's rejection of the *analogia entis*, Werpehowski's position deviates from Barth's. Take, for example, what Werpehowski says in his essay on practical wisdom: "What I have said about theological concreteness, it is essential to add now, is not only fully compatible with but requires an affirmation of an objectively valid 'natural morality' that may be attained, even in the weakness of sin, through some sort of 'acquired virtue.'"[26] Werpehowski here treats sin as a disease that weakens but does not destroy our ability to know and do the good. Such a view of sin mirrors that of Erich Przywara, which Barth rejects on the basis of a Reformed understanding of sin. For Barth, sin results in a complete break in the relationship between God and creation. His understanding is much more radical than the one provided by Werpehowski here.

To be fair to Werpehowski, he is not trying to be faithful to all of Barth's thought in his own account of practical wisdom. While he draws from Barth in that account, he is also critical of theological views that deny any natural human capacity to know the good. On the other side, he is also wary of those accounts that are overly sanguine about that capacity. Nonetheless, his middle-of-the-road position makes his account suspect on Barthian grounds.

A second concern arises regarding the basis of Werpehowski's conception of natural morality. Drawing from Col. 1:15–17, in which Christ is described as the firstborn of creation, in whom all things came into being, Werpehowski concludes,

[It follows] then the human creature's reality is in, through, and for Jesus Christ. A theological ethic of natural morality must generally but still concretely identify how the goods that human creatures seek as such are in their distinction grounded in, ordered to, and hold together with God's sovereign, reconciling, and redeeming love.[27]

Werpehowski claims that the christological pattern embedded *in creation* is the basis for humanity's grounding in and orientation toward Jesus Christ. A Barthian reading would challenge this position. For Barth God's electing decision to be God for us is the basis for the claim that our reality is "in, through, and for Jesus Christ." God elected to be God for us logically prior to his decision to bring creation into being. In this way Barth is able to maintain both the radical break between God and creature that results from human sin, on the one hand, and the assurance of God's grace, on the other. If our identity in Christ were really rooted in the fact that we were created, then sin would present a problem.

One way to resolve the problem is to view sin as a disease that impairs the relationship but does not sever it. This is the traditional Roman Catholic position and appears to be the one that Werpehowski also holds. The Reformed tradition, however, has consistently viewed sin as a radical break in the relationship. Granted, Barth's position provides a unique spin. Traditionally, Christ's work of reconciliation on the cross is the bridge that reestablishes the relationship. Barth's doctrine of election places the basis of reconciliation logically prior to creation. However, whether one holds to the classic Reformed position or Barth's modification of it, Werpehowski's position is problematic. Because of sin, our access to our identity in Christ does not come through our created identity. It is not found in us but is only possible through God's grace. Remember that for Barth the *imago Dei* is not something we possess apart from God; it is the continual work of the Holy Spirit.[28]

Finally, does Werpehowski's account manage to satisfy Barthian concerns about habitual grace? The question here is whether Werpehowski's account of grace in sanctification avoids Barth's criticisms of divinization mentioned in the last chapter and also embraces a Chalcedonian understanding of divine and human interaction. It does.

Keep in mind Barth's concern that in habitual grace we possess God's grace through our own powers. While the preceding discussion about Werpehowski's views of natural morality might call into question whether or not God's grace is intrinsic to our being, a distinction needs to be made between nature and grace in Werpehowski's account. What is objectionable above is his account of natural morality. For Werpehowski our natural capacity to know the good is not simply and irreducibly a result of God's grace in our election but rather is something we have access to through our creation. However, in relation to God's grace, Werpehowski is careful to emphasize our dependence at all times on God in receiving grace. His emphasis on Luther's *simul iustus et peccator* demonstrates his commitment to an understanding of grace that is congruent with a Reformed understanding.

Karl Barth also rejects a synergism in which we are moment by moment aided by the Holy Spirit to act on God's grace. The problem with this view of sanctification is that it minimizes our freedom to respond openly to God's grace. Werpehowski's account successfully avoids such a problem. In his essay on Barth's use of narrative he is careful to note Barth's understanding of God's relationship with creation, which is characterized by two types of freedom: freedom from us and freedom for us. Expressed in christocentric terms, they remind us that Christ is both above us and with us. He stands in judgment of both structural and personal sin, but God in Christ is also in covenant with us. We are free actors within that covenant. God does not coerce but coaxes us to acknowledge his presence and saving work in Christ.

And what of Barth's own Chalcedonian understanding of divine and human interaction? Is Werpehowski's work faithful to this understanding? Yes. In regard to the asymmetrical relationship between God and us, Werpehowski's account makes it clear that the direction of grace proceeds from Christ to the human. Integrity and intimacy follow from what was just said about the covenantal relationship between God and us made known in Christ. In this covenant we have a close relationship with God, yet our agency and freedom remain intact.

VIRTUE ETHICS WITHOUT RECOURSE
TO NATURAL MORALITY

Given the divergence between Werpehowski and Barth on natural morality, a Reformed virtue ethics on Barthian lines will have to part ways with Werpehowski's reading of Barth. Yes, to echo Werpehowski's use of Colossians 1:15–17, all things were created through and for Christ, and all things remain held together by him. But for Barth all things have also been disrupted; the relationship between God and us has been severed due to our transgression, leaving humankind both stranded and incapacitated. How, then, is there room in Barth's account of the Christian life for character formed by the biblical witness?

If the development of character in the Christian life does not come from some innate ability on our side, then it must come from God's revelation to us. And indeed that is the Barthian explanation. As Barth's ethic of divine command illustrates, God's initiating revelation not only provides the context for our proper response but also makes it possible. The Christian life, then, is construed in terms of obedience to those commands.

Barth's emphasis on God's revelation as the initiating context within which the Christian life is lived raises a set of questions about the possibilities for a virtue ethic. It appears that what is required is not some settled disposition within which character is fostered but rather a spontaneous obedience to the divine command. And if that spontaneous obedience really is just that, spontaneous, what room is there for human reasoning in the process of deciding how one should act? On the other hand, if, as Barth maintains, human freedom flourishes under the divine command, then it must be the case that we receive God's command in such a way that our human faculties of perception and reason are fully engaged rather than overthrown. But how is this different from the formulation of Thomas Aquinas that grace does not destroy but perfects human nature? If God's command is the form God's grace takes in our lives, then for Barth it seems that God's grace does in some way transform us, at least to the extent that it wakens us up to our true state of relationship with God in Jesus Christ. To a certain extent, then, Barth agrees with Thomas. But to what extent?

Answering these questions involves a consideration of what training in the virtues looks like in three different contexts: (1) the moral virtues in Aristotelian ethics, (2) the infused virtues in Thomistic ethics, and (3) all virtues in the new model for Reformed virtue ethics proposed here. By focusing on the process through which we acquire or receive the virtues in each of these contexts, it can be demonstrated that Reformed virtue ethics within a Barthian theological framework is possible. And not only is such ethics possible; it also has a unique set of characteristics that distinguishes it from other accounts. As we will see, these characteristics make Reformed moral virtue an attractive alternative to other accounts of virtue, both inside and outside of the church.

TRAINING IN MORAL VIRTUE

Aristotle's Account

Since much contemporary discussion on virtue ethics draws from the work of Aristotle, it is helpful to start with his account before proceeding to a description of virtue that presupposes a Christian moral and theological framework. For Aristotle there are two kinds of virtue: intellectual and moral.[29] The proper dispositions associated with the intellectual virtues are a result of the potential that one has at birth and the realization of that potential that comes from proper teaching. Moral virtue is a result of habit, which is contained in the name *ethikē*, a slight variation from *ethos* (habit). Aristotle notes that the products of the arts are different from the actions of the virtues in that it is enough if the products of the arts are good in themselves, but it is not enough if the actions of a person are good in themselves. To be virtuous requires that the person performing these actions do so in knowledge, consciously choosing these acts and choosing them for their own sakes. Furthermore, one's action must proceed from a firm and unchangeable character. The acts of an artist, in contrast, do not require the last two conditions but only that they result in products that are deemed of high quality.[30]

For Aristotle, becoming a person of virtue requires both luck and innate capability. In order to possess virtue fully one must be a person of practical wisdom, but such wisdom takes time to acquire; it is not an inborn trait. To a large extent its acquisition depends on the proper training at a young age. But in order to choose the right mentors one would already need to possess practical wisdom, and even then they may not be available. Therefore, whether or not one has the right teachers is a matter of luck.

Second, practical wisdom involves one's own judgments about how to act in different contexts. Aristotle defines virtue in this way: "Virtue, then, is a state involving rational choice, consisting in a mean relative to us and determined by reason—the reason, that is, by reference to which the practically wise person would determine it."[31] When we mature in virtue, it is our own judgments that count, not the judgments of our teachers. What is required is something more than the mere ability to comprehend what we have learned. A sense of judgment is required to choose the right rational principle within the particular circumstances of a given situation. Those particulars will no doubt be different from the ones we were exposed to by our teachers. There are therefore those who fail to exhibit practical wisdom, even among those who have had the right training.

How do we become persons of virtue? For Aristotle training in virtue requires more than mere obedience to commands or dictates of law. It requires that our passions and reason be transformed, which does not happen through obedience alone. We have to choose the right actions for the right reasons. In one sense this comes to us naturally since, as Aristotle notes, human beings are the most imitative animals in the world.[32] We naturally seek to imitate those around us. The people we end up imitating are those we love and, ideally, are loved by. Our parents, or those who raise us, therefore, have a tremendous influence on our formation in virtue.[33]

In the early stages of imitation our motivation for doing the right actions is to please those we love or to avoid punishment. In the former case, it is the pleasure that we derive from their enjoyment of our actions that we seek as our end.[34] At this stage, we are not yet mature in virtue, which requires that we seek virtue for virtue's sake. However, the process of imitation, or *mimesis,* is not simply an unthinking copying of someone else's behavior.[35] It involves taking note of the distinctive features of that behavior in comparison to the behavior of others. Second, the particular circumstances within which the act of imitation takes place will be different from the original act. Different actors will be involved, and the action itself will be part of a sequence of actions different from the original. Therefore imitation requires both careful reasoning and imagination put into practice. It is more complex than mimicry.

For instance, imitating a courageous person means more than simply copying the individual's actions on the battlefield. Courage looks different in different circumstances, on the battlefield and off of it, depending on the dangers one faces. Imitation then requires the assessment of what makes for courage in these different circumstances, imagination as to how it applies to one's current situation, and improvisation in terms of how to act appropriately. We grow in the virtue of courage by first imitating courageous acts where the character of such acts is most clear until, by stages, our practical reasoning in relation to increasingly complex situations involving dangers is finely honed. What develops, finally, is a stability of character that makes acting in courageous ways second nature. At the same time, our reasons for acting in that way go beyond admiration for our mentors and instead become an appreciation for and love of the virtue itself.

As Alasdair MacIntyre notes in *After Virtue,* virtuous acts are not interpretable as such in isolation. They make sense only in terms of a narrative, an account of a series of actions with a beginning, middle, and end. And since virtue, properly understood, extends to one's life as a whole, to be a person of character requires that the narrative of our lives have continuity across time and place. Since we are shaped by the social practices in which we participate, it is important that these practices be rooted in a larger narrative that links our own life stories with those of our community, past and present. Otherwise, our lives become fractured. Our narrative thus ought to be part of a living tradition in which others participate. A living tradition, for MacIntyre, is "an historically extended, socially embodied argument, and an argument precisely in part about the goods which constitute that tradition."[36] Traditions thus span generations and provide the boundaries within which an individual's pursuit of excellence takes place. However, being living traditions, they evolve over time, changing according to the accrued wisdom of those practicing the tradition. Arguments about the goods that constitute the tradition require that there is more agreement than disagreement about those goods, for the very terms within which the arguments are framed need to be familiar to all the participants, and these terms provide the framework within which the arguments are made.

Thomas Aquinas and the Infused Moral Virtues

While Thomas Aquinas did not introduce Aristotelian virtue ethics to Christianity, his baptism and his reformulation of said ethics have proved profoundly influential up to the present. In that reformulation Thomas distinguished natural from infused virtues. Thomas notes that while the natural virtues involve objects proportionate to human nature, the infused virtues involve objects that surpass our nature and can be attained only through God's power. The infused virtue of charity, for example, involves the proper love one has for God. Since it is beyond the capacity of our will and reason to love God properly, our acts of charity depend on God's grace, which works "in us without us." This is not only true of the theological virtues, for even the acquired moral virtues have their infused counterparts. And while Thomas's account of the acquisition of acquired virtue is similar to Aristotle's, his account of the infused virtues is quite different.

Since we receive the infused virtues through God's grace rather than through a process of training, we might ask whether the infused virtues really are virtues at all. Not only do they appear without training, but the whole social context within which they arise seems to make little difference, since it is God's action that is the deciding factor. What is it, then, that the infused and acquired virtues have in common such that we may include them together as two types of the same thing? The question may be addressed by looking at one particular moral virtue, prudence (also called practical wisdom), and by comparing infused prudence to acquired prudence. The similarities evident in this one virtue will demonstrate the similarities between the infused and acquired virtues as a whole. What follows is a short description of Thomas's view of infused prudence, the resulting consequences for the infused virtues in general, as well as the relationship between the infused and the acquired virtues. Once this is in place, an account of practical wisdom in line with Reformed concerns may be drawn.

Thomas's position on the infused virtue of prudence arises out of his church context. He had to affirm the church's position that infant baptism was sufficient for salvation, meaning that the infused virtues were present in the infant after baptism. Among the infused virtues was prudence. But clearly infants do not exhibit this virtue through their actions. How, then, was the virtue present? Thomas's answer relies on two distinctions: (1) the difference between prudence in relation to our salvation and prudence in relation to worldly affairs and (2) the difference between a habit that yields the appropriate action and one that does not yet yield such action. Baptized infants possess prudence in relation to their salvation but not in relation to worldly affairs. In addition, since they are not yet at the age where they possess the use of reason, the virtue of prudence exists only potentially. Still, Thomas insists that even baptized infants have all the virtues necessary for their salvation.[37]

The other infused virtues are like infused prudence in that we receive them in undeveloped form. We grow in charity, for instance, through acts of charity. Although immediately after receiving the infused virtue of charity we have what is required for our salvation, the perfection of the virtue requires repeated action. Thomas writes of infused prudence that its practice "merits increase, until it becomes perfect, even as the other virtues."[38] In contrast, acquired virtues are formed through repeated actions that eventually yield the proper settled disposition in us. Consequently, acting on these virtues comes to us easily due to ingrained habits.

The ethicist Jennifer Herdt argues that in Thomas's account the process by which the infused virtues are perfected mirrors the process by which the acquired virtues are acquired. As she notes, this is borne out by Thomas's account of charity, in which "each act of charity disposes to an increase of charity."[39] The primary difference, as Thomas points out, is that repeated action merely *strengthens* the infused habit whereas for the acquired virtues repeated action *causes* the habit. Despite this difference, the process of growth in the infused virtues requires a support system identical to that of acquired virtue: the presence of virtuous exemplars, instruction by mentors, personal motivation, and practice. Consequently, the infused virtues are more like the acquired virtues that Aristotle describes than we might at first think.

Reformed Virtue

What does training in virtue look like for my proposed Reformed moral virtue ethics along Barthian theological lines? In certain ways it resembles Thomas's account of the development of the infused virtues but with some important caveats. Thomas's account depends on his understanding that grace does not destroy but perfects human nature. As pointed out in the second chapter, this formulation runs aground for Barth. His Reformed concern for the sovereignty of God, the freedom of God's grace, and the depth of human sin make it problematic. The account of moral virtue ethics proposed here takes into consideration these concerns and in many respects is influenced by Barth's understanding of sanctification. This section begins with a description of Barth's doctrine of sanctification. Once this doctrine has been foregrounded, training in the Reformed virtues will be discussed.

Consider Barth's views on sanctification found in *CD* IV/2, paragraph 66, titled "The Sanctification of Man." For the purposes of our thesis, the questions to be addressed here have again to do with the possibility of virtue in sanctification. The overriding question, as it was with justification, is whether there is room for virtue in Barth's account. In fact there is, on the grounds that his understanding of participation in Christ has a relational dimension that perdures through time. Paul's account of Christ's relation to the church in 1 Corinthians 12 stands as the model: with Christ as the head, the community of believers participates in the holiness of Christ as his body in the world, through obedience to Christ's commands. It is only within that relational dimension that virtue is possible.

Barth views sanctification in christological terms as the exaltation of the Son of Man. This upward movement corresponds to the humiliation of the Son of God, the downward movement in which our justification is secured. In the logical ordering of justification and sanctification, justification precedes sanctification. For Barth, however, this ordering does not imply that justification is a onetime and finished event in the life of the sinner. Rather, we always stand in need of justification.

Barth objects to accounts of sanctification in which there is continuous growth in the Christian life, in which the effects of grace are partial and in which grace may be measured in quantity. Instead, his view of sanctification is faithful to Luther's "*simul (totus) iustus, simul (totus) peccator.*"[40] Notice the *totus/totus* formula here: we are *totally* justified and *totally* a sinner. As a consequence, there is within us a continual struggle. Barth is careful to note that he is not talking about a struggle between one part of us and another. Rather, we are at the same time both completely under the power of sin and completely redeemed. This double determination is not a permanent state. Ultimately, eschatologically, we are fully determined by Christ's grace. In the interim, however, we struggle. Our conversion, far from alleviating that struggle, only exacerbates it as it awakens us to the fact of our sinfulness. Christians sin as do non-Christians; what distinguishes them is the fact that Christians acknowledge their sinfulness.

Barth's dialogue partner throughout this paragraph is John Calvin. While Calvin's doctrine of sanctification has much to commend it, Barth also sees serious deficiencies. The two most significant are Calvin's doctrine of limited atonement and his overemphasis on the no of God's judgment in relation to God's yes. These two deficiencies are related. Because Calvin did not recognize that Christ's saving death had universal significance, he was unable to realize that God's yes was the overriding and determining answer to our no.[41]

Barth's affirmation raises an interesting question regarding virtue. At first glance, Calvin's doctrine of sanctification offers more room for virtue since Calvin claims there is room for progress in the Christian life, albeit slow progress. Barth's emphasis on Luther's *simul iustus et peccator* suggests a portrait of the Christian life in which progress is illusory, every step forward a false one. But consider Barth's choice of language in paragraph 66, which includes both God's twofold command to "halt" and to "proceed." The command to halt is spoken to the totally sinful determination of our humanity; the command to proceed is spoken to the new person in Christ.[42] So there is a very definite and real progress in the Christian life, but it is not described in psychological terms as if our faculties gradually came under the sway of grace and less under the sway of sin. Rather, that progress is a deepening in our relation to Christ. While Barth emphasizes the *disruptive* characteristics of Christ's grace as it comes to us and our moment-to-moment response awakened by that relation, nonetheless there is also a *continuous* dimension to that relation. True, only Christ as the Son of Man was fully open to the determination of the command of God and thus uniquely without sin. But we through our relation with Christ are also empowered to say no to sin. Of course we do not do so on a consistent basis, but nonetheless we have that power.

Is it possible in this conception of sanctification to have an account of virtue, one in which training in virtue makes sense? Consider Barth's portrait of participation in Christ found in the second section of paragraph 66. Our participation in Christ has both a confrontational and a responsive dimension. Christ confronts us in our slothful state of sin and thus begins the struggle within us between the new person as determined in Christ and the old person bound by sin. The responsive dimension consists in our raising ourselves up through our attention and focus on Christ. Christians are called to holiness: "As they are called by Him, and look to Him and therefore lift up themselves, they have a part here below in the holiness in which He is the One who alone is holy."[43] The confrontational and responsive dimensions of our participation in Christ resemble the picture of the early stages of training in Aristotelian virtue previously described. Just as a parent would, Christ points out our failings, but in this no is a yes, that contains the promise of human flourishing. We are not simply called to account; we are called to active participation in Christ as a free response to his call to holiness.

But do we remain always a toddler in Christ? Are we always at the stage in which we must hear his corrective commands in order to act in the right way? Are we, like the Corinthians, always at the point at which we are only able to digest spiritual milk? Or is there room for practical wisdom even in Barth's account, wisdom developed over time such that we internalize the commands given to us and choose the right thing to do for the right reasons at the right time, as part of a settled character? The outlines of an answer may be found in a section of *CD* IV/2 titled "The Call to Discipleship."[44]

Barth begins this section by rejecting a simple *imitatio Christi* in which we seek to follow as closely as possible the life of Christ as it is made known in the Gospels and through the commandments he gave both to his followers and to all humankind. A true notion of discipleship, as it is gleaned from the biblical witness (and here Barth's analysis is heavily weighted toward the New Testament), emerges through an examination of the use of the Greek word ἀκολουθεῖν, meaning "following after." Barth notes that this verbal form is used much more frequently in the New Testament than its substantive equivalent, ἀκολούθησις, "discipleship." Therefore, the focus of the biblical witness is on the event of following after Christ rather than a steady state of being his disciple.

Christ commands us to leave our former life behind, as he did to the first disciples. That command comes to us not once but again and again. Our faithful response is one of "simple obedience," a term Barth borrows from Dietrich Bonhoeffer. Our tendency is to put qualifications on God's commands, to look for an escape by twisting the meaning of the command rather than respond to its straightforward interpretation. But God's commands come to us clearly rather than mysteriously. We dodge them when we interpret them along lines that are more amenable to us. Here Barth quotes an example from Bonhoeffer's *Nachfolge* (*Discipleship*):

> A father says to his child: Go to bed, and the child knows what has to be done. But a child versed in this pseudo-theology might argue as follows. My father says: Go to bed. He means that I am tired. He does not want me to be tired. But I can dissipate my tiredness by going out to play. Therefore, when my father says: Go to bed, he really means: Go out to play. If this were the way in which children reasoned in relation to their fathers, or citizens in relation to the state, they would soon meet with a language that cannot be misunderstood—that of punishment. It is only in relation to the command of Jesus that things are supposed to be different.[45]

According to Bonhoeffer, when we start to rely on our own interpretations of the command, we deny Christ's sovereignty, his lordship over our lives. One of the key characteristics of the command is that it is given to us by our Lord, who in giving us the command does not act as therapist or friend but as Lord.

If it appears there is little room for practical wisdom in Barth's account of discipleship, such a conclusion should not be too hastily drawn. True, the command given to the child is simple and clear. Not only that, but obedience to the command, in terms of concrete action, requires little effort or planning. Consider, however, the long-term desires of the father. In issuing the command the father is not only seeking immediate and simple obedience. He wishes for his child to be able one day to discern for herself that she is tired and needs rest. She will need to, at times, discipline herself in this regard, knowing that although she feels wide awake now, if she does not go to sleep, she will suffer tomorrow. Such an internalization of the command is not in any way a form of dodging the command. It instead takes the command more seriously than if she were only to externalize it according to the rubric "Obedience to my father's commands requires that I obey without deliberating into his overriding intention." If this is the rubric the child lives by, at twenty-one she will still be dependent on her father to tell her when to go to bed.

Barth would no doubt object to this interpretation by noting the crucial point at which the analogy breaks down: it misses the infinitely qualitative distinction between Creator and creature that makes creaturely independence impossible. While for Barth God has elected always to be God for us, such a choice does not signal an equal partnership. The relationship between God and us is such that God is always leading and we are always responding to that lead. Independence from God is inconceivable. In contrast, the relationship between father and daughter sketched above evolves over time such that after several years the daughter's growth and change lead to a more equal relationship with her father. Perhaps even as her father ages, she begins to take care of him. Given this distinctive difference in relationship it is misleading to conclude too much from this analogy.

Nevertheless, our dependence on God does not require that our relationship with God remain immature. Barth's emphasis on the character of God's command as eliciting human freedom requires that we respond to that command with our whole being engaged, including our reasoning capabilities. To see what this means, we return to an essay by William Werpehowski that addresses concerns about human responsibility in relation to God's command and demonstrates how maturity in Christ results from our obedience.

Werpehowski's explanation of how human beings receive the divine command is of direct relevance regarding the development of practical wisdom that is fashioned by God's initiating revelation. Werpehowski makes an important distinction between the proper attitude for hearing a divine command (i.e., openness) and the mechanism of the hearing itself.[46] Barth's emphasis that we always hear the divine command anew refers to our method of preparing to hear a divine command. At the center of that preparation is openness: our past experiences must not close us off to the possibility that we will hear something new this time. But the mechanism of the hearing itself is a process of fine-tuning in which our previous experiences with the divine command help us to perceive when God is speaking to us. That is, the divine command arouses in us a moral sensibility that, though it cannot be given an independent status, is nonetheless present and not negated by the divine command.[47]

When defending our actions, we cannot simply claim that we heard the voice of God. For Barth the divine command comes from the God made known in Jesus Christ and thus bears the stamp of God's gracious, electing character. We ought to discern in the command the same gracious, elected presence. In that discernment, then, we must find reasons for why we believe that what we are hearing is in fact God's command and not a command of our own making. As Werpehowski notes in his analysis of Barth, the key feature of God's commands is that they liberate and grant permission. Werpehowski writes,

> *All* commands in the everyday world, including divine commands, ask us a question, demand our acceptance with a categorical seriousness, and aim at corresponding decisions of will. The difference is that the divine command liberates us and grants us permission as it confronts us. Commands of the everyday which bring as well "the granting of a very definite freedom" are the commands of God incarnate in and with the everyday.[48]

First, all commands (including the divine command) elicit our participation. Some interpreters of Barth, including James Gustafson, understand the recipient of such a command to be docile in response. However, Barth's understanding is that recipients are *provoked* by the command. Other modes of address such as declarations and questions about states of affairs rarely provoke an existential response from us. But commands require us to respond in action, either in obedience to the command or in rejection of it. We are required not simply to acknowledge the state of affairs or provide our opinion but to make a decision, a decision that requires that we take responsibility for that state of affairs either to maintain the status quo or to overturn it. Thus, as responsible actors we recognize our culpability and are called to account by the command. Responding to that command in an appropriate manner means that we are prepared to give reasons for our actions, reasons that extend beyond "I was commanded to do X by Y."

Second, as Werpehowski points out, the divine command in particular has a unique character in that it always grants permission and freedom to the human who is confronted by it. No doubt many other types of commands are constricting and limiting to human freedom. They involve the abusive use of power to demean and diminish our humanity. God's command in Jesus Christ does not have this character. Our obedience to that command empowers and liberates us to be who we were meant to be in Jesus Christ, free partners in the covenant initiated by God.

Training in practical wisdom thus involves exposure to God's commands again and again. It is an epistemological process in the sense that God's interaction with us affects us primarily at the level of our awareness and understanding. In contrast, for Thomas Aquinas the acquisition of the infused virtues involves an ontological process that God works "within us without us." It requires that God give us finite creatures the capacity to love an infinite being. This is why Thomas feels the need to assert that when God's grace comes to us, it does not destroy but perfects our nature. If Thomas did not see the effects of God's grace as in some way affecting us ontologically, this would not be a concern. From a Barthian point of view, God's revelation to us always comes through creaturely means and is thus veiled even in its unveiling. It does not transform us ontologically but rather raises our awareness of God's involvement in our lives and the demands such involvement places on us. That awareness reorients us in terms of how we see the world, but it does not involve an ontological change in us.

It follows that Barth's ethic of divine command places a decisive spin on the understanding of "cooperation" involved in divine and human action that is different in character from Thomas Aquinas's understanding of cooperation. For Barth this cooperation is captured by the sequence of God's giving us a command and our response. Such a sequence keeps intact the separation between Creator and creature. For Thomas cooperation entails God's infusion of grace such that we are now ontologically capable of loving God in the appropriate way. Barth's concern is that such a construal muddies the distinction between God and us.

The central question is whether or not the grace that God bestows is christological all the way down. There are enough traces of Neoplatonism and Aristotelianism in Thomas's ontology to raise concerns that grace becomes our possession, in some sense, when God infuses virtues into us. Our account of Reformed virtue avoids these concerns by maintaining the Barthian emphasis on the command of God and the epistemological changes such command effects in us.

However, Thomas's account of the development of infused prudence nonetheless provides important parallels to our account of practical wisdom. Like infused prudence, the Reformed virtue of practical wisdom begins with God's initiating action and cannot be attained through training in certain habits of discernment alone. In addition, like infused prudence the Reformed virtue of practical wisdom is nonetheless strengthened when an individual is part of a community formed around practices of spiritual discernment. A fuller explanation of how this is so will need to be made later when certain Reformed virtues are compared to their Thomistic counterparts.

This chapter has laid the grounds for Reformed moral virtue ethics within a Barthian theological frame in response to those theological concerns that most plagued Barth regarding the theology that usually undergirds Roman Catholic versions of virtue ethics. It remains to be seen what distinctive shape such ethics takes. That will be the task of the next chapter.

4

THE SHAPE OF REFORMED VIRTUE
AFTER BARTH

CHARACTERISTICS OF REFORMED VIRTUE

The following is a set of distinctive understandings about who God is and the character of the relationship between God and us, as Barth construes them, which have been touched on from chapter 1 onward:

1. God is the God who has chosen unequivocally to be God for us.
2. Our identity in Christ is marked by a struggle between old and new: *simul iustus (totus) et peccator (totus)*.
3. The relationship between God and us is unidirectional such that God's grace is given to us in revelation, not through our own natural capacities.
4. The relationship between God and us is Chalcedonian in character.
5. Grace is not separable from the God made known in Jesus Christ but is in fact identified with that person.

The Reformed moral virtue ethic proposed here shares these commitments and in that sense is faithful to the Reformed tradition as Barth understood it. Below is a point-by-point evaluation, demonstrating the congruency between Barth's commitments and the proposed ethic.

The Covenantal Context

Karl Barth and Thomas Aquinas differ regarding their understanding of how grace comes to us. For Barth grace comes to us in the form of the divine command, and its effects in us are epistemological. For Thomas, grace is infused into us. In relation to the virtues, this infusion results in an ontological change that allows us to love God properly, perfecting our nature without destroying it. One might well ask how it is that in Barth's view grace does not effect an ontological change in us at our conversion. The answer requires saying something about Barth's own ontological commitments, which are centered on the concept of God's covenant with us.

God's commands do not come to us willy-nilly out of the blue. Rather, as Barth explains, they come as a result of God's electing decision to be God for us. That decision is verified and confirmed in the life, death, and resurrection of Jesus Christ. Thus, according to Barth's objective soteriology, the terms for our salvation are already complete. Our conversion is the event in which we become conscious of our salvation. Our salvation, in an objective sense, is not dependent on our awareness, acknowledgment, or consent. Yet the logic of Barth's ethic of divine command does require that our response be a free response. To understand how this may be so, we need to examine Barth's covenantal ontology in more detail.[1]

For Barth our being is determined by God's electing decision to be with us. The chief identifying characteristic of human beings is their relation to the triune God made known in Jesus Christ. In an important sense, then, there is nothing we can do to negate or violate this covenant. Our status as creatures in relation to God is determined on God's side, not ours. We cannot through our actions or inactions overturn that status. Yet, in another sense, how we respond to God's commands is of vital importance. While our human essence is constituted by what we were chosen to be by God, our human existence is constituted by our own actions. Our essence is fully determined by God's decision and action to be in relation with us, and that continues even when we turn away from God. But when we respond to God's commands in free obedience, our existential state comes closer to the essence of who we actually are.

God's unconditional covenantal relationship with us sets the stage for our justification. One criticism of the Protestant notion of justification is that it is a legal fiction. God's declaration of our righteousness does not match the reality on the ground. How is it that we can affirm with Luther that we are *simul iustus et peccator* and yet reject this criticism? As the theologian Bruce McCormack points out, the solution is to recognize the eschatological dimensions of God's declaration that we are righteous. While our actions may not yet reflect that essence, eschatologically we have the promise that, like Jesus, there will be congruence between our existence and our essence, between our actions and God's intentions for us. Ultimately, God's declaration that we are justified effects what it declares. McCormack writes,

> The regeneration, which flows from justification as its consequence, is the initiation of a work that is completed only in the eschaton, only in the glorification of the saints. Hence, God's pronouncement of the sinner as an innocent takes place with a view towards the final purification of the sinner in the eschaton.[2]

McCormack notes that when a human judge makes a judgment, it is only a provisional assessment. The contents of that judgment may or may not reflect true guilt or innocence. That judgment affects how we are viewed by others, but it does not affect our true state of innocence or guilt. However, when God makes a judgment, it brings into effect innocence or guilt.

Although we are guilty of sin, God's judgment of innocence begins the process by which we actually become free from sin. Yet the full effects of God's verdict are only completed eschatologically, though they begin immediately at the point of justification.

Importantly this process is construed by Barth as epistemological rather than ontological. Our ontological status has been secured by God's electing decision. What changes is our awareness of that decision. When we realize God's decision applies to us as well, we become more attuned to the command of God in our lives. That perception influences the depth of our relationship with God as it develops over time. Throughout this process, our ontological status does not change.

The Reformed moral virtue ethics proposed here incorporates Barth's understanding of covenantal ontology in the following ways: First, an ethic of divine command is affirmed that is situated within the same unconditional covenantal context that Barth describes. The freeing and life-giving dimensions of God's commands become clear within this context. These commands draw us into a relationship with a loving God who has chosen to be with us regardless of how faithful we have been to God. Second, this account of Reformed virtue ethics affirms the reality that each of us is fully justified and at the same time a sinner. Such an affirmation raises complications for virtue ethics, which in its Aristotelian form would deny this sort of interior struggle in the heart of a virtuous person. These complications will be addressed shortly. Finally, this account affirms the limitations of looking for true virtue in this life and recognizes the eschatological dimensions of God's sanctifying work in us.

Simul Iustus et Peccator

According to Barth's interpretation of Luther's dictum not only are we totally justified, but we are fully determined in our new humanity just as we are fully determined in our sinfulness. Each of these claims will be examined in turn in relation to our proposal for Reformed moral virtue ethics.

Barth speaks of a new movement of one's entire being after one's conversion. It is an inbreaking of the focused attention on God's will for our lives that will be fully sustained only in the eschaton. Yet this movement nonetheless captures our whole being.[3] In relation to the virtue of practical wisdom, it is characterized by the capacity to reason rightly in a given situation about the proper course of action as well as the will to take that course of action. Our reorientation toward God, given to us by God, enables us to do just that.

The mitigating factor is, of course, that the full determination of our sinfulness is always impeding our ability to follow Christ faithfully. In

Aristotelian virtue ethics, the person of virtue has a unity of character such that this kind of interior conflict has been conquered.[4] For example, consider the distinctions among temperance, continence, and incontinence. A temperate person is one who, though his appetite is stirred, walks by an ice cream store without regret. He does so because he delights more in the rational principle of moderation than in the stimulation of his taste buds. A continent person, on the other hand, has visions of a double chocolate sundae but resists these temptations and walks on. Although he is able to suppress his desires, it is difficult for him to delight in the course he has taken, since the vision of the chocolate sundae holds more appeal. An incontinent person doesn't even have the strength to resist and rushes in to consume more than he ought. While it is clear that the incontinent person lacks virtue, it is less so with the continent one. Nonetheless, Aristotle argues that only the temperate person exhibits true virtue, since only his appetite is perfectly in line with his practical reason about what constitutes the good.

In Barth's schema, we are at the same time both temperate and incontinent. If Christ commanded us to give up ice cream, the new person would do so without any qualms while the old person would look for every opportunity to consume that double chocolate sundae. Because this inner conflict never goes away until the eschaton, Barth claims that we make a "first step" every time we obey the command of God. Such obedience is not ingrained in us whereas disobedience is. Yet the future promise is that the person of sin is dying away while the new person is destined for eternal life. Where then in this picture is there room for virtue?

That room is made in terms of the awakening of the new person, who is provoked by the command of God as it confronts him. In what does that awakening consist? It consists in the fact that he recognizes the rebellious "double chocolate sundae" voice as a foreign one to which he is no longer bound, which is dying and destined for destruction. It consists in a new recognition that he is bound by Christ alone, the Christ in whom his true freedom resides.

Practical wisdom, developed through an ongoing relationship, is required in order to recognize Christ as such. Christ is made known to us not in general and vague terms but in specific ones, just as his commands to us are specific. As we continue in the Christian life, we develop a specific history with the living God, in whom our salvation is no longer only de jure but de facto as well. Hearing that command and responding with the appropriate actions results in increasing practical wisdom on our part to the extent that it involves a deepening of relationship. That is, our growing ability to respond appropriately to the command of God is based on an increased understanding of the God made known to us in Jesus Christ. Just as with any loving relationship that develops gradually, this relationship allows us to see the depth of God's love in new and more penetrating ways over time, making our humble response to God's grace deeper and more genuine as it matures.

In this model of virtue through relation with Christ, our response to the divine command confirms who we are in Christ. That command has an unsettling effect in us, awakening our new being in Christ while at the same time challenging our old determination as sinner. From the standpoint of our capacity for virtue, our new being in Christ is similar to Thomas's notion of infused virtue: it creates in us the proper capacities to respond in the right ways, yet it requires action on our part to be fully realized. The more we act in response to God's commands, the more we come to know what it means to be in Christ, to participate in Christ. Our de jure salvation becomes our de facto salvation.

God's commands have two characteristics that are important to consider from the standpoint of virtue ethics: they are addressed to communities as well as individuals, and taken as a whole, they have a consistent character. Barth speaks of "main lines" of response to God's commands. In other words, there are certain predictable patterns to God's commands. Christians are called to obey God "by the fact that His commanding, while it does not require the same thing of everyone, or even of the same person in every time and situation, always moves along one or more of these prominent lines."[5] The consequence of this abiding character of God's commands is that communities of faith, and in particular certain exemplary individuals in that community, may help us to obey the command.

Consider Christ's command to renounce earthly possessions, which Barth names as one of the prominent lines of communication from Christ to us. This command is not understood by Barth to mean that we necessarily take a vow of poverty but that we reject the sovereignty these possessions all too often have over our lives. Here Barth quotes from certain passages of Matthew's Gospel, including Matt. 6:31: "'Therefore do not worry, saying, "What will we eat?" or "What shall we drink?" or "What will we wear?" For it is the Gentiles who strive for all these things.'" This call from Matthew's Gospel is a call to be a unique community, distinct from the Gentiles, who have a different manner of life. It has not only individual implications but also communal ones. Social context here is important, as is the command to the individual.

It turns out, then, that a virtue ethic of divine command requires more than an intimate relationship between God and an individual. Because God's commands have a communal dimension, Christian community is important. Because God's commands have a continuous dimension, those commands may be embodied in social practices and institutions. Finally, our efforts to follow God's command in our own lives are also aided by exemplary individuals who serve as mentors. In other words, all the support structures that are required for Aristotle's account of the acquired virtues prove efficacious for the development of Reformed virtue as well.

Unidirectionality

Note that in the preceding scenario, we still do not have access to God through our natural capacities but only through God's relation to us. There is no point in our account at which we may depend on those capacities to carry on the life of virtue without God. Whether on an individual or a communal level, our dependence on God's revelation remains throughout. Practical wisdom and the attendant virtues of the Christian life are thus all aimed at relation with God in Jesus Christ. The whole point of these virtues is faithful witness. Since we worship a living God whose commands come to us fresh every day, our faithful witness is dependent on our openness to God's revelation, not on the virtues that have accrued over time. On the other hand, those virtues play a significant role in the acts of witness that constitute the Christian life. Because God's command also has a continuous dimension, it follows that the life of virtue is a form of witness to God.

This conclusion is verified by the fact that for Barth one of the twelve forms of the church's ministry is the production of moral exemplars.[6] The vitality of the life of the community is strengthened by the special witness of these individuals. They attest, through speech and action, the proper ways the whole church should respond to God's grace. Barth observes,

> It does not in any way contradict the priesthood of all believers in the community, nor the equality of all Christians before God as poor and lost sinners saved and kept only by grace, that the community always needs and may point to the existence of specific individuals who, without leaving the multitude of believers within it, and therefore in relation to the world around, stand out as models or examples in their special calling and endowment, its witness being more clear and comprehensible and impressive in their persons and activity than in those of others.[7]

Two Reformed principles are maintained here: salvation by grace alone and the priesthood of all believers. Still, Barth contends that certain individuals have received special callings in the community. Such callings do not negate these important principles.

Note also in this passage that these individuals not only serve as models or examples within the community but in the surrounding world as well. Individuals outside of the community may pattern their lives after these saints of the church without entering the walls of the institution. Do we have here a glimmer of pagan virtue?

Chalcedonian Character

For Karl Barth the relationship between the divine Word and the assumed human nature in Jesus Christ, described at the Council of Chalcedon, becomes a pattern for the relationship between God and us. George Hunsinger, as noted in chapter 2, highlights three key attributes of this relationship: asymmetry, intimacy, and integrity. Barth's ethic of divine command demonstrates all three characteristics: asymmetry in terms of God's initiating action and our faithful response; intimacy in virtue of the fact that the one who commands is Immanuel, God with us; and integrity as embodied in the nature of the command, which does not coerce us but leads us into a free response.

Our account of practical wisdom and virtue ethics also has a Chalcedonian character to it. The divine command always holds center place, practical wisdom and the other virtues being the result of our human response over time to that command, which has a continuous as well as a disruptive character. However, in contrast to Thomas's account of the virtues, which focuses on their continuous character, the focus in Reformed virtue is on reform and renewal. These are really two sides of the same coin, with Thomas and Barth emphasizing different sides. For example, the virtue of prudence involves right action in a particular set of circumstances. Since circumstances are always varying, right action will take different forms accordingly. The character of that right action, however, will remain the same. Barth emphasizes the confrontational nature of the divine command, in essence focusing on the differing circumstances within which we are called to respond. Thomas focuses on its continuous character. But both need to be present in order for right action in a given situation to be ascertained correctly.

Christological Form of Grace

Our account of practical wisdom and the other virtues supports the Reformed claim that grace has a specifically christological form. Barth's main concern about Roman Catholic ethics, particularly as formulated by Thomas Aquinas's grace-nature axiom, is that the grace it articulates is too general to be considered Christian. Second, in this understanding of grace Christ might at some point become superfluous as we ourselves are perfected. Salvation, in this scenario, entails the proper ordering of human beings such that our reason is properly ordered to God, and our will is properly directed to the dictates of our reason. Barth, on the other hand, emphasizes that even in our fully redeemed state we remain dependent on Christ.

Our dependency on Christ is maintained in this account because the content of God's revelation is at all times centered on Jesus Christ. We are witnesses in response to that command, and the one to whom we witness is Christ. While God's commands perpetually challenge our ingrained assumptions, they also meet us where we are. For Barth we remain dependent on Christ for our sanctification. His concern is not violated by saying that our dependence on Christ evolves over time such that Christ's speech to us takes on a different flavor in response to a deepening relationship.[8]

A COMPARISON OF SPECIFIC VIRTUES:
THOMISTIC VERSUS REFORMED

So far the focus has been on how Reformed virtue is possible if we take seriously certain distinctive characteristics of divine and human action laid out by Karl Barth. But beyond the general contours, what does such an ethic look like? To answer that question we turn to an examination of three virtues: temperance, prudence, and love (charity). What follows is a comparison between Thomistic conceptions of these virtues and our proposed virtue ethics along Barthian theological lines. The point of the comparison is to highlight the concrete differences between the two.

For Thomas Aquinas, each of these three virtues is in a different category from the other: temperance is a moral virtue; prudence, intellectual; and charity, theological. Each of these virtues thus has been selected as a representative of its kind. While Thomas lists four cardinal virtues and three theological virtues, there is no need to come up with a comprehensive list of Reformed virtues. This section is meant to be suggestive rather than exhaustive. After a description of what these virtues look like in Thomas's account, we will consider their Reformed counterparts.

Temperance

Temperance, according to Thomas, is that habit that yields actions that restrain and tame the passions of the senses. Our passions may mislead our reason and our will through either overindulgence or avoidance. As a consequence there are two corresponding moral virtues having to do with moderating the passions: temperance and courage. The virtue of temperance deals with the former tendency (overindulgence), and the virtue of courage, with the latter (avoidance).[9]

Temperance as an *acquired* virtue is governed by its object: the desires of the senses (namely, sex, food, and drink). The rule or mean that guides this virtue is twofold: what is not harmful to reason (e.g., too much alcohol) and what is not harmful to the body. Temperance as an *infused* virtue considers its object, the desires of the senses, in relation to the good of its ultimate end, God. The rule or mean that guides the infused virtue is determined by Scripture, that a person should "chastise his body, and bring it into subjection."[10]

For a Reformed view of temperance, consider Barth's assertion regarding a Christian's proper attitude toward wealth. He claims that since the foundation of the church, God has persistently called us to divest ourselves of our money and possessions. This divestment consists in recognizing the lordship of Christ in all of our human affairs, since we cannot serve both God and money (Matt. 6:24). If necessary, we may be required to give all we have away. At the very least we should be willing to do so if called on. This attitude may be extended to created goods in general, including all those things involving desires of the touch. Thus sexual relationships also fall into this category.

Virtue, as defined by Aristotle and affirmed by Aquinas, has to do with a mean. Where is the mean in voluntary poverty? What Barth is suggesting would be considered by many a vicious extreme. Yet there is a mean here as well, but it is one determined by God's command to us in our unique situation. Jesus' command to the rich young ruler to give up everything no doubt stems from his assessment that it is the right action given the circumstances, since it is precisely money and possessions that keep the rich young ruler from following Christ. While this command appears to us to be extreme, it is exactly fitting in context. God's command to us follows similar lines but addresses us in our unique situation. Thus the form it takes will be different yet nonetheless perfectly suited. The fittingness of this form is essentially the equivalent of Aristotle's mean.

One of the marks of the Reformed virtue espoused here is that it begins and ends with God's commands. Reformed virtues thus resemble the infused virtues in Thomas's virtue ethics, since their character comes to us from God, not from our own activity. Nevertheless, like the infused virtues in Thomas, our response to God's initiating activity strengthens the virtue. It follows that the Reformed virtue of temperance resembles Thomas's infused virtue of temperance. In form, it comes to us instantaneously as the command of God. However, because of our twofold determination, we still experience a struggle to obey the command, a struggle that doesn't appear in Aristotle's description of an acquired habit.

What then becomes of the pagan (civic) virtue of acquired temperance? A full response to this question will have to wait until later in the chapter when we examine the role of the state in the formation of virtue. An argument will be made there that since the commands of God are mediated through a variety of communities, institutions, and practices, pagan virtue is possible as a response to the commands of God as they come to us through these media. We have need of food, drink, and sex. God's commands recognize those needs and affirm them through, among other means, the established ordering of the state. For those who recognize those commands as God's commands, our needs are superseded by our identity in Christ as witnesses to the gospel. That witness may require that we abstain from such goods when called to do so.

Prudence

In Thomas's schema, prudence is a virtue unique among the intellectual virtues in that it requires a good will to be complete. As an acquired virtue it has as its object right action in relation to practical matters in worldly affairs. Right action requires not only that our reason make the proper assessments but that our will yield to reason's dictates in the appropriate ways. Prudence as an infused virtue has a different objective: right action in the fellowship of the saints.[11]

Prudence for Thomas consists of three acts: inquiring, judging, and commanding. First, we seek counsel and inquire into the best course of action. Second, we weigh the information we have received and judge which course is best. And finally, our reason issues commands that yield particular actions we willingly take. The moral virtues depend on prudence to provide the means to their respective ends. Although acquired prudence relies on the application of a small set of general principles, it takes time to develop since these principles themselves provide only very broad direction. A good deal of experience is needed not only to draw from the relevant principles but also to apply them rightly in a given context. As stated above, not all saints have this ability in relation to worldly affairs. But they do at least have the proper form necessary to act in prudent ways in relation to their salvation.

What does the pagan virtue of prudence look like for Thomas? Regarding this question, he points out that there are three different types of prudence: false, imperfect, and perfect. False prudence is exemplified by the parable of the Shrewd Manager (Luke 16:1–8) and entails right action in relation to a bad end (e.g., the actions of a skilled thief). Imperfect prudence is either prudence in relation to an end that is good but particular (e.g., running a successful business) or the failure to execute properly a course of action concerning life as a whole (concerning one's chief end), on which one has inquired into rightly and judged rightly. This is true but imperfect prudence. Finally, there is true and perfect prudence, in which all three acts of prudence are performed rightly in respect to a good end concerning life in general.[12] Pagans may exhibit the first two types of prudence but not the third, since only Christians correctly ascertain the chief end of human beings.

Through a reading of William Werpehowski's essay "Command and History," an account of Reformed practical wisdom (prudence) has already been sketched. The primary task of such prudence is to hear the commands of God as *God's* commands. How do we know that it is God speaking to us? The three acts of prudence that Thomas speaks of fit into the Reformed conception of prudence as follows. We inquire into whether a given command is God's command. Next, we make judgments about the evidence. We then act on that command simply and obediently if in fact it is God's command (or if we consider it to be a good command in general). While the outline is simple enough, in practice discerning God's command requires that we are attuned to the continuities in that command as well as to the unique particulars of our own situation. Many times such discernment best takes place within the context of the life of a Christian community, where we are reminded again and again of God's great love for us and of our indebtedness to God.

In comparison, the pagan virtue of practical wisdom looks quite different. Such wisdom in relation to just management of one's own affairs involves honesty, industry, and ingenuity. But godly virtue often has a very different look, that of prodigality, wherein we give up that which has been given to us with no hope of earthly return. Consider Jesus' parable of the Great Banquet in Luke 14:12–14:

> "When you give a luncheon or a dinner, do not invite your friends or your brothers or your relatives or rich neighbors, in case they may invite you in return, and you would be repaid. But when you give a banquet, invite the poor, the crippled, the lame, and the blind. And you will be blessed, because they cannot repay you, for you will be repaid at the resurrection of the righteous."

Note that godly righteousness is radically different from worldly righteousness; it has the look of magnanimity since it involves a disproportionate giving. According to Aristotle, human standards of commutative justice center on giving according to what is due to another. Heavenly righteousness, as it reflects God's gracious act of justification, is giving over and above what is due to another.

Here important parallels may be made to the infused virtue of prudence in Thomas's schema. The truly virtuous person is the one who recognizes God as the proper end and whose generosity is proportionate not to what is due to the neighbor but to what is due to God. Practical wisdom in this godly virtue looks very different from practical wisdom as it applies to worldly affairs in and of themselves.

Charity

According to Aquinas, charity is an infused virtue that, like the other infused virtues, "God works in us without us."[13] The theological virtues of faith, hope, and charity work in a person toward a supernatural end in a way similar to that of the intellect and the will toward a natural end. The intellect starts first with universal principles and then, aided by the light of natural reason, reaches speculative and practical knowledge. The will tends naturally to good according to reason. In terms of the supernatural end, our intellect is aided by divine light to grasp the truths to be believed by faith. The will is also aided by God to adapt to the supernatural end. Hope is the will reaching out for that end as a movement of intention toward what is attainable. Charity is spiritual union with that end.[14]

The way Aquinas describes it, the growth of charity in us is much like the sprouting of a plant that is activated by the warmth of the sun. We are on a journey toward God. Our progress is marked not by physical movements but by movements of the soul's affections that are activated by the charity that unites us to God. Growth is in fact a part of the very nature of charity: the more our soul grows into unity with God, the greater the capacity for growth.[15] To extend Thomas's analogy, imagine this increased capacity as being like the difference between a small sapling and a giant oak—the oak has a much greater capacity for harnessing the sun's energy for its own growth due to its extensive foliage. God increases charity in us by deepening its hold on us so that our soul more perfectly shares in the likeness of the Holy Spirit, which is the love of the Father for the Son and of the Son for the Father. The deeper charity penetrates our will, the more our will becomes fixed on our ultimate supernatural end.

Yet our hold on charity is fragile. When we choose a created good over God, we lose it. Such a failure originates in the will, the seat of charity. Because our wills are free, we can choose to follow some other form. Such temptation exists on earth, but it won't in heaven. Charity won't be lost where everything that accords with it necessarily strikes us as good. Thomas argues that in heaven, where we see God in his very essence, the essence of goodness itself, there is no possibility that we will lose charity.[16]

How does Thomas reconcile charity's fragility with God's initiating and sovereign grace? On the one hand, he affirms that charity is infused—we cannot simply gain it by doing the works associated with it. As an infused habit it depends on God's infusing and preserving it, like the sun lighting up the atmosphere. And just as the atmosphere darkens the moment an obstacle blocks the sun, so charity immediately ceases to exist in the soul the moment anything impedes this action. All mortal sin contradicts God's commandments and thus is an obstacle to the infusion of charity. Aquinas writes, "From the very fact that a man by his own choice prefers sin to the divine friendship, which requires him to follow God's will, it follows that by one act of mortal sin he immediately loses the habit of charity."[17] In contrast, the acquired virtues cannot be lost by one disordered act. Since they have been built up over time, through numerous actions, it likewise takes numerous actions to undo the proper settled disposition.[18] Thomas's position has the advantage of both affirming God's sovereignty in the act of infusing charity in us and at the same time upholding human free will in accepting that gift. However, it has the disadvantage of placing God's grace at the mercy of human free will, a position that Luther and other Reformers came to challenge.

In order to adopt charity as a Reformed virtue, two concerns must be met. The first regards an objection Luther raises about the role of love in shaping faith. In Thomas's system, our faith in God depends on our love for God. Without it, our faith founders. Luther rejected such a notion and claimed our salvation comes from faith alone. The second concern involves Anders Nygren's assessment that charity is an improper synthesis of two very different forms of love: agape and eros.[19] Whereas agape is self-sacrificing love, eros is love motivated by selfish desires. Nygren argued that a right understanding of Christian love requires eliminating the erotic element. After both of these concerns are explored, their ramifications for Reformed moral virtue will be addressed.

Luther objected to the medieval conception of charity on autobiographical grounds. According to Roman Catholic doctrine at the time, faith was formed by love (*fides caritate formata*). Luther reasoned that if our faith is contingent on our love for God, then our justification depends on it. But he did not see enough empirical evidence of transformation in his own life to substantiate the truth of the doctrine. As a monk, Luther felt no assurance of his salvation. Faith formed by love depends on the quality of love one exhibits, and he was only too aware of the ambivalence of his own motives in living out the Christian life. He perceived that although the doctrine was based on God's grace alone, in practice it revolved around works righteousness. It reassured those whom it should have challenged and let down those whom it should have reassured. Those who didn't take the church's doctrine of sin seriously enough assumed their acts of love were meritorious while folks like Luther were plagued by their own shortcomings.

Luther's understanding of justification and the role that grace plays in it is influenced by his reading of Galatians. In his commentary on Galatians, Luther employs the image of Christ wrapped in our sins as if in a blanket to describe the nonimputation of our sin and God's gracious imputation of Christ's sinlessness to us. Commenting on Galatians 3:13, Luther writes the following:

> For the papists dream about a kind of faith "formed by love." Through this they want to remove sins and be justified. This is clearly to unwrap Christ and to unclothe him from our sins, to make Him innocent, to burden and overwhelm ourselves with our own sins, and to behold them, not in Christ but in ourselves. This is to abolish Christ and make Him

useless. For if it is true that we abolish sins by the works of the Law and by love, then Christ does not take them away, but we do. But if He is truly the Lamb of God who takes away the sins of the world, who became a curse for us, and who was wrapped in our sins, it necessarily follows that we cannot be justified and take away sins through love. For God has laid our sins, not upon us but upon Christ, His Son.[20]

While for Thomas charity is an infused virtue that God "works in us without us," for Luther, charity consists of works of love that depend on human initiative for their efficacy. The whole notion of cooperation that Thomas depends on is suspect for Luther both from a psychological and an empirical point of view. For one thing, as previously noted, it produces anxiety over the security of one's salvation. But empirically it is also suspect because no one appears to demonstrate the requisite works of love that should follow from the change in form that takes place with the infusion of charity.

The second main concern regarding historical understandings of charity regards its composition. Is it in fact a composite of two very different forms of love? This is the view of Anders Nygren, who argued in *Agape and Eros* that these two forms of love, conjoined in the concept of charity, represent fundamentally opposing attitudes to life. According to Nygren, eros is an attitude toward life that is selfish in orientation, in which human beings are thought to overcome the distance between themselves and God through their own efforts. Agape, on the other hand, is theocentric in orientation. In this view of love, the distinction between human beings and God is an absolute one, a border that can't be crossed on our side but can be on God's. God's love for us expresses the purest form of agape. Since God is already complete in Godself, there is no taint of selfishness in God's expressions of love toward us. In contrast, the love that human beings express, as fallen creatures, always has a dimension of eros.[21]

Nygren traces the problematic use of *caritas* in Christian history back to Augustine. He argues that Augustinian *caritas* is essentially eros, since it is fundamentally acquisitive love marked by longing for certain desirable features of the object of love. Here Augustine was too heavily influenced by the Neoplatonic quest for the highest good.[22] *Caritas*, according to Augustine, is an upwardly directed love in which we make progress toward God through our desire for God. The work of grace in this schema is to help us overcome our natural sloth and resistance and propel our souls toward God.[23]

Nygren argues that the Augustinian view of love was dominant in Western Christianity until Luther restored agape to its proper place. It was Luther's revolutionary thoughts on justification that led him to a very different understanding. Luther argued, contra Augustine, that fellowship with God does not consist in our ascent to God's level of holiness but rather in God's descent to ours. This was "fellowship with God on the basis of sin, not of holiness."[24] The Roman Catholic Church's adaptation of *fides caritate formata* placed stress on love rather than on faith. Luther's *sola fide* did the opposite. What then became of love in Luther's theology? Nygren argues that by leaving love out of the formula of justification Luther freed it from eros. God's justification of us is an act of agape, with no ground in any good in us that God might seek. On the human side, our motives for loving God no longer include a desire for our own salvation, since that salvation is no longer dependent on that love.[25]

In volume IV/2 of *Church Dogmatics*, Karl Barth shares the concern that the use of *caritas* (charity) in the Middle Ages is a deceptive synthesis of eros and agape and argues that the terms ought to remain separate. While there is still some dissonance evident in their medieval synthesis, the tension is understated and the benefits of maintaining the contradictory elements of agape and eros are lost.[26] Barth eschews the use of *caritas* language and prefers to speak of agape and eros, thus ensuring that these different forms of love remain distinct. Here Barth's doctrine of justification guides his doctrine of love, following his embrace of Luther's dictum *simul iustus (totus) et peccator (totus)*. As total sinner, a human being's quest for God is eros driven and self-centered. Yet at the same time the person who is justified by God is identified eschatologically as the one who demonstrates agape. Here and now, both identities and both forms of love coexist. But eschatologically, the one who is declared just is made just and is enabled to love God agapically.

The relationship between eros and agape in Barth's account is complicated by the multiple forms of erotic love to be found in the Greco-Roman world. While certainly such love pertains to sexual desire, that is only one of many meanings attached to the word.[27] Nonetheless, Barth maintains that even in its noblest form erotic love is opposed to the gospel. In *CD* IV/2, Barth notes that throughout the Bible the use of eros is eschewed in favor of agape.[28] What connotations had eros accumulated that these Greek translators wanted to avoid? Barth observes that across a variety of Greek literature, from poetic, to mythogical, to philosophical, eros "is always a matter of man hovering but in some sense moving upwards between a lower world and a higher, a world of darkness and a world of light."[29] Barth thus affirms Nygren's position on the matter that eros, as self-centered love, is opposed to the biblical conception of love as self-giving and other centered. The contrast is stark, for agape recenters us on God's agenda rather than our own. Barth writes of the person who exhibits such love,

> It [*agape*] consists in the fact that he is determined and ready to live from and to God to the best of his knowledge and capacity: not raising any claim; not trying to control God; not with the ulterior motive of winning

God for himself or demanding anything from Him; but simply because He is God, and as such worthy to be loved.[30]

This love that places the other at the center includes both love for God (vertical dimension) and love for neighbor (horizontal dimension). Importantly, Barth sees such love as completing our human nature rather than negating it, as may seem the case with Nygren's account.

More recent scholarship has since challenged Nygren's depiction of agape, which influences Barth's own account. Amy Laura Hall, for example, calls for a "polyphonic" description of agape in order to correct for Nygren's description of God's love as unmotivated and spontaneous in character. Hall draws from a variety of texts to demonstrate that biblical descriptions of love are more complicated than Nygren's account allows.[31] Citing Exodus, Hall points out that while God's decision to embrace Israel was at first unmotivated by any merit on the part of the Israelites, to say that such love remained "spontaneous" is misleading. God's loving acts toward Israel reflect an ongoing relationship that deepens with time. This characteristic of God's love is not captured by Nygren's description. As Hall observes,

> While God is not required to act on behalf of Israel, to say that God's actions toward Israel are spontaneous misses the temporality of the narrative and threatens to isolate each of God's acts and commands as arbitrary moments of divine whim. Temporality need not mean causality, but it does imply memory, motive, and affective connection.[32]

Nygren's attempts to characterize agape as spontaneous thus miss the covenantal context within which God's love is portrayed.

Hall notes that the term "unmotivated" is also challenged by the biblical witness. Jesus' command to love those typically considered outside of the covenant (e.g., one's enemies) is in fact an echo of God's gracious love found in the Old Testament. God's love toward Israel, despite its flaws, sets the precedent for our loving in this way. Such love is dramatically depicted in the prophetic writing of Hosea, in which the relationship between Hosea and his adulterous wife mirrors God's love for Israel. As Hall observes, by extracting such love from its covenantal context, Nygren suggests that loving our enemies is in fact a warrantless action. She concludes that when the covenantal history is in full view, there is abundant warrant for us to act as God did.[33]

What conclusions, then, may be drawn regarding a Reformed moral virtue ethic of charity? The Reformed emphasis on the sovereignty of God and the depth of human sinfulness casts suspicion on an account of charity that forms the basis of our faith. As with justification, a Reformed view of love must take into account the fact that we are totally sinner as well as totally justified. Barth's account of agape and eros presents an appropriate tension that must always exist in the life of the Christian here and now. On the other hand, the dramatic contrast between agape and eros in Anders Nygren's account needs to be modified to bring a more accurate account of Christian love into view. Nygren's emphasis on the spontaneity and groundless character of God's agapic love falls short of describing the character of God's love toward us. That covenantal love makes the category of history critically important for understanding the content and form of Christian love.

Our Reformed virtue ethic of charity takes this history seriously. It has as its basis a covenantal ontology in which the ground of our being (and our salvation) is secured by God's electing decision to be God with us no matter what. As God makes God's presence known to us there is a continuous as well as a disruptive character to the grace imparted to us. Our response to God's divine command is part of a chain of responses (sometimes faithful, sometimes not) that reflects God's steadfast love and our continuous need to be guided. Just as in Thomas Aquinas's conception, in which God's grace works "within us without us," we recognize that the source of this agapic love is God's revelation to us rather than some intrinsic capacity on our part. Unlike Thomas's conception, the relationship between God and us is portrayed as a lively dialogue guiding us toward virtue, rather than as an organic process.

God's grace also comes to us in the form of the Christian community, which through its communal life offers examples of agapic love. As Barth affirms in his account of agape, there is a horizontal dimension to agape that is constituted by a caring love for our neighbor. Such love treats the neighbor not as a means to one's own self-fulfillment but rather as a person to whom one is bound through a relationship that mirrors one's fundamental relationship with God.[34]

THE ROLE OF THE CHURCH IN THE FORMATION OF VIRTUE

The acquisition of virtue does not take place in isolation. It requires a process of formation in which individuals are guided by those who are virtuous themselves. Thus it requires a virtuous community. In what ways is the church such a community in our Reformed understanding of virtue ethics? Earlier in this chapter we discussed the key role that revelation plays in the formation of Reformed virtue. God's commands mold us into the persons we ought to be through our hearing and our obedient response. At first glance, this process of virtue formation appears to minimize the role of any community outside of the relationship between God and a particular individual. But in fact this is not the case for two reasons. First, the Christian community is important because our hearing and responding to God's commands take place within a social context. How we hear and understand God's revelation to us are determined in large measure by that context, by the norms and expectations of those with whom we are surrounded. The contents of God's revelation to us will also be determined by that context as God calls us to respond in a particular way, keeping in mind our own gifts as well as the needs of our community. Second, God's commands have a continuous character that has shaped the Christian community over time. Even Barth, who often emphasizes the disruptive nature of such commands, also attests to the fact that there are main lines of communication and continuities in God's commands over time. For these two reasons it is important to consider the role of the church in the formation of Reformed virtue.

To understand that role, consider Barth's account of church practices, those activities of the church that have been part of its faithful witness since its inception. Here, as elsewhere, it should be noted that these practices in and of themselves do not lead one into virtue. The Holy Spirit, as it comes to us in the doing of these activities, makes them efficacious. But, on the other hand, God has clearly chosen these tasks not only for the upbuilding of the Christian community but also for the sake of the world.

In his analysis of the church in *CD* IV/3.2, Barth asks, "What is it that always takes place when its ministry is performed in accordance with the purpose of its existence in the world and task towards it?" The answer is "witness."[35] But this response needs to be given content and explanation. Barth elucidates three elements here: (1) declaration, (2) proclamation (exposition and address), and (3) explication and application of the gospel as the Word of God entrusted to it. The church is called not only to proclaim and explain the gospel in words but also in its actions. There is therefore a twofold form in all Christian witness.[36]

The church's witness may also be more concretely spelled out in terms of twelve forms of ministry, which in contemporary discussions of Christian virtue ethics are referred to as church practices. Rather than attempt a vast historical survey and critical analysis of the church, Barth turns to the Gospels and to the letters of Paul to discern forms of ministry and witness that have persisted into the present. He hopes in this endeavor to come up with a "general law of the differentiation of the Church's ministry."[37]

The first six of these twelve forms focus on speech acts and include praise of God, proclamation of the gospel in worship, as well as communication of the gospel to those beyond the Christian community. The latter six focus on active ministry in which speech acts play a part but not as prominent a role. These include the cure of souls, the diaconate that attends to those at the margins of society both within and outside the church, the production and existence of exemplary individuals within the community, and those activities that build up community life in general.[38]

What is the correspondence between these practices and the formation of Christian virtue? A couple of thoughts come to mind. First, Barth's emphasis does not concern the pursuit of sanctification for its own sake. Rather, his interest is in describing the life of the church. When he writes about exemplary individuals who mirror in their actions the love of Christ, he is careful to note that the purpose of God's work in these individuals in a special way is for the upbuilding of the church, and none is immune from sin. Barth writes,

> None is by a long chalk a second Christ. But each in his particularity is a witness of Christ to be greeted with particular thanksgiving. For what would the community be if it were referred only to the Christian mediocrity in which all these possibilities might finally be open in a mild form to all? What would it be if it had no place for shining exceptions? What would its external witness be if there were only that Christian mediocrity and none of these lights which, even if only transitorily, shine with particular brilliance?[39]

Second, these practices indicate the renewal aspect of Reformed virtue. A call to praise God, to minister to others, and to proclaim the gospel outside of the Christian community all point to the reality that virtue is not a steady state in which we rest. Rather it is an activity in which we participate.

Take the example of Christian love. The twofold form of speech and act identified by Barth is represented both in the church's proclamation to love one's neighbor and in the practices of the diaconate who minister to those in need. And what of eros and agape? These two aspects of love will always be at work and at war with each other, influencing the motives of clergy and laity alike. While certain individuals will stand out for the love they demonstrate toward others, these individuals nonetheless stand in need of reform and repentance. They also turn away from God's love for selfish reasons. Yet their example serves the church as a model, however flawed, of God's gracious love in our midst.

THE ROLE OF THE STATE IN THE FORMATION OF VIRTUE

Given the emphasis placed on God's revelation in the formation of Reformed virtue, it is not clear what the role of the state would be in this process. Two possibilities can be ruled out. First, there is the possibility that God's revelation does not touch on the state, at least not directly. Rather, God's revelation is directed toward the church, and only through the work of the church is God's revelation made manifest in a public manner. This view limits God's direct engagement with the world to the life of the church. It also fails to distinguish adequately between the visible and invisible church, between the church as an institution and the church as the body of Christ. The second possibility is that God's revelation is closely identified with the activities of the state. The dangers of such a view became manifestly evident in Nazi Germany during the 1930s and 1940s, when the German Protestant Church capitulated in endorsing Adolf Hitler as the spiritual leader of the state as well as its political leader.[40]

Barth's reflections on the church and the state offer a helpful guide to navigate around these two pitfalls. In regard to the first possibility, Barth's reflections on the role of the church in the salvation of the world demonstrate that God's revelation is not to be narrowly identified with the church. The practical consequence of this position is that God's revelation comes to us in many contexts and communities, including those ordered by the state. Barth's reflections on the role of the state, written after his work on the Barmen Declaration and after the devastation of World War II, both affirm that God's intentions for creation make the state a secular parable of the kingdom and warn of the dangers of an overidentification of the state with the kingdom of God.

Is the church necessary for the salvation of the world? If the answer is yes, then the possibility of civic virtue is negated. For if the church is considered to be necessary for the salvation of the world, then it follows that it is the church that is the seedbed of virtue. In this view, the Christian community alone provides the representative forms of life and action that are truly salvific. Second, how one determines the relationship of the church and the state to each other guides one's account of civic virtue. For civic virtue to be possible, there must be an understanding of the state such that it offers grounds to some extent for virtuous life apart from the influence of the church. This in turn means that the state has a function to play in the shaping of individuals. It also raises the question of what God's intention is for civil authority. To analyze the role of the state in the formation of virtue, we will begin by examining the first issue. An alternate view will then be considered, followed by a defense of the position to be taken up. This alternate view is represented by Stanley Hauerwas, specifically in his critique of Karl Barth's ecclesiology.

When it comes to the place of the church as the home of Christian witness, Hauerwas has argued that the church must play an important role. However, his views here diverge from Barth's. A close examination of their differences helps reveal Barth's own views on the role the church plays in the world. While Hauerwas's view on the church makes pagan virtue difficult to explain, Barth's view leaves more space for pagan virtue.

In his Gifford lectures, published in 2001 under the title *With the Grain of the Universe*, Hauerwas criticizes Barth for arguing that God does not need the church in order to effect the salvation of the world. As evidence to back this claim, Hauerwas cites the following passage from *Church Dogmatics*:

1. The world would be lost without Jesus Christ and His Word and work;
2. The world would not necessarily be lost if there were no Church; and
3. The Church would be lost if it had no counterpart in the world.[41]

The item of contention here is point 2: Barth's claim that the church is not *necessary* for the salvation of the world. Because Hauerwas is committed to the view that the church is a necessary part of God's work in the world, he does not envision what place the church would have in God's work if it were not "necessary." What is the concern behind Barth's claim that "the world would not necessarily be lost if there were no Church"? Barth is adamant here, and rightly so because this is where the church is most likely to stumble in its ministry to the world. If the church construes itself to be necessary to the work of God in the world, then there is a clear violation of the ordering between divine and human acts: God becomes bound to the church rather than the other way around. One can almost hear Barth's "Nein!" to such a conception as he writes the following: "It is an act of free grace that Jesus Christ wills to claim its [the church's] service in this matter. He is not bound to it in His prophetic action. He is not restricted to what He can and does accomplish by means of its ministering work. Who is to prevent Him from going His own direct way to man without it in His self-declaration?"[42] For Barth it is imperative to bear in mind the Chalcedonian logic of divine/human action when recognizing the contours of the church's ministry: if it is violated the ministry of the church becomes an idol under which even Christ's work is subsumed.

The church, nonetheless, does have a vital role to play in God's work in the world. While Christ does not *need* the church in order for Christ's Spirit to reach the world, still Christ chooses the church as a means of witness to the world. It is not the only means, but it is still an important one. In addition, since the church is freed *from* the impossible task of supplementing Christ's work, it is correspondingly freed *for* the task of prophetic witness to Christ that is its designated task in the world.

Hauerwas's concerns about the limits of Barth's ecclesiology arise out of his own commitments in regard to Christian witness. Broadly speaking, both men share much in common in their emphasis on such witness and their rejection of a theological approach to God that minimizes the role of revelation. But there are important differences in their specific conceptions of what constitutes Christian witness. Hauerwas's dependence on church practices to lay the groundwork for Christian character formation ultimately hinders the church's conception of its witness. Barth's understanding places the efficacy of the church's witness in God's hands. Because of Barth's objective soteriology, he can claim that the church is not necessary for the salvation of the world.[43] That has already been accomplished in Christ. But the church nonetheless plays a vital role in announcing that victory to the world so that the world may become aware of its true status.

Because the church is not necessary for the salvation of the world, God is free to choose the means by which God's command is heard, both inside and outside the church. The implication of Barth's position in relation to virtue ethics is clear. There is more room for pagan virtue in Barth's ecclesiology than there is in Hauerwas's. If we extrapolate Barth's views on the church within the context of virtue ethics, pagan virtue may be explained in terms of a human response to God's command as it reaches the world outside of the church. Such a view is not possible in Hauerwas's ecclesiology, where the cradle of virtue is found almost exclusively in the church.[44]

But how do we avoid the opposite problem, in which the activity of the state is too closely identified with God's revelation? To answer that question, I turn to Barth's understanding of the role of the church and state as it is found in an essay written in 1946, "The Christian Community and the Civil Community." Barth viewed the state as a parable of the coming kingdom of God. Its role is temporary until the kingdom of God is established in the eschaton, but the church is nonetheless significant in that it provides a certain tenuous order in a sinful world. Since even corrupt governments have been given this task to perform, Barth affirms such governments insofar as they take up that task responsibly. This qualification is an important one. For example, Barth's interpretation of Romans 13, in which Christians are to be subject to governing authorities, indicates that such subjection is qualified by the state's own (often unrecognized) subjection to its Lord, Jesus Christ. Since Christians' greater allegiance is to Christ, where obedience to the state conflicts with obedience to Christ, Christians are ordered to obey Christ.

In "The Christian Community and the Civil Community," Barth highlights the roles of the church and the state as well as the relationship between them. The special task of the state is "to provide for the external and provisional delimitation and protection of human life."[45] Political systems are human inventions, to be tested experimentally to see if, through law and peaceful order, they provide for human flourishing (albeit in a provisional and fragile manner). The divine purpose for the civil community is to create a safe place for the preaching and hearing of the Word. But such opportunities are only made possible through secular and profane means of protecting freedom and peace.[46] While the state cannot be identified with the kingdom of God, it should be seen as a parable/analogue of the kingdom. If, in the mind of Christians, there is either a complete identification or a complete separation between the state and the kingdom of God, problems will ensue since either the state is worshiped or religion becomes completely privatized. By viewing the state as a parable of the kingdom of God, Christians are called to participate in the political sphere to call the life of the state into account when necessary.[47]

The special task of the church is to proclaim "the rule of Jesus Christ and the hope of the kingdom of God."[48] But again, this should not lead to a privatization of religion or a focusing on inward piety. Barth explains,

> The object of the promise and the hope in which the Christian community has its eternal goal consists, according to the unmistakable assertion of the New Testament, not in an eternal Church but in the *polis* built by God and coming down from heaven to earth. . . . Bearing all of this in mind, we are entitled and compelled to regard the existence of the Christian community as of ultimate and supremely political significance."[49]

The goal of the church is not to perpetuate its own existence but to point to and anticipate God's coming. Its witness is a public witness but not a coercive one. That is, it does not seek a theocratic state: "Its own position, influence and power in the state are not the goal which will determine the trend of its political decisions."[50] Here Barth quotes John 18:36: "'My Kingdom is not of this world.'"[51]

By calling the church the "Christian community" and the state the "civil community," Barth indicates he is less interested in the institutional dimensions than he is in the webs of relationships among individuals in these two different contexts. As he points out, individuals quite often are involved in both communities; thus a line of separation cannot be too distinctly drawn as if individuals only belonged to one or the other. Instead, Barth speaks of two concentric circles, in which the Christian community forms the inner, and the civil community forms the outer. At the center of both, informing and guiding both bodies, are Jesus Christ and the kingdom of God. The church, as the center of the civil community, has a special task to witness to the need for human flourishing. The church is called especially to minister to those who are poor. And in its efforts to uphold the law, it should seek a fashioning of the law, "as will make it impossible for 'equality before the law' to become a cloak under which strong and weak, independent and dependent, rich and poor, employers and employees, in fact receive different treatment at its hands: the weak being unduly restricted, the strong unduly protected. The Church must stand for social justice in the political sphere."[52]

The following conclusions can be made about the role of the state in the formation of virtue. First, following Barth's claim that the church is not necessary for the salvation of the world, God uses whatever means God chooses to reach individuals and draw them to God. The instruments of the state would be one means of doing so. There is room for pagan virtue in this position, since it opens up the possibility that communities of virtue exist outside of the church. Barth confronts both the arrogance and the indolence of the institutional church that claims to have a corner on the Holy Spirit yet fails to live accordingly. In relation to the immediately preceding discussion, we saw that in Barth's view both the church and the state have Christ at the center. While the state is blind to that reality, it nonetheless is established as a parable of the kingdom of God. God is working through the state to create the conditions within which order and peace may reside. Thus the church needs the state in order to fulfill its function as witness to the world of the love of Jesus Christ.

What happens when the church fails in its task of witness? If pagans are unaware of the Holy Spirit's interactions with them, how do they participate in Christian virtue? In Barth's ecclesiology ignorance need not be an impediment. God's commands may address individuals without their recognizing them as such. These commands will be mediated through a set of circumstances in which a choice is necessary. Such circumstances afford an opportunity for the individual to act in line with God's commands. Their acting will bring them more into line with God's will for their lives, yet they may not be aware explicitly of God's presence in the situation. Before choosing how to act, they will have to engage in the same deliberative process as Christians but without a conscious awareness of the relationship that exists between themselves and God. While this puts them at a relative disadvantage, God's awareness of who they are is such that God may speak through the Holy Spirit in a persuasive way nonetheless.[53]

The state has a role in the formation of virtue because God's revelation extends to all. As Barth notes, God's care for creation includes proper governance, which involves a coercive enforcement of civic law as well as the defense of the community against violent intrusion. Barth is not claiming that such governance is predetermined by orders of creation (e.g., universal natural laws evident to the light of reason). He categorically rejects that notion. Any resemblance to the kingdom of God evident in the workings of the state is a gift of grace:

> If there were and still are good as well as bad States—no doubt the reality is always a curious mixture of the two!—then the reason is not that the true "natural law" has been discovered, but simply the fact that even the ignorant, neutral, pagan civil community is still in the Kingdom of Christ, and that all political questions and all political efforts as such are founded on the gracious ordinance of God by which man is preserved and his sin and crime confined.[54]

That the state has such a character is a reflection of the twofold nature of human existence. It is not simply the case that human beings, taken individually, stand before God both as justified and sinner. It is also the case that the *arrangement* of human relations reflects this twofold state.

The ordering of the civic community is both disrupted by human sinfulness and restored to health through its Creator and Redeemer. The eschatological ordering of the kingdom of Christ is continuously breaking into the life of the civic community even though this process remains largely invisible to human eyes.

Practically speaking, how does this view of the state yield the communities of virtue, practices, and moral exemplars needed to promote individual virtue among its citizens? An exhaustive answer to this question is beyond the limits of this book, but an example from Scripture proves illustrative. Both Matthew 8 and Luke 7 contain the story of a centurion in the Roman army who comes to Jesus asking him to heal his servant. Rather than ask Jesus to follow him back to his house, the centurion asks only that Jesus give the command and trusts that it will be enough to heal his servant. Both versions of the story recount that Jesus is amazed by such faith, exclaiming in Luke 7:9, "'I tell you, not even in Israel have I found such faith.'"

Where does the centurion's faith come from? The rhetorical force of Jesus' exclamation points to the expected conclusion that such faith comes from within the ranks of God's people, the Israelites. They, after all, have been special recipients of God's revelation since Moses. Instead, the source is a Gentile whose training in faith comes from his experience in the military. His understanding of how commands work in that context prepares him to believe in a God whose commands take effect without our having to be there. No doubt such preparation was the work of the triune God engaged in that man's life even before he was cognizant of that work.

The kind of obedience and faith learned in military training, however, can often have a distinctly different cast than that which is identified with Christ. As Werpehowski notes, the character of God's commands is shaped by a loving-kindness that makes those commands merciful and just. When obedience and faith are blind or motivated by fear of reprimand or reprisal, they take on a character distinctly different from our obedience to God's commands when properly understood. Nonetheless, this example provides a window into how an institution of the state such as the military may provide the training grounds for Christian virtue. It demonstrates how the practices of such an institution, which inculcate obedience and faith, help form an individual's disposition to that virtue. And it provides a case study of an exemplary individual whose actions embody that virtue.

CONCLUSION

Reformed virtue after Barth is grounded in God's revelation to us rather than in our natural capacities to ascertain and do the good. This key feature stems from Barth's concerns about natural morality, which presupposes an overly optimistic view of the effects of sin on humankind. The result is that all of the virtues come to us not through our own efforts alone but through our response to God's commands that both confront and enable us to respond accordingly. The virtues that Thomas Aquinas describes as moral, intellectual, and theological retain their labels, but the distinction between acquired and infused virtues is dropped. To use Thomas's terminology, all Reformed virtues are infused virtues. However, to avoid any confusion over the term *infused*, which implies that God's grace comes to us as a gift that we take possession of, it is more accurate to say that all Reformed virtues are shaped by grace that has the following characteristics: it is covenantal, Chalcedonian, christological, and unidirectional, and it works to justify us even as we are resistant to it (*simul iustus et peccator*). This chapter's examination of three virtues, each representative of their respective types, reflects how these characteristics mold Reformed virtue in particular ways. Here the church plays a vital role in promoting virtue although it is not the only community-forming institution that does so. The state also plays a significant role, as God's revelation uses both media to communicate God's commands to us.

This chapter identified general characteristics of Reformed virtue along Barthian lines. The next step is to demonstrate how such an ethic would operate in the life of the church. This will be the task of the following chapter, where the social witness of one Reformed institution, the Presbyterian Church (U.S.A.), will be examined in order to see, in more concrete terms, what such an ethic would look like. Specifically, we will look at the denomination's efforts to challenge injustices that arise when globalization goes awry. The Reformed moral virtues already discussed in this chapter will be highlighted to demonstrate what they add to the issues raised by the pressures of globalization.

5

LIVING OUT THE REFORMED VIRTUES

To what extent should churches seek to change society, and how should they go about doing it? Reformed responses to the first question have been shaped by John Calvin's third use of the law. For those who already have the Spirit of God in their hearts, the law acts as a guide to God's will regarding how to act in the world. Calvin called this the principal use of the law.[1] Lutherans also recognize this use, which is stated in article 6 of the Formula of Concord. However, in the Lutheran tradition the third use of the law is more contested because of anxieties over works righteousness. In comparison, Reformed thinkers have placed greater stress on the role of sanctification in the Christian life. This difference is most stark in Reformed depictions of Christian vocation. Calvin writes that "each individual has his own kind of living assigned to him by the Lord as a sort of sentry post so that he may not heedlessly wander about throughout life."[2] For Calvin this calling is the basis of all good action. To follow one's calling, no matter how humble, is every Christian's duty.

While Calvin imagined a rather stratified society, his doctrine of vocation had profound effects on social transformation. Before the era of the Reformation, the notion of vocation was associated with the religious, those who became priests, monks, or nuns. By broadening out the notion of vocation, Calvin and other Reformers empowered the laity to think about their work as a part of God's calling in their lives. This new conception transformed society from the ground up. Consider Max Weber's argument for the roots of modern rational capitalism. Weber famously argued that Protestant anxiety over salvation led seventeenth-century English Puritans to view success at work as a sign of God's favor. In response they established new patterns of working and spending that led to the form of capitalism we experience today.[3] Weber argued that Calvinists practiced a form of worldly asceticism marked by frugality. They worked harder because work was their means of demonstrating their faith. They saved because they perceived the fruits of their labor were in the life to come. As a result, their frugality provided the excess capital they needed for their entrepreneurial interests.[4] Whether or not one agrees with all of Max Weber's claims, it is easy to see in his argument the ways in which Reformed conceptions of vocation have the power to shape society by creating new habits and virtues.

In what ways might Reformed moral virtues shape society in the future? The question seems an audacious one, given the declining influence of institutional mainline denominations. Yet moral virtue ethics after Barth looks beyond as well as within institutional walls in order to grasp the ways that the Holy Spirit is at work in the world. This chapter will investigate one set of issues where such ethics stands to make an impact. Those issues arise within a context of global development in which some players have vastly more resources than others. While economic globalization is not a new phenomenon, thanks to technological advances the ability to transfer resources (physical and intellectual) from one side of the globe to the other has increased dramatically in the last half century. Jagdish Bhagwati defines economic globalization as the "integration of national economies into the international economy through trade, direct foreign investment (by corporations and multinationals), short-term capital flows, international flows of workers and humanity generally, and flows of technology."[5] These phenomena have been embraced by some and pilloried by others. While Bhagwati unabashedly celebrates the advances made in developing countries as a result of globalization processes, Amartya Sen's assessment is more lukewarm. Sen argues that the rich and powerful in every country tend to enjoy the benefits of globalization more than do the poor and oppressed. According to Sen, justice demands that those benefits be spread more evenly.[6]

In the context of this case study on the Presbyterian Church (U.S.A.)'s social witness policies regarding just and sustainable human development, the focus will be on the impact of economic globalization on developing countries, first on the people who live in these countries but also the animal and plant life that dwell there. The PC(USA) is a Reformed body whose social witness is shaped by Reformed confessions and polity. Historically, that social witness is guided by a tradition that emphasizes practical wisdom on the part of individuals to determine for themselves what course of action to take. Since the 1960s, however, the social witness of the PC(USA) has focused on addressing justice concerns at an institutional and structural level, crafting recommendations aimed at national and international bodies to promote systemic change.

The change in strategic focus is evident in the PC(USA)'s response to globalization from 1996 through 2006. Starting in 1996, when the 208th General Assembly adopted the report *Hope for a Global Future: Toward Just and Sustainable Human Development*, the Advisory Committee on Social Witness Policy, a committee of the PC(USA), was directed to monitor the effects of trade policy, particularly on the poor and on the natural environment, as well as to track the distribution of power among the primary actors driving economic development.[7] It also was requested to report back its findings to the General Assembly and its member bodies on a periodic basis. An examination of the ACSWP's work and its reception by the General Assembly provides a picture of the church's response to globalization.

Despite its emphasis on structural reform, the church's position on globalization also depends on private virtue. As stated in the social policy of the PC(USA), an ethic of frugality is integral to the satisfaction of the church's commitments to sufficiency, sustainability, and eco-justice. This ethic requires an account of habits and practices of individuals and congregations that fits well with a virtue ethic. However, a framework for developing such behavior is never explicitly articulated in the church's documentation.

FRUGALITY AND SOCIAL JUSTICE

Even taking into account the recent recession, public interest in frugality over the last twenty-five years has tended to be brief and intermittent. Yet throughout that same period it has received sustained interest in social policy papers of the PC(USA) dedicated to environmental concerns and globalization processes.[8] In both the 1990 General Assembly report "Restoring Creation for Ecology and Justice" as well as the 1996 *Hope* policy statement, frugality is seen as a significant companion piece to the social policy initiatives aimed at ensuring sustainable development. As these documents indicate, social policy initiatives that stress sufficiency and sustainability need to be complemented at the individual level by modified consumption and lifestyle patterns.

The 1990 report points out that such a norm is needed because of the inequality of distribution among nations. Modern industrialization has placed a severe strain on natural resources while at the same time poverty plagues developing countries. Given this context, "sufficiency for all will be achieved and sustained only if the good things of God's creation are shared according to a keen sense of what is needful." The report calls for a new norm for the "good life" that involves "a wide range of lifestyle changes that move toward frugality in the affluent sectors of society, and arrangements whereby all may participate in the community and the economy."[9]

Hope is even more explicit about the link between frugality and social justice: "An interpretation of justice and sustainability is incomplete without an emphasis on frugality as a norm for all, a norm particularly incumbent upon those 'to whom much has been given.'"[10] In its own description of frugality, *Hope* incorporates both individual and societal dimensions of the virtue:

Frugality denotes moderation, temperance, thrift, cost-consciousness, efficient usage, and a satisfaction with material sufficiency—similar to the "contentment" celebrated in the first letter to Timothy (6:6–10). As a norm for the economic activity of both individuals and societies, frugality means morally disciplined production and consumption for higher ends, such as the common good.[11]

For Calvin frugality was both a personal virtue that shapes our character toward the final end of worshiping God and an attitude of stewardship that involves love for one's neighbors. *Hope* affirms both dimensions of frugality, extending love for the neighbor globally. However, the explicit context for this type of frugality is the global marketplace, with its emphasis on production and consumption. As a result, *Hope*'s treatment of sustainability and sufficiency tends to confirm rather than to challenge the framework within which frugality as a personal virtue operates. In this regard, Calvin's discussion of stewardship, which presupposes that all we have is a gift from God, provides a more radical challenge to the economic presumptions of our time.

The link between frugality and sustainability demonstrates the interconnection between individual norms, societal norms, and social policy. James A. Nash, former executive director of the Churches' Center for Theology and Public Policy, observes that frugality may be both a personal virtue and a social norm.[12] As Nash reminds his readers, for Aristotle and Aquinas the virtues are both personal as well as political since human beings are social beings. When frugality is considered as merely a social norm, the emphasis is placed more on social ends and consequences rather than on individual motives. It is more structural in its character than personal. If we apply Nash's insights to frugality in the Reformed tradition, we see that historically Calvin's notion of frugality is focused on the individual whereas current discussions about frugality and the PC(USA) focus on its social benefits. There is nonetheless an interconnection between these two aspects that is mutually reinforcing.

The most recent resolution by the General Assembly of the PC(USA) on globalization issues, "Resolution on Just Globalization: Justice, Ownership, and Accountability," roots the church's commitment to just and sustainable globalization theologically in a doctrine of creation that emphasizes the need for stewardship rather than "rapacious dominion," as well as in a doctrine of sin that both affirms and delimits our capacity to be good stewards.[13] While the report itself is heavily weighted toward social policy initiatives, there is nonetheless recognition that these initiatives need to be buttressed by different patterns of individual consumption. The section on the environmental impact of globalization, for instance, provides startling statistics: the average American consumer consumes 309 times what the average Ethiopian uses, twenty-six times what the average Indian consumes, and twice as much as the average German.[14] Unfortunately for the environment, the trend is for individuals in developing countries to copy American patterns of consumption rather than the reverse.

In 2008 the PC(USA) revised its social policy statement on U.S. energy policy and again affirmed its commitment to the norms of sustainability and sufficiency. The author of this policy statement, James B. Martin-Schramm, writes that the norm of sufficiency "repudiates wasteful and harmful consumption, emphasizes fairness, and encourages virtues of humility, frugality, and generosity."[15] Frugality thus stands together with a family of virtues that shape our dispositions such that our love for neighbor and our love for God's creation are expressed in tangible ways.

What does a virtue ethic approach to the problem add to the church's position on globalization? The virtue tradition has much to offer in the debate about how we are to respond to our growing environmental crisis. First, its emphasis on habit formation is a welcome resource in a discussion about how we are to change our lifestyle patterns of consumption. Second, moral virtue ethics recognizes both individual virtues that have their own unique excellences as well as a unity of the virtues that is characterized by practical wisdom. Ideally, participants in disagreements over environmental concerns will exhibit a host of virtues: love, justice, and courage among them. But what is needed most of all are persons of practical wisdom. For no matter what arrangements are made, there will be a need for individuals who can identify both proximate and long-range goods and who have the capacity to achieve both kinds of goods through their own labor and through their interactions with others.

Finally, Reformed moral virtue ethics offers an account of tradition that is chastened at its best. That is, rather than a belligerent traditionalism that seeks to perpetuate itself at all costs, this tradition is characterized by an ongoing, open-ended understanding of the excellences that constitute a good life. Given the changing political, economic, religious, and environmental circumstances of the twenty-first century, traditions that foster the collective wisdom of those who have gone before us are needed. But we also need wineskins that are supple enough to take new wine. Thus the Reformed tradition, with its emphasis on course correction over time, holds promise.

But does this proposal for an ethic of frugality, appealing as it is, go far enough? Hypothetically, is it enough that committed Christians adapt an attitude toward created goods that involves delight in those goods in moderation along with the recognition that these goods are given by God for their needs as well as for their enjoyment? Does such a change at the individual level really make a difference? Empirically, the answer would seem to be no. The U.S. military, for example, spends between $55 billion and $100 billion a year on oil. If there are roughly 220 million drivers in the United States, each would have to cut their personal consumption of oil by $250 to $455 a year to make up that amount. It would seem an easier task to target defense spending and pass legislation to safeguard against excessive consumption of a nonrenewable resource.

As convincing as this argument is, its conclusion does not require the abandonment of virtue. The need for individual frugality and the need for social policy initiatives regarding U.S. energy policy go hand in hand. What is needed is a both/and approach. The synergy between individual changes of lifestyle and changes at the systemic level is clear. When people commit themselves to the virtue of frugality, they are more attuned to abuses of natural resources and are more willing to speak out against those abuses that challenge a deep investment that has already been made in God's creation. On the other hand, changes made at the systemic level provide incentives to change individual behavior such that the benefits of an ethic of frugality become greater.

SOCIAL JUSTICE INFORMED BY PRACTICAL WISDOM

What does practical wisdom have to do with social justice? And what distinctive advantages does Reformed moral virtue add to an understanding of practical wisdom? The illustration above regarding energy consumption provides a ready answer to the first question. Practical wisdom is required for the exercise of all the moral virtues because it determines the proper level of response to any given situation. Such wisdom is not only necessary for the practice of moral virtue at the individual level, but it is also imperative to good decision making in regard to public policy. The second question requires further investigation into the PC(USA)'s commitment to personal liberty, which places a high degree of importance on practical wisdom in the Christian life and in the church's social witness.

Freedom of conscience has characterized the PC(USA)'s social witness policy from its inception. It is enshrined in the set of principles known as the "Preliminary Principles of Church Order," which were drawn up in 1788 in anticipation of the formation of the first U.S. General Assembly of the Presbyterian Church. They are stated in the first chapter of the *Book of Order*, one of two books that forms the constitution of the PC(USA).[16]

This commitment to freedom of conscience is bounded by a tradition of confession. The second source of enduring influence on social witness policy is a body of confessional statements that contain the church's affirmation of its faith at various times. The Westminster Confession stood, for many years, as the principal confession of Presbyterian churches in the United States. Only in the latter half of the twentieth century were other confessions officially recognized as influential for the faith of the church.[17]

As a result, the Westminster Confession cannot be seen as dogmatic truth that is best left untouched. The addition of other confessions highlights the importance of historical context in interpreting the place these documents have for today's church. It makes explicit the need for practical wisdom to discern God's changing relationship with the church.

The church's recognition and support of these principles and confessions provides continuity to its witness over time and across issues and helps to define the uniquely Presbyterian dimensions of the Reformed approach to social concerns. Understanding these two sources of reflection is critical for the purposes of this chapter because they place limits on how a moral virtue ethic could be implemented in the PC(USA). In addition, they help to explain the conditions under which the policy statement on globalization was crafted, its intended audience, as well as its prescribed implementation within the church. What follows is a brief examination of social witness policies dating back to the late eighteenth century that focuses on the role that the Preliminary Principles of Church Order, the Westminster Confession, and formation of the *Book of Confessions* had in shaping these policies.[18]

A Short History of Social Witness in the PC(USA)

The development of the social witness policy of the PC(USA) may be divided into three stages: from an emphasis on personal conscience, to a recognition of the limitations on personal conscience imposed by social arrangements, to an institutionalized approach.

Regarding the first stage, consider the first of the historic eight principles of church governance:

> 1 (a) That "God alone is Lord of the conscience, and hath left it free from the doctrines and commandments of men which are in anything contrary to his Word, or beside it, in matters of faith or worship."[19]

> (b) Therefore we consider the rights of private judgment, in all matters that respect religion, as universal and unalienable: we do not even wish to see any religious constitution aided by the civil power, further than may be necessary for protection and security, and at the same time, be equal and common to all others.[20]

The original context for this principle is important. First crafted as a part of the Westminster Confession of Faith, in an England where political and religious powers were often mixed, it offers protection against political influence in the lives of individual believers on two levels: within the politics of the church as well as in the church's dealings with the state. The American context is also important to consider. While several members of the Presbyterian Church held influential positions in colonial America, the church itself did not benefit from any legal establishment that promoted it, nor did it seek such promotion.

The first shift in the church's social witness, from an emphasis on freedom of conscience to a greater recognition of the limits on that freedom, took place as a result of the church's response to American slavery. In some ways, the response of the Presbyterian Church was exemplary. The General Assembly, with representatives of the church from the North and the South, declared in 1818 that slavery was a "gross violation of the most precious and sacred rights of human nature . . . utterly inconsistent with the law of God, fully irreconcilable with the spirit and principles of Christ." The Assembly went on to say that it was the duty of all Christians "to use their honest, earnest, and unwearied endeavors to obtain the complete abolition of slavery."[21] However, such proclamations were rarely if ever enforced among either congregants or clergy. The issue was ignored in the General Assembly for the next eighteen years, having been deemed in practice a matter decided by one's own conscience. During that time the practice of slavery became entrenched and was seen by many in the South to be an economic necessity.

The split between the northern and the southern Presbyterian churches began in earnest in the 1850s when New School Presbyterians, located predominantly north of the Mason-Dixon line, demanded that possession of slaves be treated as an offense subject to the church's *Book of Discipline*. Lincoln's declaration of war in 1861 finally forced the issue. The General Assembly meeting in that year passed a resolution committing the assembly to uphold the federal government and its constitution. Dr. Charles Hodge of Princeton Seminary lodged a formal protest arguing against the assembly's decision to make allegiance to the federal government a requirement of church membership, because it violated the constitution of the church.[22] James D. Hudnut-Beumler, in his analysis of the Presbyterian Church's social witness policy, notes a major shift in that policy after the Civil War. Because of the slavery issue, a critical distinction was made to restrict the protections ensured by the freedom-of-conscience principle: in matters where one individual's behavior threatened the well-being of another, the principle could not be used to support that person's behavior.[23]

Historically, the public nature of the PC(USA)'s advocacy of social issues has varied. In the nineteenth century, the church was cautious about seeking an end to the institution of slavery by political means, even when it condemned the practice. Yet it was very much involved in supporting legislation that would protect the observance of a Sunday Sabbath.[24] However, the motivation behind this legislative effort was less a matter of social justice (ensuring a day of rest for all) and more a matter of the church's seeking to protect Sundays as a day of worship. In both cases, the church was careful to defend its own interests.

The church's strategy underwent a second major change in the 1960s, in concert with the social upheaval of that era. The focus of the church's social witness moved in the direction of addressing unjust economic and social policies. This move is nicely summarized in a denomination report on transnational corporations: "Overall, the report sees the fundamental strategy shift that has marked the church's witness from the 1960s forward as a movement from the *exhortation of individuals* to change society to the church's own *engagement as an institution* in social change efforts."[25] Interestingly, at the same time the church was modifying its approach to social witness, it was also making key changes to its theological witness. These changes were motivated in no small part by the theology of Karl Barth.

Ordered by Confession

Churches in the Reformed tradition have relied on confessions of faith to order their communal life together. Behind the claim to be a church *semper reformanda* lies the understanding that the church is a human institution, liable to sin and constantly in need of reform. While the basic tenets of the faith remain constant, a fresh confession of faith is needed periodically. Prior to the 1960s and for over 250 years, the American Presbyterian Church was guided by the Westminster Confession. Initially the church sought to update the confession, but in the process it was decided by the northern UPCUSA that a new confession be drafted, the Confession of 1967, and that a book of confessions consisting of a number of historically important confessional documents be compiled. The result, the *Book of Confessions*, became the first half of the denomination's constitution.[26]

The Confession of 1967, hereafter referred to as C67, helped reshape the social witness policy of the UPCUSA after its adoption. One of the distinctive marks of this confession is its explicit mention of certain social-ethical issues that needed to be addressed by the church: issues of race, poverty, and hunger. C67 does not explicitly call for the institutional approach to social witness that emerged in the 1960s, but because it made social justice issues explicitly a part of Christian confession, it helped promote the church's lobbying efforts to right these wrongs. The confession has since provided support for the efforts of the church to address a number of other social witness issues, including those affected by globalization.

The emphasis on reconciliation in C67 is a direct result of its theological commitments. Many of its drafters were influenced by Barth's theology, particularly in his emphasis on Christ as the concrete expression of who God is for humankind. A comparison between the beginning of the Westminster Confession and the beginning of C67 is instructive here. Westminster begins with a statement on the infallibility of Scripture: "The infallible rule of interpretation of Scripture, is the Scripture itself; and therefore, when there is a question about the true and full sense of any Scripture (which is not manifold, but one), it may be searched and known by other places that speak more clearly."[27] C67, on the other hand, begins with an account of Jesus Christ and his primary work as reconciler of the world to God. Our faith is the result of this work. The Bible also points to it: "The one sufficient revelation of God is Jesus Christ, the Word of God incarnate, to whom the Holy Spirit bears unique and authoritative witness through the Holy Scriptures, which are received and obeyed as the word of God written."[28] While Scripture is unparalleled in its witness, its role is to direct us to the sole content of our faith, which is God revealed to us in Jesus Christ by the power of the Holy Spirit.

This theological shift in emphasis has a noteworthy impact on the mission of the church, which is now construed as a reconciling body.[29] Just as Christ has healed the division between God and us, so our mission is to proclaim that message of reconciliation to the world:

> The life, death, resurrection, and promised coming of Jesus Christ has set the pattern for the church's mission. His life as man involves the church in the common life of men. His service to men commits the church to work for every form of human well-being. His suffering makes the church sensitive to all the sufferings of mankind so that it sees the face of Christ in the faces of men in every kind of need. His crucifixion discloses to the church God's judgment on man's inhumanity to man and the awful consequences of its own complicity in injustice. In the power of the risen Christ and the hope of his coming, the church sees the promise of God's renewal of man's life in society and of God's victory over all wrong.[30]

The consequences for social witness policy flow from the fact that such witness is construed primarily in terms of reconciliation. The common thread that runs through its discussion of specific social issues that are in need of address (e.g., the threat of warfare, the problems of poverty, and confusion over human sexuality) is concern for the healing of divisions that both cause and are exacerbated by these problems.

Practical Wisdom as a Reformed Virtue: Distinctive Attributes

Presbyterians do things decently and in order. It is in many ways a fitting stereotype, considering the emphasis given to order in the denomination's confessions and *Book of Order*. That stress on order both depends on and enriches practical wisdom. It presupposes the collective wisdom of the church, for the purpose of establishing such order is to grant voice to that wisdom. But it also *fosters* practical wisdom by providing leadership opportunities in conjunction with clear protocols for group decision making.

Practical wisdom entails knowing how to act in a fitting way when faced with difficult circumstances where the proper response is not obvious. The key to acting appropriately is to make an accurate assessment of the circumstances. Such assessment involves knowledge of the particulars as well as a way of thinking about those particulars that yields a course of action leading to human flourishing. The Reformed tradition provides a history of how individual churches with a common heritage have handled difficult situations in the past. The continuities in that history provide guidelines for those confronting difficult situations today.

In the last chapter, five characteristics of Reformed virtue were outlined based on theological commitments of Karl Barth's that are also central to Reformed thought. There the shape of practical wisdom was provided in general terms. In what follows that virtue is considered again in the context of what has been said specifically about the PC(USA), its principles of church order, and the confessions that guide its social witness policy.

Covenantal Character

The UPCUSA's move from the Westminster Confession to the *Book of Confessions* demonstrates a historical consciousness on the part of the church in relation to faith. Such consciousness requires that the content of our faith as it has been expressed over time be taken up and examined in light of the circumstances in which it was first articulated. No one statement of faith, even that as basic and fundamental as the Nicene Creed, is impervious to historical review.

To be a church committed to *semper reformanda* means fundamentally to be a body always in the process of improvisation, seeking in time to ascertain and express God's truth today. Practical wisdom thus becomes a key virtue. Such improvisation does not neglect the tradition out of which it springs but embraces it. Contrary to critics who charge that such a contextual approach relativizes and minimizes God's truth, the *Book of Confessions* actually expands an awareness of what the church has stated and practiced in relation to its faith. Rather than seek to replace an "outdated" confession with a current version, like an old software program whose date of obsolescence rapidly approaches as soon as it is released, the church in its wisdom recognizes that certain key confessions have something important to say that necessitates their inclusion along with the most current statements of faith. Radical relativism would jettison older confessions as outmoded and thus of no value.

At the heart of this attention to context is a covenantal understanding of theology that recognizes the historical aspects of God's relationship with us. This covenantal relation has continuous as well as disruptive characteristics. God's character is revealed to us in familiar as well as surprising terms. The church's social witness is in tune with what the church has said before while also attentive to what God is saying to the church today. The virtue of practical wisdom, then, becomes preeminently valuable.

Simul Iustus et Peccator

How the church views its role in relation to moral issues reflects an epistemological humility that is in keeping with the Reformation guideline that Christians are simultaneously declared just even though they remain sinners. By providing middle principles in its social witness policy, the church offers guidelines for thinking about these issues without presuming to have the definitive answer. It calls on the practical wisdom of its congregants to make choices that correspond with God's command to them in particular.

The PC(USA)'s social witness statements on globalization reflect this attitude of humility. In light of the freedom-of-conscience principle, the *Hope* policy statement and the *2006 Resolution* point to the need for individual congregants to examine their patterns of consumption without compelling change. Recognizing that individual differences in wealth and opportunity are exacerbated by local/national/international systems of trade, these same documents also seek to make changes at the systemic level through legislative change. Therefore, recognizing the truth of *simul iustus et peccator* does not lead to quiescence in the face of injustice. Instead, it leads to a combination of self-reflection and suspicion regarding the underlying motives and forces that make up our natural/social/cultural/ economic environment. Luther's dictum properly understood, then, has an effect that is opposite to that of an opiate that satisfies our need for inward peace; instead it directs us outward to seek the transformation of a sin-ridden world.

Unidirectionality

The characteristic of unidirectionality follows from the Barthian claim that we do not have access to God and God's will through any natural capacities (e.g., our reason) but must depend on God's revelation to us for knowledge of God. Two important consequences follow from this understanding. First, because we cannot make any claims about God apart from God's revelation to us, the church's social witness cannot state that it is speaking on God's behalf unless it can root its pronouncements in Scripture. And even where it does root its pronouncements in Scripture, it recognizes that God's Word is living, and like anything living it always holds the capacity to surprise us. Thus the proper interpretation of Scripture depends on the Holy Spirit, who is characterized by movement rather than fixed location. What God is saying in that Word here and now is always new in some way even as it also has a consistent character. Second, God's commands override our own claims about God's character and will. Again, this is affirmed by the PC(USA) through its embrace of the *Book of Confessions*, which recognizes that dogma is eschatologically driven rather than written on stone tablets. God's word and action are always prior to our own and determine the constraints for our free and faithful human response.

Chalcedonian Character

The nature of God's relationship with us is further distinguished by these three characteristics: asymmetry, intimacy, and integrity. The social witness policy of the PC(USA) demonstrates the characteristic of asymmetry by recognizing certain constraints placed on freedom of conscience, namely, those imposed by the Word of God. As Calvin notes, our conscience stands as a reminder of our status as sinners in need of redemption. For Calvin a good conscience consists of an uprightness of heart marked by a "lively longing to worship God and a sincere intent to live a godly life."[31] He adds here that, properly speaking, a good conscience refers only to our relation with God. However, the benefits of that right relation flow outward so that its effects are deeply felt in our relationships with other people.

These constraints on our freedom also reflect God's intimacy with humankind. It is for the sake of others that God's Word binds our conscience. As the Presbyterian Church recognized after its own failure to stand up to the moral horrors of slavery, freedom of conscience does not apply when our actions are harmful to other individuals. Such actions demonstrate that we are not in right relationship with God; here our conscience ought to convict us of our sin rather than condone our actions.

That God calls the church to be responsible to the world as well as to God indicates that the human side of this relationship is given its own integrity. Such integrity reflects the enhypostatic characteristic of the union between the Son of God and a particular human nature in Jesus Christ. Consider the third principle of order, found in the PC(USA)'s *Book of Order*:

> That our blessed Savior, for the edification of the visible Church, which is his body, hath appointed officers, not only to preach the gospel and administer the Sacraments, but also to exercise discipline, for the preservation of both truth and duty; and that it is incumbent upon these officers, and upon the whole Church, in whose name they act, to censure or cast out the erroneous and scandalous, observing, in all cases, rules contained in the Word of God.[32]

As the body of Christ, the church receives its commands from its head, the God made known in Jesus Christ. But Christ has graciously given authority to the officers of the church to preach God's Word, to administer the sacraments, and also to exercise discipline so that the whole church may flourish.

What does the Chalcedonian character of our relationship with God add to the notion of practical wisdom as a Reformed virtue? Namely, the understanding that our witness as individual Christians, and the church's witness as the body of Christ, take direction from its Lord and head. If we receive the command of God obediently, we are called away from the safety of disengagement, under the false pretext of preserving individual liberty, to engage the world in ways that are not always going to be judged politically correct.

Christological Form of Grace

Clearly if Christians are to be wise individuals regarding matters of the Christian life, they cannot do so on their own. They need to have God's grace as a guide every step of the way. God's character shows through in the kind of grace they receive. Such grace is reflective of the relationship that exists within the Trinity. The love that characterizes that relationship overflows onto us as evidenced by the life, ministry, death, and resurrection of Jesus Christ. Jesus' ministry of reconciliation continues through the work of the Holy Spirit, building up a community of faith that gives glory to God. In acknowledgment of that ministry the church, Christ's body, also engages in the task of promoting reconciliation.

The PC(USA) recognizes this ministry as a mission of special importance for the church, as affirmed in C67. Here specific social issues are lifted up in light of the ministry of reconciliation that Jesus Christ imparted to the church. The Reformed virtue of practical wisdom, in relation to social witness, thus has a christological dimension because its prescriptions reflect underlying relationships that need to be mended. While sin is named and confronted, those responsible for sin are called to repent, not doomed to ultimate condemnation and punishment. Causes of social ills are also traced back to failures to recognize and attend to relationships that already were broken. However, the finality of this brokenness is relativized by the fact that Jesus Christ is the triumphant Lord of all creation, not just of the church.

A good deal has just been articulated about the shape of practical wisdom in the Reformed tradition. But is there really a need to call it a virtue? What does such language add that isn't already present and operating in the communal life of the PC(USA)? The benefit comes from making explicit an ability that is implicitly presumed in the approach the PC(USA) takes to its own governance as well as its social witness. Labeling the process of deliberation that leads to the flourishing of the church "practical wisdom" alerts the church to what it is looking for in its congregants and leaders. When practical wisdom is claimed as a virtue to be fostered by the church, certain misuses of the church's principles of order are less likely to occur. Such misuses include a wooden application of Scripture to determine solutions to the problems the church has faced (e.g., the slavery issue). By naming practical wisdom a virtue, the church endorses the importance of discernment in reading Scripture and interpreting it as a guide for God's people. Such identification also helps to clarify what the church is looking for in its leaders and congregants. Personal charisma and good preaching alone do not a pastor make; church leaders ought to be persons of practical wisdom as well. As Scripture attests, wisdom is a key quality for all Christians to possess.[33]

CHARITY AS THE GROUNDS FOR SOCIAL JUSTICE

Two arguments for the virtue of charity constitute this section. The first claims that acts of Christian charity on the part of individuals and congregations provide a necessary complement to the PC(USA)'s policy prescriptions for more just and sustainable human development found in the *Hope* report. The church's demands for justice at the national and international level can only go so far. The church has limited powers. It does not, for example, have the power to enact civil laws that are binding on its congregants or those outside its doors. Its demands for justice have appeal only insofar as they stoke the consciences of their hearers. It must then depend on its power of persuasion. But even if the church's legislative appeals to the U.S. government and the United Nations are successfully heard, changes in laws and intergovernmental treaties must be made in such a way as to preserve human freedom. The freedom of people to act according to their own consciences also needs to be recognized and balanced against the inherent rights of at-risk human and animal populations.

This balancing act raises the question of how far justice claims may be extended in relation to concerns about globalization. On what basis may appeals to human rights be made? On what basis may appeals be made for the rights of other living beings? *Hope* contains a robust conception of justice that extends rights to all life-forms. The foundation for these rights is, however, variously described. In some parts of the report the rationale for human rights is rooted in the mutual concern of nations who are participating members of the United Nations. In other parts, it is rooted in God's covenantal love toward all of creation. The report is strongest where it points to the latter basis. Even here, though, a more robust account of Reformed charity as a virtue would add to the report's conception of justice. To demonstrate this, we will examine the *Hope* report's analysis of just and sustainable human development and then provide a sketch of what Reformed charity adds to the picture.

The second major argument in this section makes the case that charity provides the context and basis for the church's justice claims. Such claims recognize that all life has certain inherent rights. These rights are not based on human agreement or on any characteristics particular to these life-forms. Rather, they are rooted in God's gracious love toward all of creation. That love is definitively expressed in Jesus Christ and his reconciling work on our behalf. The value of each living being is thus rooted in the worth that God bestows on that being. A Reformed understanding of charity properly recognizes that who we are is constituted by our relationship with God in Jesus Christ through the Holy Spirit. This understanding of charity successfully defends moral virtue ethics against those who argue that it is too agent centered to provide for an account of justice based on inherent rights.

The Problem of Grounds in the Hope Report

The *Hope* report's primary concern is that global development in its current form is unjust and unsustainable. The goal of the document is to offer a substantive alternative to current trends in globalization by critiquing those trends and providing the characteristics of a more just and sustainable human development process. The first half of the report eloquently critiques injustices in the current economic system that exacerbate global poverty as well as generate large sums of money for a small elite; in addition, it addresses sustainability issues raised by overconsumption and overpopulation. However, problems crop up in the second half of the report, which provides a blueprint for just and sustainable human development. While the prescriptions given here are well-meaning, they are nevertheless problematic for two reasons. First, their ramifications are so pervasive that they could not be implemented purely on the basis of legislation, for such legislation would be highly invasive. While *Hope* emphasizes the need for systemic change through modifications in existing legislation, it also requires a ground-up change in habits that requires some form of virtue. Yet that debt to virtue is not adequately stated nor are steps laid out for how to foster such virtue. The second weakness of these prescriptions is that they rest on conflicting conceptions of justice. At some points the rationale for human-rights claims comes from U.N. discourses that have no theological basis; at other points the rationale comes directly from theological presuppositions about the universe as God's creation.

The *Hope* report's recommendations revolve around three key concepts: sustainability, justice, and humanity. In regard to sustainability, the report builds on the work of U.N. bodies, but not uncritically. Two U.N. papers are examined: the 1987 report of the United Nations World Commission on Environment and Development, titled *Our Common Future*, as well as a summary document of the 1992 United Nations Conference on Environment and Development (UNCED), titled *Agenda 21*. While *Hope* commends the stress on participation and reduced inequality found in these documents, it is nonetheless suspicious of the reports' accepting position on the sovereign right of nations to exploit their resources as well as the reports' emphasis on economic development without attention to other forms of development.[34] Seeking sustainability alone does not go far enough. As *Hope* states, "It must be accompanied by other norms of comparable value, particularly distributive justice, defined broadly enough to include equal rights to participate in public life."[35] Such a conception of distributive justice requires that the rights of individual persons as well as the rights of *all life-forms* be respected, especially when these rights are threatened by the agenda of national governments.

Having elaborated just and sustainable development, the *Hope* report then examines the third key concept: human development. Such development is defined across six dimensions: economic, social, political, cultural, full-life paradigm, and ecological soundness. Five of the six of these dimensions are borrowed from a list compiled by human development theorists and practitioners who met at the Marga Institute in Sri Lanka in September 1986. In its description of all six of these dimensions, *Hope* relies on an article by Dennis Goulet, "Development: Creator and Destroyer of Values."[36] *Hope* merely summarizes Goulet's description of each dimension instead of reworking Goulet's terms within a theological context.

The need for virtue comes right out of the *Hope* report's summary statement on human development:

> Just and sustainable human development, in whatever form it is undertaken, is the comprehensive enhancement of the quality of life for all (present and future), involving the integration of the economic, social, political, cultural, ecological and spiritual dimensions of being. It reflects the understanding that human development is a universal need and is the business of the whole human family. It cannot be achieved without the kind of solidarity among all of God's children that recognizes and uses the gifts of all.[37]

The solidarity described in this passage is contingent on factors that go beyond legislation. These factors include a sense of shared destiny, compassion and caring toward those less fortunate, an awareness of the current state of need, and a belief in God that sustains commitment to one another despite differences, tensions, and the suffering we inflict on one another.

Prescriptions for just and sustainable human development must depend on individual charity as well as legal remedies, as the last part of the summary statement attests. While the aforementioned demands for frugality are no doubt based on God's justice, which measures intentions as well as actions, when implemented according to human law they would become excessive. The best motivation for citizens of developed countries to reduce voluntarily their patterns of consumption would be agape: self-sacrifice of material goods for the sake of the well-being of others, including all living beings.

The report's prescriptions also fail to provide consistent grounds for its rights claims. On one hand, the report presupposes a liberal democratic framework that emphasizes universal human rights as found in the U.N. documents noted above. On the other, its concerns for biotic rights depend on a theological description of nature as a part of God's creation. It is not clear why this latter description does not also serve as the sole basis for the report's examination of just and sustainable human development. Instead, the framework laid out by the U.N. documents takes over. As a result, the basis of the report's justice claims rests almost entirely on humanistic grounds.

Yet a theological conception of justice is there in the report, in the chapter immediately preceding *Hope*'s analysis of just and sustainable human development. This conception is rooted in God's covenantal love toward all of creation. The proper response of human beings, in turn, depends on self-sacrificing love that is tuned into what they owe to God, neighbor, and the rest of God's creation. Why *Hope*'s justice claims don't rely on this conception is a mystery.

Hope espouses a doctrine of creation that is affirmed by the early creeds of the church and is noteworthy in many respects. First, it grants God sovereignty over all of creation and gives God special status that nothing else in creation can have since all of creation is dependent on God for life. Second, with divine sovereignty comes the reassuring belief in divine providence over the universe. Believers in a Creator God have hope that God's concern for creation leads God to act to restore and heal the damage done to it. Third, such reassurances do not leave humans off the hook for their part in the damage done to creation. Human beings thus have a special responsibility when it comes to caring for the earth.[38]

The second part of this doctrine of creation has to do with the special status that human beings are granted by God at creation, as highlighted in Genesis 1:26. Human beings have been created in God's image. Subsequently all humans have dignity and worth and are deserving of rights, including the right to participate in political and economic life. This unique status comes with special responsibilities toward God's creation. Genesis 1:26 is closely followed by 1:28, where human beings are commanded by God to have dominion over all of creation. *Hope* interprets "dominion" in terms of stewardship of nature rather than license to plunder. Just as God uses God's dominion for creation's good, so we are to do the same. When we oppress others and use natural resources without due consideration, we distort the image of God within us. As noted in this section, Christ is the perfection of the image of God, which is made evident through his reconciling love. The nature of this reconciliation is not articulated in any depth here, but weight is placed on living out our love by tending to creation. We are called to just relations with others, human and nonhuman alike.

In this chapter of *Hope*, justice is rooted in covenant. God's love for creation forms the basis of justice. God's care begins at creation and continues in the New Testament with the reign, or kingdom, of God. *Hope* highlights God's covenant with Noah over the Deuteronomic covenant with Moses. The latter is more narrowly focused on the Israelites while the rainbow covenant emphasizes God's commitment to all of creation. *Hope*'s accent on God's promises to Noah is meant to compensate for a historical imbalance: "Although the ecological covenant was infrequently emphasized in Israel's life (Deut. 22:6–7, 10; Exod. 23:12), it needs emphasis in contemporary Christian life, as the 'always-reforming' community of God seeks new understanding of the theological meaning of ecological degradation."[39]

Human sin and God's judgment reflect the difficult part of this relationship. God's justice is manifested as judgment on the wrongs done by human hands, but even here it is God's love that shapes God's condemnation of human behavior. God confronts humankind and labels their behavior "sin" in order to call them to repentance. Sin is described as a rebellion against God based on an illusion of self-sufficiency. The result is self-centeredness, which views the world in such a way that we "value things over people, measuring our worth by the quantity of goods we acquire and consume, rather than by the quality of our relationships with God and with others."[40] Sin turns us inward and places our interests above the welfare of others, which leads not only to our own corruption but to the corruption of creation as well. Sin is thus a form of injustice, perpetuated by individuals and systems that fail to recognize the interconnectedness of God's covenant of justice with all of the created order.

The mission of the church in this context is to do justice. Here, too, the work of justice is dependent on a particular kind of love. The document notes, "God's goal of a just and reconciled world is not simply our final destiny but an agenda for our earthly responsibilities. We are called to be a sign of the Reign, on earth as it is in heaven, to reflect the coming consummation of God's new covenant of shalom to the fullest extent possible."[41] While the present state of the world, with its injustices and ecological crises, is cause for grave concern, it is not cause for despair. The document notes that although the power of sin should keep us on guard against being too optimistic, we nonetheless have good cause to hope for change in the future. The resurrection of Christ offers a reminder of that hope. In addition, we have hope that our God never ceases in the work of healing and empowering us.

Reformed Charity: Grounds and Context for Proper Development

Charity provides the proper grounds and context for just and sustainable human development. Where the *Hope* report seeks a different basis, rooted in U.N. documents, it falters. Its claims for extensive human rights are frustrated by the U.N. commitment to the sovereign right of nations, nations that sometimes do not recognize human rights. Its claims for extensive biotic rights are even shakier, since U.N. documents provide even fewer provisions for nonhuman life. In effect, these documents depend on shared agreements among member nations as the basis for rights talk. The theological commitments of the *Hope* report, however, place the grounds and context for rights claims in God's initiating and loving relationship with all of creation. Christian talk about rights then depends not on mutual self-interest but charity as it is exhibited first and foremost by our Redeemer, who is also our Creator.

Clearly, charity plays a key role in the church's reflection on globalization issues. But what does a Reformed definition of charity add to the discussion? An emphasis on covenant is one place to start. Reformed charity presupposes that human beings' relationship with God has been given particularity through the covenants that God has made with creation and humankind as presented in Scripture. God's charity already possesses a distinctive form and context that is expressed in different ways as it is lived out in historical relation.

Relationality is the hallmark characteristic of Reformed virtue that saves it from broader criticisms leveled at accounts of virtue ethics in general regarding human and other biotic rights. Such criticisms have been made by Nicholas Wolterstorff, a Reformed thinker.[42] Wolterstorff argues that virtue ethics, or eudaimonism, has two key features that mitigate against inherent rights talk. He claims (1) that eudaimonism's conception of the good life as the well-lived life places an emphasis on the agent's activity rather than on a state of justice or injustice in relation to one's rights and (2) that eudaimonism preferences the flourishing of the agent over the protection of the inherent rights of others. Wolterstorff's argument presupposes, then, that the kind of love endorsed by eudaimonists is inherently a self-centered love.

What follows is an elaboration of Wolterstorff's argument, followed by a counterargument that Wolterstorff's concerns are addressed in Reformed virtue after Barth. Such virtue only flourishes when it is lived out eccentrically, not egocentrically. It is grounded in God's polyphonic agapic love made known in Jesus Christ, rather than in some selfish desire to achieve happiness through moral excellence.

No Room for Inherent Rights in Virtue Ethics?

Wolterstorff's argument presupposes that modern versions of virtue ethics are rooted in the ancient Greek notion of *eudaimonia*, translated into English as "happiness" or "flourishing." While there are notable contemporary eudaimonists, these proponents rely heavily on ancient philosophers who developed the concept such that it grew into two schools of thought: the Stoic and the Peripatetic. Most modern thought on the subject focuses on the Peripatetic school. Surprisingly, Wolterstorff focuses on the Stoic school with only minor attention given to the Peripatetic when he deems the differences between the two schools to be significant. Even more surprising, Wolterstorff only minimally considers Thomistic virtue theory. When he does speak of Thomas's conception of justice as possibly including a theory of rights, he concludes that the addition of such rights violates the basic principles of eudaimonism.[43] Let us see why he thinks this must be the case.

Wolterstorff bases his conception of inherent rights on the notion of worth. Whether one is talking about human beings or other life-forms, the requirement that we are bound to treat them in a certain way is predicated on the notion that they have intrinsic worth. Take away that concept of worth, and the basis for inherent rights disappears. Wolterstorff argues that eudaimonism does just that. It does so by defining well-being in terms of a life centered on properly ordered activities. Proper order depends on the flourishing of an individual; while eudaimonism isn't pure egoism, it is agent centered. Whereas a crude egoist seeks short-term answers to the question "What do I have to gain?" a eudaimonist engages in certain kinds of activities, such as friendship, with a broader notion of the good life. For the latter, the good life does not simply depend on getting something personally beneficial from each action; instead it requires that we engage in activities that lead to a fulfilling life as a whole. According to Wolterstorff's account of eudaimonism, while friendship may entail making personal sacrifices for a friend, at some point the overall benefit of the friendship outweighs these consequences.[44] In this conception, even a friend doesn't have intrinsic worth: his or her worth is always tied to the value added to the agent's life. That value could always, potentially, disappear.

Second, for Wolterstorff eudaimonism's emphasis on activities as opposed to states of affairs also undermines inherent rights. One of the characteristics of such rights is that we may enjoy them without having to act. Wolterstorff calls them "passivities."[45] He mentions, as an example, my right not to be assaulted as I walk across a park. In order to enjoy such a right I should not have to appear menacing, brandish a gun, and so forth. I should simply be able to walk as I normally would as if no threat were present. But for the eudaimonist such rights cannot be considered a constitutive part of the good life since they are not in themselves activities.

Wolterstorff argues that they are not even instrumental goods for a eudaimonist. This is easy enough to see for the Stoic, who argues that virtue does not depend on one's circumstances, including how one is treated by others. But Peripatetics do consider such circumstances to be important. For Aristotle and his followers, true happiness requires some amount of good fortune. Why would rights not be considered instrumental goods for them? Again, Wolterstorff provides a helpful example to illustrate his point. Imagine that a person is ridiculed behind his back. Since the target of ridicule never finds out, his virtuous activity is unaffected. His rights not to be ridiculed have been violated, but it makes no difference to him in leading a flourishing life.[46]

If one agrees with Wolterstorff, then those versions of virtue ethics promulgated by ancient Stoics and Peripatetics do not provide the requirements necessary for supporting inherent human rights. However, an argument can be made that Reformed virtue after Barth does satisfy Wolterstorff's concerns about virtue. That argument centers on the Reformed virtue of love. It is God's love that bestows inherent worth on all of creation. The character of that love is demonstrated through the life, death, and resurrection of Jesus Christ. God's love comes to us in the form of a command; our faithful response to that command entails loving others as we have been loved, bestowing equal worth on our neighbors just as we have had it bestowed on us. In answer to another of Wolterstorff's concerns, such a conception of love places as much emphasis on states of affairs as it does on the activity of loving others.

How Reformed Charity Resolves the Problem

Wolterstorff worries that eudamonian reasons for choosing one activity over another are based on calculations regarding our own flourishing. Those activities that most benefit our long-term happiness are to be chosen over those that are not as beneficial. According to the Reformed virtue ethics proposed here, that is not the case. Since our true identity is as creatures in relation to the triune God, there is no way to separate our own flourishing from that relationship. And that relationship, in turn, leads us to recognize the intrinsic worth and rights of all other human beings as well as all other forms of life found in God's creation. Their worth comes not from anything intrinsic to them but rather is based on what is bestowed on them by God. God has blessed them, called them good, and so they are.[47] Our lives are lived out obediently in response to God's commands. Yet because those commands have a consistent dimension, and because our relationship with God develops and grows over time, the Christian life may be described in terms of virtue. From our perspective, *eudaimonia* is not the goal of the Christian life; worshiping God is. Yet out of love for us, God does wish us to experience *eudaimonia*. Divine command ethics and virtue ethics are not mutually exclusive, nor does a framework of virtue ethics need to exclude inherent rights. In responding to God's commands we ask not, "Will this lead to a more flourishing life?" but rather, "Is this indeed the command of God?" The consequence of our obedience is, nonetheless, a life of virtue.

What about Wolterstorff's concern that the eudaimonian focus on activity over states of affairs rules out eudaimonism as a framework for inherent rights? A curious lacuna in Wolterstorff's treatment of Aristotle's ethics looms large here. He never once mentions Aristotle's *Politics*. Whenever he is discussing Aristotle's notion of justice, he always points to passages in *Nicomachean Ethics*. The same holds for Aristotle's account of virtue in general. Why is this lacuna significant? For Aristotle the good of the political community represents the highest good of all, and a proper constitution is required if that good is to be realized. That form of government in which every man (and here Aristotle is specifically thinking of men) can "act best and live happily" is the best.[48] So while individual activity is the basis of the good life, certain states of affairs must be in place in order to make that life possible. The framework for virtue depends as much on these states of affairs as on the activity of each individual. Is Aristotle arguing for equal rights for everyone? No, he is thinking specifically about equal rights only for citizens of a political community. In his context, slaves and women would not be a part of such a polity. But rights of some kind are indeed explicitly a part of his political schema.

An objection could be made that the type of rights in this account are political rather than inherent human rights. Political rights are those bestowed on us through some human agreement or law. Inherent rights, in contrast, derive from our worth. That worth may be based on intrinsic characteristics or in terms of relationships. However that calculation is made, the rights that follow are connected to that worth rather than being given by some political body. This distinction between political rights and inherent human rights is crucial because unjust political regimes may very well not recognize the political rights of the oppressed. The appeal instead needs to be to inherent rights. Is such an appeal possible within a eudaimonian framework? The concern may have some merit in relation to

Aristotle's conception of virtue, but it certainly doesn't hold for Reformed virtue after Barth. Because of the worth bestowed on all creatures by God, all such creatures have corresponding inherent rights. Therefore our account withstands the objection.

Reformed moral virtue ethics based on God's covenantal love, as such love is depicted in the theological sections of *Hope*, extends rights to all life-forms. These rights become an intrinsic part of God's command as it comes to us. Since God honors God's covenants with us consistently, we recognize that God's command to us is voluntarily constrained and conditioned by those covenants. Christians are then called to act proactively when the rights of human beings and other life-forms are violated. God's covenantal love forms the basis of these rights as well as the context within which they are realized. Christians acknowledge that not everyone in the public square recognizes God's presence, let alone the existence of these covenants. Yet they also recognize that something must be done. We may debate the best means to bring about change in the political community, but the call to act in some way is unequivocal. Thus it is entirely appropriate that the church's official policy statement on globalization include specific recommendations to the U.S. government and U.N. bodies to change existing laws to bring about a greater recognition of human and biotic rights and to safeguard such rights. It is entirely consistent, within the proposed version of Reformed moral virtue ethics, to affirm the need for the protection of biotic rights as part of the Reformed virtue of charity.

REFORMING SOCIAL WITNESS

Two changes in the life of the PC(USA), both taking place in the 1960s, have had a significant impact on its social witness. The first was the shift from a single confessional standard, the Westminster Confession of Faith, to a collection of confessions that became the first part of the church's constitution. This transformation took place in full view of the church and was debated extensively before it was finally approved. The second change was not so purposeful, brought on more by broader currents of unrest occurring throughout society rather through the initiative of the church. That change involved a strategic shift on the part of the denomination in its engagement with social issues. The focus of the church's history of social engagement up to that time was directed at changing individual behavior to bring about change from the bottom up.[49] From the 1960s onward the strategy of the church has been to engage in social change as an institution. The social policy formulated since that time, by the ACSWP and other denominational bodies, has been built on the assumption that the voice of the denomination as a whole carries some weight in changing the political structures that perpetuate social injustices.

Such a change in strategy has its benefits as well as its pitfalls. Institutional pressure can bring about structural changes that would not happen otherwise. For example, in the 1970s the PC(USA)'s efforts to divest board of pension money from certain corporate holdings placed pressure on those corporations to change the way they did business, pressure that could not be applied by individual stockholders. On the other hand, the PC(USA)'s strategy shift away from changing individual behavior risks a one-sided approach to social justice issues. The denomination needs to incorporate both strategies to promote social change. Otherwise, the concerns and responsibilities of individual congregants and local churches become divorced from the concerns and responsibilities of the national body.

Therefore, the social witness of the church depends on strong lines of communication between those who craft social witness documents and the local leadership of the church. The Reformed moral virtue ethics proposed here provides one means to ensure such communication. Practical wisdom, frugality, and charity are already presupposed and embedded in the PC(USA)'s governing principles and in its social witness policy. The first step is making these commitments explicit. The next is integrating an institutional focus on social injustices with concern for individual moral change. Virtue ethics, with its link between the flourishing of society and the flourishing of individuals, provides rich resources for this integrative task.

CONCLUSION

While the place of virtue in the Reformed tradition is evident if one knows where to look, Reformed virtue has been largely neglected over the last thirty years even though other Protestant traditions returned to virtue ethics during that same time. Where should the process of reclamation begin? One does not need to look too far or dig too deeply to discover that the social witness of Reformed churches like the PC(USA) already presumes moral virtue in its congregants. What is implicitly assumed ought to be explicitly recognized. That it is not indicates either neglect on the part of the church or suspicion over virtue's claims about human capacities. Neglect, once identified, may be easily reversed. Overcoming suspicion, on the other hand, requires more work.

The source of that suspicion flows from Reformed understandings of human sinfulness. In the wake of Eden, the tradition assumes that humans are incapable of knowing and doing the good apart from God's direction. Where virtue is depicted as a purely human accomplishment, the tradition is rightfully skeptical. John Calvin and Jonathan Edwards addressed this suspicion by emphasizing the role of God's grace both in the origination of virtue and in its continuance. Humility was, for both, a key virtue. Without it, they argued, one would focus on the fruits of one's own virtue rather than on its source. Thus, as pointed out in chapter 1, Reformed virtue offers an alternative vision of virtue to that of Aristotle or even Thomas Aquinas, one that acknowledges the sovereign work of God's grace in our sanctification as well as our justification. The result is a picture of the Christian life that incorporates virtue in its view of Christian vocation while at the same time attesting to the radical human need for God's grace.

Yet the work of Calvin and Edwards, as well as the theology of the Westminster Standards, presents difficulties for a twenty-first-century account of Reformed virtue. They all presume true virtue is possible only for Christians who have begun to experience the healing effects of regeneration. In addition, they also assume the church has pride of place in the affairs of the state. Both of these presumptions are challenged in today's environment, where Christianity represents just one of many religions and where democratic polities intentionally separate the institutions of church and state. Such a diverse world even challenges presumptions about a common basis for ethical decision making grounded in natural law. In this context, the work of Karl Barth offers resources for an updated account of Reformed moral virtue. While Barth himself never proposed his ethics of divine command as a basis for moral virtue, his own theological commitments provide surprisingly fertile ground for it. Barth's doctrine of election extends virtue's reach to those outside the church as well as to those within it. His reflections on the relationship between church and state, shaped by Germany's involvement in two world wars, offers a vision of social justice that makes the church a key witness without tying it too closely to the apparatus of the state. His doctrine of revelation also establishes Reformed moral virtue ethics on viable ground without tying it to natural law. Such ethics offers exciting possibilities for addressing the unique set of challenges faced by today's churches, whether they are Reformed or not. Getting a grasp of how expansive this vision of virtue is requires comparison to another image of virtue's place in the world, sketched three decades ago by Alasdair MacIntyre.

VIRTUE AMONG THE RUINS?

At the end of his landmark *After Virtue*, Alasdair MacIntyre paints a dreary landscape of the impending Dark Ages, in which those seeking the vestiges of moral virtue find them in, of all places, a new Benedictine monasticism.[1] Throughout *After Virtue* MacIntyre argues that moral discourse has fragmented to the point that consensus regarding moral concerns is impossible. With the fracturing of society that ensues, the only solution appears to be Nietzschean: those who have the will to power make their own way while the rest get trampled on. *After Virtue* is not all bleak. MacIntyre heralds the Aristotelian tradition of virtue as a viable alternative to the morass that is modern moral philosophy. While certain features of Aristotle's thought, like his metaphysical biology, are outdated, MacIntyre argues that it is possible to construct a workable account of Aristotelian virtue for today using narrative, social practices, and tradition in place of Aristotle's teleology.

MacIntyre's book is a philosophical text, but his mention of St. Benedict at the end suggests that a theological premise is also at work. MacIntyre's own journey toward the Roman Catholic faith is more than hinted at here. But why St. Benedict? As the founder of a rule for monastic life that outlasted the Dark Ages, Benedict is the prototypical purveyor of the life of virtue that MacIntyre espouses. Benedict's rule avoids the extreme austerity of the desert fathers and at the same time the laxity of those orders that had no cohesive rule. Through a mixture of prayer and work, it seeks a balance between the active and the contemplative life. It provides order for community life together, structure through the person of a spiritual

father, but also freedom preserved through the rule itself. With a prophetic flourish worthy of John the Baptist, MacIntyre's book ends with a
call for a new Benedict, one who will presumably establish in the secular
realm what the old Benedict did in the religious one.

But how does one jump from the controlled environs of the monastery
into the multicultural milieu of the twenty-first century, where opposing religious and secular visions of the good life collide? According to
MacIntyre, the modern nation-state has become hopelessly bureaucratic,
too big and too diverse to foster communities of virtue. Jeffrey Stout's
book *Democracy and Tradition* challenges MacIntyre's diagnosis of the state
of moral discourse and his picture of modern democracy as toxically individualistic.[2] Stout argues that democracy itself is a tradition with certain
virtues that foster and are fostered by the process of practical deliberation
over the goods that ought to be pursued. As such, democracies provide
the context for discursive practices that seek compromise where differing visions of the good life collide. Citizens of modern democracies cannot afford to be too individualistic, since the health of such democracies
depends on their active and collaborative participation.

Stout argues that tight-knit religious communities with their own distinctive narratives should also not retreat from the public square. If they
do, their vision of the public good is lost, and their participation in democratic discourse is missing. They risk becoming more insular, radical, and
disenchanted with the modern state, despite the fact that there are available avenues through which their concerns may be addressed.

Stout's prescriptions involve more than just talk. In his follow-up book,
Blessed Are the Organized, he investigates the process by which grassroots
movements help promote change from the bottom up by engaging in a
variety of democratic practices. Stout highlights the work of one such organization, Jeremiah, which works with churches and synagogues, unions,
parent-teacher associations, and other nongovernmental agencies. He
tracks Jeremiah's community organizers as they help rebuild New Orleans
after Hurricane Katrina. These organizers aid existing organizations in
identifying volunteer leaders and then train them to think strategically
about the best way to effect change. The process takes time and a great
deal of patience. In New Orleans, the rebuilding process is complicated
by the fact that powerful business interests see the decimation caused
by the storm as an opportunity to develop areas once claimed by low-
income communities. Courage is needed on the part of grassroots workers
to stand up to such powers in order to represent the interests of the folks
whose houses have been destroyed.[3] It helps if these organizations already
promote the kind of moral virtue required for the task. Because so many
such organizations are churches, the health of grassroots democracy in the
United States depends on them. Without them, these efforts would fail.

While Stout's own commitments stem from an American pragmatist tradition that runs from Emerson through Dewey, his prescriptions for religious involvement in the public square ought to be heard by all persons of faith, regardless of their tradition. The Reformed tradition, with its emphasis on social reform, seems particularly suited to the task of addressing social justice concerns wherever they arise. Reformed churches like the PC(USA) already endorse the requisite moral virtues in their social witness policy. In addition, Reformed churches have for centuries mimicked the process of grassroots democracy through their ecclesial, presbyterial polity. Making Reformed commitments to certain moral virtues more explicit, such as temperance and agape, would help further the church's social witness in this regard.

What is it that MacIntyre, baptized in a Presbyterian church, does not see in the Reformed tradition that he does see in Thomism? Thomas Aquinas's incorporation of Aristotelian virtue within a Christian worldview provides MacIntyre with the framework he needs as he elaborates his account of virtue in the years following *After Virtue*. MacIntyre's examination of Reformed views, in contrast, yields a different outcome. His assessment is found in his historical exploration of Scottish philosophy in his follow-up book, *Whose Justice? Which Rationality?*[4] MacIntyre finds traces of Aristotelian virtue in this philosophical tradition, but these rest on an unstable alliance between Augustinian notions of sin and Aristotelian conceptions of *phronēsis*, or practical wisdom. The health of any tradition, posits MacIntyre, depends on its adherents' ability to recognize outside challenges and to provide coherent and convincing responses. Thus while all rationality is deeply shaped by the distinctive language and practices of a particular tradition, the reasons provided by any one tradition are accountable to others. If members of that tradition fail to provide such reasons, the tradition becomes unintelligible to outsiders and loses its influence in society at large.

Adherents to the Scottish philosophical tradition, being members of the Reformed faith, were caught between two opposing parties. On the one hand, they needed to adhere to the Westminster Standards and answer to those Calvinist clergy who condemned the use of philosophy in theological matters. On the other hand, they had to answer to those deists, and later atheists, who regarded with suspicion their appeal to God's miraculous intervention in the world as attested in Scripture. Frances Hutcheson, MacIntyre's chosen standard-bearer for the tradition, resolved this tension by postulating a common moral sense in place of Aristotelian *phronēsis*. Hutcheson's understanding of justice was similar to Aristotle's: competing claims to certain goods should be awarded according to merit rather than mutually agreed-on self-interest. One of the problems of such a conception of justice is "buy-in," our tendency to look out for our own self-interests and the interests of those like us. What motivates us to look beyond such self-interests and agree to a system of awarding goods based on merit? Aristotle resolved the problem by arguing that practical wisdom helps us ascertain that a merit reward system leads both to the flourishing of individuals and to society. In contrast, Hutcheson argued for a universal moral sense that calls to question our tendency toward self-interest. He claimed arguments over distributive justice occur as a result of faulty reasoning from the same moral sense rather than from incompatible understandings of justice itself.[5]

Hutcheson's solution was initially received with enthusiasm in Scotland. It satisfied the Calvinists, who understood God's revelation to have an immediate and obvious appeal to one's consciousness, without resort to philosophical reasoning about what constitutes justice. It also appeared to answer the concerns of those outside the Reformed tradition since it did not resort to revelation but to a universal feature of human nature.

But Hutcheson's solution collapsed in the generation that followed him. Its collapse may be explained by the incompatibility of different cultural conceptions regarding justice and other moral concepts. Because the culture of early eighteenth-century Scotland was relatively insular, consensus regarding moral concepts was high. In this respect, Scotland resembled many other premodern societies. However, as modernity brought with it more social interaction among groups of different premodern societies, resort to the self-evident nature of moral concepts no longer proved persuasive.[6] Newly aware of the incompatibility of moral intuitions, philosophers rejected Hutcheson's claim that a common moral sense was a feature of all human existence.[7]

MacIntyre's cautionary tale about the conflict between reason and revelation in Scottish moral philosophy highlights a tension that runs throughout the Reformed tradition and stands in need of address if a viable account of practical wisdom is to be proffered. It cannot be answered by resorting to natural theology without a more suitable resolution to the tension between Augustinian accounts of original sin and Aristotelian assumptions about human capacities. It also cannot be answered by turning to a common moral sense, the solution Hutcheson offers. Looking to a new spiritual sense, originating at the point of conversion, is also problematic, as pointed out in our evaluation of Edwards's work. What is left?

The ethics of divine command, such as that offered by Karl Barth. remains as a viable alternative, yet such ethics also raises problems. While these problems have been addressed extensively throughout this book, one more example will serve as an illustrative summary. Gerald McKenny has criticized Karl Barth's account of Christian ethics for providing insufficient guidelines for recognizing God's commands. McKenny argues that although Barth highlights the need for rational inquiry into whether the promptings we hear come from God, Barth also claims that rational reasons alone will not suffice. God's commands may require that we act in contrast to reason in certain boundary cases. Thus the attentive listener is stuck with insufficient guidelines as to how to interpret God's direction in those cases that are particularly vexing.[8]

McKenny's argument rests on a distinction Barth makes between God's activity and ours. He maintains that while Barth's explanation of God's activity in issuing divine commands is insightful, his account of how humans perceive these commands is inadequate. Yet McKenny fails to take into account the living relationship between God and us. Just as with any relationship between two individuals, there are three terms to take into account, not two. Besides the individuals involved, the relationship between them stands as a reality that is constantly being shaped by present circumstances, but it is one that nonetheless grows deeper over time. Only if we remove that living relationship from the equation does there appear to be insufficient guidance on the human side. When that relationship is taken into account, something new emerges.

God knows us best. Just as all human reasoning is shaped by tradition, every relationship has its own logic that becomes richer and more fine-tuned with time. It is in itself its own tradition. While there are certain ground rules for a loving relationship, such as integrity, intimacy, and mutuality, the forms these characteristics take will vary from relationship to relationship. Relationships that extend through many years develop their own insider language. When God speaks to us, God speaks as an insider, using the means of expression required for the circumstance. God is thus the master rhetorician. Should everyone wish to have a Damascus experience such as Paul's? No. Paul's personality was such that he needed to hear a thundering voice in order to be convinced that his views on God were wrong. Many of us need only a still, small voice to make a course correction. God does not waste breath.

Such a picture of God's dealings with us appears too intimate to be helpful for the purposes of promulgating social justice claims in public forums. "Because God told me to," is not always the most persuasive reason for convincing others to agree on a course of action, even in Christian circles. Yet God's command comes with clothes on, dressed up to meet the circumstances at hand. There are a good many reasons that organizations in New Orleans, post-Katrina, stand up for the rights of the poor and the oppressed. Among them is the one echoed in the pronouncement of the Old Testament prophet Jeremiah: "Seek the welfare of the city, for in its peace you will find your own" (29:7).[9] Regardless of whether such organizations hear that message as a call from God, they can still rally around a message that includes their own collective welfare. As Jeffrey Stout argues, religious groups should not have to leave their religious convictions at the door when they engage in public discourse, even when such convictions will not be shared by everyone.[10] Agreement on a course of action does not require agreement on principles.

Times have changed since the mid-eighteenth century. Attempts to ground rights in appeals to universal reason are now viewed with suspicion. While MacIntyre's work warns of the attendant dangers of abandoning something like Thomistic natural law, other avenues for forging common agreement on justice matters based on mutual consent exist. A Reformed moral virtue ethics inspired by Karl Barth's theology, grounded in the divine command rather than in natural law, offers an attractive alternative. God speaks to all, not a select few. God speaks consistently in favor of upending systems of oppression that favor the few over the many. And while God's speech comes in a variety of forms and elicits from us a variety of responses, in every mode it calls forth acts of self-giving love patterned after Christ. When God speaks in this way, we would do well to have the courage to respond accordingly.

FROM VIRTUAL TO VIRTUOUS COMMUNITIES

What does Reformed moral virtue ethics look like in the information age? How does such ethics change when the very notion of what constitutes community changes? The latter question is not a hypothetical one. The rise of social media allows for users to create selectively the communities within which they operate. No longer are our communities restricted to the physical space we inhabit. We may in fact belong to numerous virtual communities, with each of our online avatars reflecting different aspects of ourselves. How does such participation affect a life of the virtues that aims for integrity? Do the moral virtues remain in the digital realm, or are they somehow transmogrified into vices when our physical communities give way to their virtual counterparts?

Of course human beings have been in contact with others far away for thousands of years. The New Testament, written during the Pax Romana, reflects an era in which commerce throughout the Mediterranean brought together disparate societies. It is thus no surprise that most of the books of the New Testament are letters addressed to distant communities. What has changed recently is the ability to communicate with large numbers of people and receive almost instantaneous feedback.

This change in the nature of community comes at a time when young adults, who came of age around the turn of the millennium, are increasingly turning away from the church. A 2010 Pew research study finds that 25 percent of young adults under the age of thirty are "unaffiliated, describing their religion as 'atheist,' 'agnostic' or 'nothing in particular.'"[11]

Approximately 20 percent of these young adults grew up going to church or to some other religious institution. Their decision to leave organized religion altogether ought to give the church pause. They have not merely switched denominational brands; they have dropped the faith almost entirely.[12] They were members of a faith community, and they abandoned it in favor of something else. But what?

One of the defining characteristics of Millennials is their pervasive use of technology. The Pew report notes, "It's not just their gadgets—it's the way they've fused their social lives into them. For example, three-quarters of Millennials have created a profile on a social networking site, compared with half of Xers, 30% of Boomers and 6% of Silents."[13] Could there be a relationship between the way Millennials see the church today and the way they interact with technology? If so, how should the church respond? What type of community should the church provide for the plugged-in generation, and how might the moral virtues play a part?

Virtual communities raise certain challenges to the formation of moral virtue. Long before the existence of such communities, Aristotle noted that moral and intellectual virtues are acquired differently. While intellectual virtues are attained through education, moral virtues are acquired through habit formation.[14] Aristotle's distinction between education and habit formation hinges on the use of the body. While the intellectual virtues may be mastered without training the body, moral virtues do require training our responses to the passions that are expressed through our bodies. The mathematics involved in calculating the trajectory of an incoming projectile may be learned through careful study of the relevant textbook. But developing the courage to respond appropriately to such a threat requires experiencing dangers with those who already know how to deal with them. For Aristotle this process required a community whose moral exemplars were physically present.

Does the Reformed moral virtue ethics described in this book require a physical community? Such ethics has a different view of habit formation than the typical Aristotelian and Thomist positions. In line with Karl Barth's doctrine of revelation, these virtues arise out of a relationship fostered by God's initiating interaction with human beings. God mentors us in the moral virtues, and out of that relationship we develop practical wisdom in the discernment of God's commands. This kind of interaction does not require God's bodily presence. Or does it?

In the Gospels discipleship begins with the command "Follow me." The command is made much simpler, though not necessarily easier, because Jesus has a body to be followed. This is not the first time in the Bible that God is manifested in order to shepherd a group of people. When Moses leads the Israelites out of Egypt, God accompanies them for forty years as a pillar of cloud by day and a pillar of fire by night. Still, the incarnation marks a whole new level of God's involvement with the world. It provides the basis for a new form of community that requires God's embodiment. God has decided it is not enough to issue commands from on top of Mount Sinai. Finding a new Moses to serve as proxy won't do. God's teaching regarding this new community must instead be embodied by God himself. Such teaching involves great risk, to the point of death. However, the message cannot be conveyed in any other way, since absolute commitment is intrinsic to its content. That risk has never really gone away. Communicating the gospel and following it still require courage. But what does such courage look like in the digital age if embodiment is intrinsic to the gospel message?

Paul's image of the church as the body of Christ in 1 Corinthians 12 is an inspiring one. Through a variety of gifts, Christians in their very heterogeneity both embody God to the world and perform God's work in the world. No part of that body is superfluous; each part is necessary for the functioning of the whole. But to the untrained eye, actual Christian congregations leave something to be desired. A quick look around on any given Sunday morning reveals a motley assortment of people, many of them with gray hair, who just as often display looks of boredom as they do joy. C. S. Lewis captures this less-than-inspiring reality in his book *The Screwtape Letters*, where he describes the following experience of a recent Christian convert:

> When he goes inside, he sees the local grocer with rather an oily expression on his face bustling up to offer him one shiny little book containing a liturgy which neither of them understands, and one shabby little book containing corrupt texts of a number of religious lyrics, mostly bad, and in very small print. When he gets to his pew and looks around him he sees just that selection of his neighbors whom he has hitherto avoided.[15]

Who isn't tempted to seek out a more perfect church online, where the sermons are always inspiring and the people you interact with share your politics and belong to the same age demographic? Given this appealing alternative, the simple act of walking or driving to church on a Sunday morning can be an act of courage.

That two-thirds of Millennials actually are engaged in organized religion suggests there is still something to be said for brick-and-mortar-housed religious communities. Maybe Christ *is* found in the faces we see, the touch of hands, the sounds of praise, the smell of sweat, and the taste of bread and wine. We are here, these churchgoers seem to say; we made a commitment to be here, despite all of the appealing alternatives. What we find, hopefully, is embodied grace.

Recently our local church served communion by intinction. Parents with small children lifted them up so they could dip their bread in the grape juice. A long line of people waited patiently while a 106-year-old man stood up and came forward with the aid of a walker. I was reminded that from the youngest members of our congregation to the oldest, we are the body of Christ together. And isn't it also wonderful that those at home, who could not make it for whatever reason, also have a virtual alternative? Yet I can't help wondering if that alternative makes the impetus to visit those who were not there just a little smaller. The mission of the church requires that we keep up the courage to do so in the face of other, more comfortable options.

Every form of technology has built-in biases. One of the biases of digital media is nonlocality. By simplifying information into a sequence of zeros and ones, such media symbolically reformats the complexity of physical reality into a series of signals that is quickly replicated and distributed across thousands of miles. Douglas Rushkoff, a commentator on social media, points out that the Judeo-Christian tradition also has a bias toward the nonlocal. In contrast to the local deities of other ancient Near Eastern religions who dwelt in rivers and trees, the Judeo-Christian God was understood to be universal.[16] This bias perhaps explains why the tradition embraced the printed word, another technology with a nonlocal bias. And while Judaism was rooted in the experience of a particular ethnic group, Christianity's universal message expanded to include all peoples. Its message was inherently nonlocal in a way that other world religions, such as Hinduism and Confucianism, could not be. Thus Christianity proved more transportable from one place to the next. But its very portability and universality also came with the risk of neglecting the local environment. Since its adherents did not see nature as itself sacred, they were more open to the idea of abusing it.

Reformed moral virtue ethics provides helpful resources to address the problematic dimensions of the nonlocal bias found both in Christianity and in digital media. As demonstrated by the case study in the last chapter, such ethics provides a comprehensive vision of social justice, grounded in agapic love, that extends to all living things. Such an account is deeply needed, since another one could be heard in its place. Lynn White, in a now classic essay, argued in the 1960s that the roots of our ecological crisis derive from problematic views of nature embedded in the Judeo-Christian message. Both religions share a narrative in which human beings alone are made in the image of God, which has led to a narrow anthropocentric focus in the Judeo-Christian tradition. White claims that this focus, coupled with an account of a God who stands over and against nature rather than within it, has led to ways of thinking that have been deeply destructive to our environment.[17]

The early chapters of Genesis can and should be read another way. Genesis 1:28 should be read as a requirement to care for the earth, not as permission to destroy it.[18] The covenant God makes with all of creation in the presence of Noah can and should be read as evidence that God not only stands above creation but is also deeply involved in its care. In the face of environmental degradation, Christians ought to be committed to an ethic of frugality as a form of good stewardship toward creation and as a response to their covenantal relationship with God.

Barth's doctrine of revelation helps to capture the ways in which the Christian gospel is both local and universal. The Word of God in Scripture attests to Christ, the Word of God in human flesh. This Word is at the same time universal and local. God's Chalcedonian relationship with creation may be asymmetrical, but it is also intimate. God has, after all, chosen to be a part of creation through the hypostatic union of Christ's human nature, a nature that continues to be inseparably united to the Word of God. In line with the rest of the Reformed tradition, Barth attests to the fact that the body of Christ cannot be in more than one place at one time. In addition, God's word in Scripture is a living word, which through the Holy Spirit is interpreted in the preaching of the gospel message afresh at different times and in different localities.

The missiologist Lamin Sanneh points out that the Bible's translatability from the original Hebrew, Greek, and Aramaic into other languages indicates the flexibility of the Word of God. Again and again, the Bible has been influenced by local cultures, whose thought forms reshape the gospel message in light of their particular contexts. As one example, Sanneh notes the experience of missionaries working with a native tribe in Mexico. These missionaries wanted to translate the idea of the Word being "full of grace and truth" (John 1:14). In this passage grace is taken to mean "gift of life" or, more literally, "a living gift." However, since the only living gifts people exchanged in the culture were chickens, they understood the phrase to say the Word was "full of chicken and truth."[19] No doubt this translation also communicates a word of truth to chicken lovers everywhere!

Living in the digital age requires a new kind of translation project. The gospel message must now be communicated in such a way that it speaks a word of grace and truth to those whose commitments spread across both virtual and physical space. As embodied agents of God's grace, Christians need the moral virtues now more than ever. They need the courage to reach out to those who are different from themselves through face-to-face contact, not just via online chat rooms. They need a vision of social justice that addresses the rights of all living things, locally and globally. They need practical wisdom to discern what to make of all the information at their disposal. And perhaps most of all, they need to know how to embody the agapic love of their savior Jesus Christ, who came and died in the flesh that they might have life and have it abundantly. As they tackle this translation project, Reformed churches would do well to embrace a version of virtue ethics that is rooted in their own tradition.

NOTES

PREFACE

1. Nicholas Wolterstorff, *Justice: Rights and Wrongs* (Princeton, NJ: Princeton University Press, 2008), 155.
2. The quote is taken from the Barmen Declaration, 8.14. Presbyterian Church (U.S.A.), *Book of Confessions: Study Edition* (Louisville, KY: Geneva Press, 1999), 311.
3. Barmen Declaration, 8.23, *Book of Confessions*, 312.

INTRODUCTION

1. Stanley Hauerwas, *The Peaceable Kingdom: A Primer in Christian Ethics*, 2nd ed. (London: SCM Press, 2003), 27.
2. Ibid., 62.
3. Dorothy C. Bass and Craig Dykstra, eds., *Practicing Our Faith* (San Francisco: Jossey-Bass Publishers, 1998), xiii.
4. Craig Dykstra, *Growing in the Life of Faith,* 2nd ed. (Louisville, KY: Westminster John Knox Press, 2005), 76.
5. Ibid., 76–77.
6. Richard Muller, *Post-Reformation Reformed Dogmatics: The Rise and Development of Reformed Orthodoxy, ca. 1520 to ca. 1725*, vol. 1, *Prolegomena to Theology*, 2nd ed. (Grand Rapids: Baker Academic, 2003), 29.
7. Stephen A. Wilson, *Virtue Reformed: Rereading Jonathan Edwards* (Boston: Brill, 2005), 4.
8. See Elizabeth Cochran, *Receptive Human Virtues: A New Reading of Jonathan Edwards's Ethics* (University Park: Pennsylvania State University Press, 2011).
9. As we will see in chapter 1, it may be possible to pull together an account of civic virtue in Edwards's work. Such virtue would be based on Edwards's view of common morality, which has affinities to Thomas's notion of natural law. However, the fact that Edwards labels pagan virtue as false virtue ought to raise a red flag.
10. Muller, *Post-Reformation Reformed Dogmatics*, 65. See also Richard Muller, *After Calvin* (Oxford: Oxford University Press, 2003), 133–36.
11. See Bruce L. McCormack and Thomas Joseph White, eds., *Thomas Aquinas and Karl Barth: An Unofficial Catholic-Protestant Dialogue* (Grand Rapids: Wm. B. Eerdmans Publishing Co., 2013).
12. See Karl Barth, *Church Dogmatics*, II/2, *The Doctrine of God*, ed. G.W. Bromiley and T. F. Torrance (Edinburgh: T. & T. Clark, 1957), 647.
13. This criticism is not new. See James M. Gustafson, *Protestant and Roman Catholic Ethics: Prospects for Rapprochement* (Chicago: University of Chicago Press,

1978), 71. See also Stanley Hauerwas, *Character and the Christian Life: A Study in Theological Ethics* (San Antonio, TX: Trinity University Press, 1985), 176.

14. John Webster, *Barth's Ethics of Reconciliation* (New York: Cambridge University Press, 1995).

15. William Werpehowski, "Practical Wisdom and the Integrity of Christian Life," *Journal of the Society of Christian Ethics* 27, no. 2 (2007): 68.

16. Hereafter referred to as PC(USA).

1. THE REFORMED TRADITION ON MORAL VIRTUE

1. The period of Protestant Scholasticism, stretching over 150 years from the late sixteenth century through the early part of the eighteenth, is one example of an era where lists of virtues were examined for use in the church. Richard A. Muller's massive reconstruction of this period is one example of attempts at retrieval. Muller, however, focuses little attention on virtue per se. See Richard Muller, *Post-Reformation Reformed Dogmatics: The Rise and Development of Reformed Orthodoxy, ca. 1520 to ca. 1725*, vol. 1, *Prolegomena to Theology*, 2nd ed. (Grand Rapids: Baker Academic, 2003).

2. John Calvin, *Institutes of the Christian Religion* 1.1.2, vol. 20, Library of Christian Classics, ed. John Thomas McNeill, trans. Ford Lewis Battles (Philadelphia: Westminster Press, 1960).

3. See Serene Jones, *Calvin and the Rhetoric of Piety* (Louisville, KY: Westminster John Knox Press, 1995), 23–25.

4. Calvin, *Inst.* 1.1.1.

5. Ibid., 3.6.1. For an interesting exposition of this passage, see Raymond K. Anderson, *Love and Order: The Life-Structuring Dynamics of Grace and Virtue in Calvin's Ethical Thought* (Chambersburg, PA: Wilson College, 1973), 84ff. One of the few monographs on Calvin and virtue, this work is based on a dissertation directed by Karl Barth!

6. St. Augustine, *De Gratia et Libero Arbitrio* 17, ed. J. P. Migne, vol. 22, *Patrologiae cursus completus, series latina* (Paris, 1844–55), 901. For the influence of Augustine's formulation on medieval conceptions of grace, see Bernard Lonergan, *Grace and Freedom*, ed. J. Patout Burns (New York: Herder & Herder, 1971), 3ff.

7. John Calvin, *The Bondage and Liberation of the Will: A Defence of the Orthodox Doctrine of Human Choice against Pighius*, ed. A. N. S. Lane, trans. Graham I. Davies (Grand Rapids: Baker Books, 1996), 123–24; text translated from volume 6 of *Ioannis Calvini opera quae supersunt omnia*, ed. J. W. Baum et al. (Brunswick, 1863-1900), hereafter *CO*; *CO* 6.317.

8. For a helpful interpretation of Calvin's understanding of participation, see J. Todd Billings, *Calvin, Participation, and the Gift* (Oxford: Oxford University Press, 2007), especially chap. 2.

9. Calvin, *Bondage and Liberation*, 210; *CO* 6:379.

10. Cicero, *De Natura Deorum* 3.36, trans. H. Rackham, vol. 19, *Academica* (Cambridge: Harvard University Press, 1979), 373. A different translation of this passage is quoted in Calvin, *Inst.* 2.2.3.

11. Calvin, *Inst.* 2.2.4.

12. The one exception being Augustine, whom Calvin treats favorably in *Inst.* 2.2.8. Calvin's assessment here is a touch overdrawn, as he admits in a later section (2.2.9). It is not that the early church fathers never mention the deleterious effects of sin on the will but that they do so on an inconsistent basis, which leads to confusion if one is to take them as authorities on the matter.

13. Calvin, *Inst.* 2.2.9.

14. Augustine, *The City of God against the Pagans* 29.25, ed. R. W. Dyson (Cambridge: Cambridge University Press, 1998), 961. For a fuller explanation of Augustine's thoughts on pagan virtue, see Jennifer Herdt, *Putting on Virtue: The Legacy of the Splendid Vices* (Chicago: University of Chicago Press, 2008), 45–71.

15. This economy of grace is stated more than once in Thomas's treatise on grace. For one example see *ST* 1-2. q.113. a.6. Unless otherwise indicated, quotations of the *Summa Theologiae* come from the Blackfriars translation, *Summa Theologiae: Latin Text and English Translation, Introductions, Notes, Appendices and Glossaries*, 60 vols. (New York: McGraw-Hill, 1964).

16. Found in the preamble to question 113 on justification, in *ST* 1-2, q.113.

17. John Calvin, *The First Epistle of Paul the Apostle to the Corinthians*, ed. David W. Torrance and Thomas F. Torrance, trans. John W. Fraser (Grand Rapids: Wm. B. Eerdmans Publishing Co., 1989), 283–84.

18. Calvin, *Inst.* 2.3.9.

19. Augustine, *Psalms*, Ps. 70:1–2, ed. J. P. Migne, vol. 36, *Patrologiae cursus completus* (Paris, 1844–55), 876, quoted in Calvin, *Inst.* 2.2.11.

20. Calvin, *Inst.* 3.3.5. See Anderson, *Love and Order*, 302ff.

21. Calvin, *Inst.* 3.6.3.

22. John Calvin, *The Epistles of Paul to the Romans and the Thessalonians*, ed. David W. Torrance and Thomas F. Torrance, trans. Ross MacKenzie (Grand Rapids: Wm. B. Eerdmans Publishing Co., 1980), 106–7.

23. *Corpus Reformatorum* 8:412, cited in Bard Thompson, "Historical Background of the Catechism," in *Essays on the Heidelberg Catechism*, ed. Bard Thompson, Hendrikus Berkhof, Eduard Schweizer, and Howard G. Hageman (Philadelphia: United Church Press, 1963), 34.

24. Presbyterian Church (U.S.A.), *The Constitution of the Presbyterian Church (U.S.A.), Part I, Book of Confessions: Study Edition*. Louisville, KY: Geneva Press, 1999, 162–63. The Erastians held that civil authorities had the final say in church affairs.

25. Ibid., 165.

26. Frederick III supervised the meetings of the theological faculty that examined the Heidelberg confession, and wrote a preface to the completed product. Ibid., 52.

27. Ibid., 170.

28. Westminster Confession 6.093, ibid., 191. The quote is taken from the UPCUSA *Book of Confessions*; the PCUS wording is slightly different.

29. Westminster Confession 6.092, ibid., 191.

30. Westminster Confession 6.076, ibid., 189.

31. W. van Vlastuin, "Personal Renewal between Heidelberg and Westminster," *Journal of Reformed Theology* 5 (2011): 62.

32. T. F. Torrance, *The Scottish Theology* (Edinburgh: T. & T. Clark, 1996), 128. See Westminster Confession (chap. 12), and Calvin, *Inst.* 2.16.3–4.

33. Westminster Confession 6.106, *Book of Confessions*, 194.

34. Calvin, *Inst.* 2.7.11.

35. In Torrance's view the legalism of the Westminster Confession belies a central tenet of the Reformation: *sola gratia*. See Torrance, *Scottish Theology*, 140.

36. Westminster Confession 6.075, *Book of Confessions*, 188.

37. Karl Barth, *The Theology of the Reformed Confessions*, trans. and annotated by Darrell L. Guder and Judith J. Guder (Louisville, KY: Westminster John Knox Press, 2002), 141–42.

38. Calvin, *Inst.* 3.3.9.

39. Ibid., 3.3.10.

40. Barth's views, as I will demonstrate in subsequent chapters, are in fact amenable to virtue once one reads them in light of his emphasis on the eschatological perspective of God's dealings with human beings.

41. Westminster Confession 6.118, *Book of Confessions*, 196. See Barth, *Reformed Confessions*, 145.

42. Westminster Larger Catechism 7.112, *Book of Confessions*, 249. See Barth, *Reformed Confessions*, 146.

43. Barth, *Reformed Confessions*, 137.

44. See George Marsden, *Jonathan Edwards* (New Haven, CT: Yale University Press, 2003), 275.

45. Mark Noll, *America's God: From Jonathan Edwards to Abraham Lincoln* (Oxford: Oxford University Press, 2002), 262–63.

46. Charles Hodge, for instance, commended Edwards's *Religious Affections* but expressed reservations about his emphasis on conversion. See Charles Hodge, *Systematic Theology*, 3 vols. (Grand Rapids: Wm. B. Eerdmans Publishing Co., 1986), 3:3–40, 213–58. See also Michael J. McClymond and Gerald R. McDermott, *The Theology of Jonathan Edwards* (Oxford: Oxford University Press, 2012), 377.

47. McClymond and McDermott, *Theology of Jonathan Edwards*, 634–35.

48. See H. Richard Niebuhr, "Religious Realism in the Twentieth Century," in *Religious Realism*, ed. D. C. Macintosh (New York: The MacMillan Co., 1931); and Richard R. Niebuhr, *Streams of Grace: Studies of Jonathan Edwards, Samuel Taylor Coleridge, and William James* (Kyoto: Doshisha University Press, 1983). For an evaluation of Edwards's influence on the Niebuhr brothers, see Amy Plantinga Pauw, "The Future of Reformed Theology: Some Lessons from Jonathan Edwards," in *Toward the Future of Reformed Theology*, ed. David Willis and Michael Welker (Grand Rapids: Wm. B. Eerdmans Publishing Co., 1999), 460–61.

49. See, for instance, Perry Miller, *Jonathan Edwards* (New York: Meridian Books, 1949), 121, 147, 257.

50. Roland A. Delattre, *Beauty and Sensibility in the Thought of Jonathan Edwards: An Essay in Aesthetics and Theological Ethics* (Eugene, OR: Wipf & Stock, 2006 [1968]).

51. See William C. Spohn, "Union and Consent with the Great Whole: Jonathan Edwards on True Virtue," *Annual of the Society of Christian Ethics* 5 (Waterloo, ON: Council on Studies of Religion, 1985), 19–32; Paul Lewis, "The Springs of Motion: Jonathan Edwards on Emotions, Character, and Agency," *Journal of Religious Ethics* 22, no. 2 (1994): 275–97; and esp. Stephen A. Wilson and Jean Porter, "Taking the Measure of Jonathan Edwards for Contemporary Religious Ethics," *Journal of Religious Ethics* 31, no. 2 (2003): 183–99. The 2003 summer issue of the *Journal of*

Religious Ethics has a number of essays dedicated to Edwards's ethics in honor of the tercentenary of his birth.

52. Stephen A. Wilson, *Virtue Reformed: Rereading Jonathan Edwards* (Boston: Brill, 2005), 4–6.

53. Jonathan Edwards, *The Nature of True Virtue*, ed. Paul Ramsey, vol. 8, *The Works of Jonathan Edwards*, gen. ed. John E. Smith (New Haven, CT: Yale University Press, 1989), 47, 540. This is the second of two related dissertations. The first, *Concerning the End for Which God Created the World*, provides the explicitly Christian doctrine of creation that is presupposed in the second. The end to which the first refers is true virtue. See Paul Ramsey's introduction to this volume, 5.

54. Edwards, *Nature of True Virtue*, 541.

55. Ibid., 552–53.

56. Elizabeth Agnew Cochran, *Receptive Human Virtues* (University Park: Pennsylvania State University Press, 2011), 64.

57. Jonathan Edwards, *Religious Affections*, ed. John E. Smith, vol. 2, *The Works of Jonathan Edwards*, gen. ed. Perry Miller (New Haven, CT: Yale University Press, 1959), 106–7.

58. Edwards, *Religious Affections*, 120–21.

59. Ibid., 118–19.

60. Cochran, *Receptive*, 22.

61. Ibid., 111.

62. Ibid., 119–120.

63. Aquinas, *ST* 1-2, q.113, a.3.

64. Edwards, *Religious Affections*, 200.

65. Ibid., 201–2.

66. Ibid., 205.

67. Paul Helm, for example, argues that this sense should be sharply distinguished from the natural senses. Perry Miller, in contrast, sees more continuity. See Paul Helm, "John Locke and Jonathan Edwards: A Reconsideration," *Journal of the History of Philosophy* 7 (1969): 51–61; and Perry Miller, "Jonathan Edwards and the Sense of the Heart," *Harvard Theological Review* 41 (1948): 123–45. For an overview of this debate, see McClymond and McDermott, *Theology of Jonathan Edwards*, 316ff.

68. Ramsey, intro. to Edwards, *True Virtue*, 33.

69. Ibid., 34.

70. Edwards, *True Virtue*, 587.

71. Ibid., 589.

72. Ibid., 43.

73. Ibid., 33. Ramsey uses the term in reference to Edwards's conception of ordinary morality.

74. Aquinas, *ST* 1-2, q.109, a.2. See Aristotle, *Nicomachean Ethics* (New York: Cambridge, 2000), 1139.a27. Augustine's claim may be found in Augustine, *De Correptione Et Gratia* 2, ed. J. P. Migne, vol. 44, *Patrologiae cursus completus, series latina* (Paris, 1844–55), 2.917.

75. Aquinas, *ST* 1-2, q.109, a.2, reply to obj. 3.

76. See Brian Shanley, "Aquinas on Pagan Virtue," *The Thomist* 63 (1999): 553–77. As Shanley notes, Aquinas believes, in contrast to Augustine, that a life of political virtue is possible. Such virtue is, nonetheless, imperfect because it is not

directed toward the ultimate end: God. Shanley writes, "Where Augustine could only see the dichotomy of perfect virtue and sham virtue, Aquinas recognizes a third kind of virtue—true but imperfect." More recent scholarship, however, challenges the view that there is no room for pagan virtue in Augustine's thought. See Eric Gregory, *Politics and the Order of Love: An Augustinian Ethic of Democratic Citizenship* (Chicago: University of Chicago Press, 2008).

77. See Aquinas, *ST* 1-2, q.10, a.1.

78. For a good explanation of how Thomas uses the concept, see Eleonore Stump, *Aquinas* (New York: Routledge, 2003), chap. 9. Regarding the will as a moved mover, Stump writes, "For this reason the intellect is said to move the will not as an efficient cause but as a final cause, because its presenting something as good moves the will as an end moves an appetite." (278)

79. McClymond and McDermott, *Theology of Jonathan Edwards*, 313.

80. Marsden, *Jonathan Edwards*, 30.

81. Ibid., 31–32.

82. See Calvin's comments on 1 Cor. 10:16–17 in Calvin, *Corinthians*, 216. See also Billings, *Calvin, Participation, and the Gift*, 98–99.

83. See Jonathan Edwards, *End of Creation*, vol. 8, *Works of Jonathan Edwards*, gen. ed. Perry Miller (New Haven, CT: Yale University Press, 1959), 433. See also McClymond and McDermott, *Theology of Jonathan Edwards*, 122–30, 212–14.

2. BARTH'S OBJECTIONS

1. For support of the claim that Barth's ethics was ignored for quite some time, see the introduction to Nigel Biggar, *The Hastening That Waits: Karl Barth's Ethics*, Oxford Studies in Theological Ethics (Oxford: Clarendon Press, 1993), 1. Here Biggar documents the dearth of studies (written in English) on Barth's ethics up until the early 1990s.

2. Sheila Greeve Davaney, *Divine Power: A Study of Karl Barth and Charles Hartshorne*, Harvard Dissertations in Religion (Philadelphia: Fortress Press, 1986), 232. I was made aware of Davaney's critique through John Webster's work. My evaluation is indebted to his brief assessment in John Webster, *Barth's Ethics of Reconciliation* (New York: Cambridge University Press, 1995), 6ff.

3. Karl Barth, "Evangelical Theology in the Nineteenth Century," in Karl Barth, *The Humanity of God* (Richmond, VA: John Knox Press, 1960), 14. Bruce McCormack notes that Barth's account here (written in 1957) is somewhat misleading. As McCormack documents, Barth's public addresses in the years leading up to and including 1914 indicate that his misgivings regarding German liberal theology were years in the making. See Bruce McCormack, *Karl Barth's Critically Realistic Dialectical Theology: Its Genesis and Development, 1909–1936* (New York: Oxford University Press, 1995), 78ff. I am indebted to McCormack for my account of Barth's early development.

4. Idealistic in the sense that it was indebted to Kantian idealism.

5. Once the possibility of direct access to God's acting in history is conceptually eliminated, claims about knowledge of God become dubious. Such a view validates Ludwig Feuerbach's criticism that our conception of God is the result of the projection of human characteristics stripped of all limitations onto a transcendent,

nonexistent being. God thus becomes nothing more than a human construction. See McCormack, *Karl Barth's Critically Realistic Dialectical Theology*, 106.

6. Ibid., 57.

7. Ibid., 66.

8. Ibid., 80.

9. Karl Barth and Christoph Blumhardt, *Action in Waiting* (Rifton, NY: Plough Publishing House, 1969), 23–24.

10. McCormack, *Karl Barth's Critically Realistic Dialectical Theology*, 124.

11. Consider this quote from a speech Barth gave in 1911: "I really believe that the social justice movement of the nineteenth and twentieth centuries is not only the greatest and most urgent word of God to the present, but also in particular a quite direct continuation of the spiritual power which, as I said, entered into history and life with Jesus." Karl Barth, "Jesus Christ and the Movement for Social Justice," in Clifford Green, *Karl Barth: Theologian of Freedom* (San Francisco: Collins, 1989), 99.

12. McCormack, *Karl Barth's Critically Realistic Dialectical Theology*, 124.

13. Karl Barth, *The Epistle to the Romans*, trans. Edwyn Hoskyns, 6th ed. (Oxford: Oxford University Press, 1933), 74.

14. Aquinas, *ST* 1-1, q.8. The sentence reads, "Grace does not destroy nature but perfects it, which is why natural reason ministers to faith and the natural inclination of the will ministers to charity." The consequences of this position are far-reaching, as this grace-nature axiom is of central importance in Thomas's theology. One of the most significant consequences is that justification of the sinner occurs at an ontological level. That is, it involves a restoration at the level of being that leads the human creature toward moral and spiritual perfection. This constitutes our salvation according to Thomas.

15. Barth, *CD* II/1, 411.

16. Barth's concern is that Thomas's axiom places too much emphasis on the triumphal dimensions of grace and does not give proper weight to the negative moment of grace in its radical rejection of sin that is at the depths of human nature. See ibid., 411ff.

17. Webster, *Barth's Ethics of Reconciliation*, 55. While Webster's interpretation still holds court, the work of two scholars presents a new challenge to the efficacy of Barth's description of human action. Gerald McKenny argues in *The Analogy of Grace* that Barth's description of the human appropriation of God's divine commands leaves inadequate guidance for ascertaining whether or not the commands we hear actually are God's. McKenny contends that Barth both demonstrates the need for rational inquiry in this matter and shows that such inquiry is insufficient to the task. In a recent essay, John Bowlin frames McKenny's critique in terms of two burdens from which Barth's account suffers: hyper-Augustinianism and actualism. McKenny's critique touches on Barth's actualism, which recognizes that God's commands always come in new and surprising form, such that any continuities with previous commands are insufficient to predict the shape of the new revelation. In addition, Bowlin tags Barth with the hyper-Augustinian label. Hyper-Augustinians question whether any progress may be made in the Christian life prior to our eschatalogical resurrected existence. The prototypical hyper-Augustinian is Luther. Bowlin places the label on Barth as well. See Gerald McKenny, *The Analogy of Grace: Barth's Moral Theology* (Oxford: Oxford University

Press, 2010), 267ff.; and John Bowlin, "Barth and Aquinas on Election, Relationship, and Requirement," in *Thomas Aquinas and Karl Barth: An Unofficial Catholic-Protestant Dialogue*, ed. Bruce McCormack and Thomas Joseph White (Grand Rapids: Wm. B. Eerdmans Publishing Co., 2013), 256ff. McKenny's and Bowlin's concerns are directly addressed in chapters 2–4. McKenny's criticisms are specifically noted and refuted in the conclusion of this book.

18. Webster, *Barth's Ethics of Reconciliation*, 88. The interior quote comes from *CD* IV/1, 6.

19. Karl Barth, *The Christian Life: Church Dogmatics IV/4: Lecture Fragments* (Grand Rapids: Wm. B. Eerdmans Publishing Co., 1981), 22.

20. John Calvin, *Institutes of the Christian Religion* 3.19.16, vol. 20, Library of Christian Classics, ed. John Thomas McNeill, trans. Ford Lewis Battles (Philadelphia: Westminster Press, 1960).

21. Ibid. 3.19.4.

22. For Barth's debate with Brunner, see Emil Brunner and Karl Barth, *Natural Theology: Comprising "Nature and Grace" by Emil Brunner and the Reply "No!" by Karl Barth* (Eugene, OR: Wipf & Stock, 2002).

23. See Amy Marga, "Partners in the Gospel: Karl Barth and Roman Catholicism, 1922–1932" (PhD diss., Princeton, NJ: Princeton Theological Seminary, 2006). See also Keith L. Johnson, "*Analogia Entis*: A Reconsideration of the Debate between Karl Barth and Roman Catholicism, 1914–1964" (PhD diss., Princeton, NJ: Princeton Theological Seminary, 2008).

24. Erich Przywara, "*Gott in uns oder über uns?*" in Erich Przywara, *Ringen Der Gegenwart: Gesammelte Aufsätze 1922–1927*, 2 vols. (Augsburg: B. Filser-Verlag, 1929), 553–54. See also Johnson, "*Analogia Entis*," 60ff.

25. See Etienne Gilson, *Being and Some Philosophers*, 2nd ed. (Toronto: Pontifical Institute of Medieval Studies, 1952), 175. See also Johnson, "*Analogia Entis*," 97.

26. Thomas Aquinas, *Questions on the Soul [Quaestiones De Anima]*, trans. James H. Robb, Medieval Philosophical Texts in Translation (Milwaukee: Marquette University Press, 1984), q. 6, ad 9, 96. Thomas writes of God that if there is "something which is its own existence . . . there will not be potency and act in it, but pure act. And it is because of this . . . that in all things other than God the to-be (*esse*) and that which is differ."

27. Erich Przywara and Alan Coates Bouquet, *Polarity: A German Catholic's Interpretation of Religion* (London: Oxford University Press, 1935), 32.

28. Przywara writes, "That is equally the basis from which, in considering the problem of essence, Catholicism finds no contradiction between the supernatural and the Incarnation, on the one hand, and *natural* forms of divine revelation and impartation on the other, and yet again finds that in God, as 'all in all,' there is no duality of grades, but a unity." Przywara, *Polarity*, 33.

29. See Johnson, "*Analogia Entis*," 129 as well as Marga, "Partners in the Gospel," 213–20.

30. See Przywara, *Polarity*, 73.

31. See Karl Barth, *The Holy Spirit and the Christian Life: The Theological Basis of Ethics*, Library of Theological Ethics, trans. R. Birch Hoyle with foreword by Robin W. Lovin (Louisville, KY: Westminster John Knox Press, 1993), 1. It should be noted that Barth's conception of the *imago Dei* evolves over time. For a good

account of Barth's views in the earlier volumes of *Church Dogmatics*, see Herbert Hartwell, *The Theology of Karl Barth: An Introduction* (London: G. Duckworth, 1964), 73, 130, and 238. Paul Nimmo summarizes Barth's views in vol. III of *Church Dogmatics* as follows, "For Barth, then, the *imago Dei* of the ethical agent is constituted by the fact that the ethical agent is a being in encounter with God. This *imago Dei* is construed by Barth actualistically: it is not a quality of the ethical agent, nor does it consist in anything she is or does. Moreover, the participation of the ethical agent in the *imago Dei* does not rest primarily on her decision, nor is it something which she possesses. By contrast, Barth writes, 'the image of God is exclusively the affair of God Himself in His disposing of man in incomprehensible mercy,' and rests on the transformation which has happened to her as a result of God's decision concerning her. The *imago Dei* is therefore something to which she is called to respond, and rests only secondarily on her own decision and action" (see Paul T. Nimmo, *Being in Action: The Theological Shape of Barth's Ethical Vision* [New York: T. & T. Clark, 2007], 91). The quote comes from *CD* III/1, 202.

32. Lovin, in Barth, *Holy Spirit*, 5.

33. Ibid., 5–6.

34. Barth makes the point that Augustine can even in his *Confessions* talk about reaching toward God through moral attributes. See Lovin, in Barth, *Holy Spirit*, 5.

35. Barth's embrace of actualism is at the same time a rejection of the substance ontology found in Thomas Aquinas. See Adam Neder, "A Differentiated Fellowship of Action: Participation in Christ in Karl Barth's Church Dogmatics" (PhD diss., Princeton, NJ: Princeton Theological Seminary, 2005). Neder's dissertation points to places in vol. IV of *Church Dogmatics* that demonstrate how important Barth's rejection of substance ontology is for his rejection of virtue ethics in the Roman Catholic tradition. Neder writes that Barth objects not so much to virtue ethics per se, as to the ontology of the theology that supports virtue ethics. This ontology suggests that grace becomes our possession through the infusion of virtues or habits. But because grace is solely identified with Christ, it can't become our possession. According to Barth, Roman Catholicism tries to divide grace by postulating the operation of God's grace in us followed by a habitual grace. But for Barth grace can't be divided because Jesus Christ cannot be divided. See Neder, "Differentiated Fellowship," 211–13, and *CD* IV/1, 88.

36. See Gilson, *Being and Some Philosophers*, 158.

37. Ibid., 160.

38. *ST* 1-2, q.113, a.5. Matthew Lamb writes, "No one insists more strongly than Aquinas on the sinner's absolute dependence on God to justify him; but he equally insists that God's justifying word effects what it says." Thomas Aquinas, *Commentary on Saint Paul's Epistle to the Ephesians*, trans. Matthew L. Lamb, Aquinas Scripture Series, vol. 2 (Albany, NY: Magi Books, 1966), 272, note 14.

39. Even so, there is also for Barth a sense of movement in justification from unrighteousness to righteousness. See *CD* IV/1, 545, and Bruce McCormack, "*Justitia aliena*," in Bruce L. McCormack, *Justification in Perspective: Historical Developments and Contemporary Challenges* (Grand Rapids: Baker Academic, 2006), 188.

40. Gottlieb Söhngen and other Catholic theologians have argued that Barth misunderstood the *analogia entis* and that the Roman Catholic position was in line with his doctrine of the *analogia fidei*. However, Keith Johnson's argument to the contrary is persuasive. A close reading of *CD* IV/2 demonstrates that even here

where Barth treats the upward movement of the Son of Man (and with his humanity also ours) toward God, he is always very cautious to maintain the qualitative separation between God and us. See Gottlieb Söhngen, *"Analogia Fidei: Gottänhlichkeit Allein Aus Glauben?," Catholica* 3, no. 3 (1934): 113–36. For Keith Johnson's position, see Johnson, *"Analogia Entis,"* 240ff.

41. *CD* IV/2, 36. In the English translation the section under review is found on pages 36–116.

42. Ibid., 106.

43. Barth first learned of the anhypostatic/enhypostatic distinction while reading Heinrich Heppe, *Die Dogmatik der evangelisch-reformirten Kirche: dargestellt und aus den Quellen belegt* (Elberfeld: R.L. Friedrichs, 1861).

44. *CD* IV/2, 89–90.

45. In an earlier section he refers to the "sinister leaven" of Roman Catholicism. This statement does not reflect Barth's complete view of Roman Catholic tradition, for which he had profound respect. *CD* IV/2, 9.

46. For an online copy of the Chalcedonian formula, see "Chalcedonian Formula," http://anglicansonline.org/basics/chalcedon.html.

47. *CD* IV/2, 66.

48. Ibid., 69.

49. Ibid., 70.

50. Ibid., 77.

51. Ibid., 81.

52. Ibid., 81–82.

53. Ibid., 88.

54. Ibid.

55. Ibid., 88–89.

56. In July 2008 I asked George Hunsinger what he thought would be Barth's main objection to virtue ethics. He said that while Barth may not be opposed to certain aspects of virtue ethics, his main concern would be that a focus on the anthropological would crowd out the focus on God. He noted Barth's metaphor for thinking about the relationship between God and us: for Barth the proper way to do theology is to think about the relationship in terms of a circle with Christ at the center rather than an ellipsis with two foci, one focus representing God and the other human beings. When theology is done in the latter way, the human focus tends to take center stage, and attention on God recedes. It is better to do theology with one focus on God. In a more recent e-mail exchange, Hunsinger added, "Barth's actualism points away from the idea of developing virtuous habits as something central to Christian ethics. It points instead toward constancy in prayer and toward a God who can and does use his servants again and again despite their fallenness rather than more and more because of their real or apparent increase in virtue" (Hunsinger, personal communication, October 2009).

57. George Hunsinger, *How to Read Karl Barth: The Shape of His Theology* (New York: Oxford University Press, 1991), 59.

58. Ibid., 174–75. The second quote is from *CD* IV/3.1, 594.

59. Hunsinger, *How*, 186–87.

3. OBJECTIONS OVERCOME

1. William Werpehowski, "Command and History in the Ethics of Karl Barth," *Journal of Religious Ethics* 9, no. 2 (1981): 334–53.

2. See James M. Gustafson, *Protestant and Roman Catholic Ethics: Prospects for Rapprochement* (Chicago: University of Chicago Press, 1978), 71.

3. See Stanley Hauerwas, *Character and the Christian Life: A Study in Theological Ethics* (San Antonio: Trinity University Press, 1985), 176. Here Hauerwas defines character as, "The qualification of man's self-agency through his beliefs, intentions, and actions, by which a man acquires a moral history befitting his nature as a self-determining being" (11).

4. Werpehowski, "Command and History," 300.

5. Ibid., 303.

6. *CD* II/2, 647.

7. Ibid., 647.

8. Ibid., 646, quoted in Werpehowski, "Command and History," 307.

9. Werpehowski, "Command and History," 308–9.

10. Ibid., 315. In support of this conclusion, Werpehowski quotes Barth: "To live a holy life is to be raised and driven with increasing definiteness from the center of the revealed truth [that God is for the person and the person for God] and therefore to live in conversion with growing sincerity, depth, and precision" (*CD* IV/2, 566).

11. William Werpehowski, "Narrative and Ethics in Barth," *Theology Today* 43, no. 3 (1986): 334–53.

12. Ibid., 339.

13. Ibid., 341.

14. Ibid., 348.

15. Ibid.

16. Ibid. The German word used here is *Auseinandersetzung*, translated "falling out," but this translation does not fully capture the meaning of the German. What Barth is describing is the tension between the old and new self that takes place in a person's movement of conversion. He affirms Luther's *simul iustus, simul peccator* here. We are fully justified, yet we are fully sinners. Therefore we have a twofold determination, but in an eschatological sense God recognizes us as saints, rather than as sinners. Existentially, we are aware of the constant struggle between our new and old selves. See *CD* IV/2, 570–74.

17. George Hunsinger raises concerns about using narrative as a category. He observes that Barth's use of narrative is always from the particular to the general. If we try to use a general category of narrative and then apply it to the particulars of Scripture, we may miss the radical claims that Scripture has over us. See George Hunsinger, "A Response to William Werpehowski," *Theology Today* 43, no. 3 (1986): 354–60.

18. See William Werpehowski, "Practical Wisdom and the Integrity of Christian Life," *Journal of the Society of Christian Ethics* 27, no. 2 (2007): 55–72.

19. Ibid., 61.

20. Ibid.

21. Ibid., 65–66.

22. The quote is as follows: "The principle of necessary repetition and renewal, and not a law of stability, is the law of the spiritual growth and continuity of our life. It is when we observe this law that we practice perseverance (ὑπομονή) in the biblical meaning of the term, a perseverance corresponding to the steadfastness of God Himself, which does not signify the suspension, but the continuing and indestructible possession and use of His freedom." Barth, *CD* II/2, 647. This is the same quote that Werpehowski referred to in his 1981 article, "Command

and History." Clearly this quote serves as an important interpretive key for Werpehowski.

23. Werpehowski, "Practical Wisdom," 67.

24. Ibid., 68.

25. See Nigel Biggar, *The Hastening That Waits*; John Webster, *Barth's Ethics of Reconciliation* and *Barth's Moral Theology* (Grand Rapids: Wm. B. Eerdmans Publishing Co., 1998); and Paul Nimmo, *Being in Action*. In response to Werpehowski's reading of Barth, Stanley Hauerwas has retracted some of his earlier criticisms of Barth on this front. See Hauerwas, *Peaceable Kingdom*, 23–24.

26. Werpehowski, "Practical Wisdom," 63.

27. Ibid., 64. Col. 1:15–17 reads, "He is the image of the invisible God, the first-born of all creation; for in him all things in heaven and on earth were created, things visible and invisible, whether thrones or dominions or rulers or powers—all things have been created through him and for him. He himself is before all things, and in him all things hold together."

28. See chap. 2, note 31.

29. Aristotle, *Nicomachean Ethics* 1103a, trans. and ed. Roger Crisp (New York: Cambridge University Press, 2000), 14.

30. Ibid., 1105a, 27ff.

31. Ibid., 1107a, 1.

32. Aristotle, *Aristotle's Poetics*, 48b (New York: Hill & Wang, 1998), 5.

33. Aristotle, *Nicomachean Ethics*, 1180b, 5–7.

34. See Jennifer A. Herdt, *Putting on Virtue* (Chicago: University of Chicago Press, 2008), 30.

35. See Nancy Sherman, "The Habituation of Character," in *Aristotle's Ethics: Critical Essays*, Critical Essays on the Classics (Lanham, MD: Rowman & Littlefield, 1999), 240.

36. Alasdair C. MacIntyre, *After Virtue: A Study in Moral Theory*, 2nd ed. (Notre Dame, IN: University of Notre Dame Press, 1984), 222. Susan Moller Okin argues that MacIntyre's account actually plays off of two different understandings of tradition that conflict with each other. The first understanding is tradition *as a set of binding constraints* on human behavior by means of recourse to authoritative texts. The second is tradition *as an evolving narrative* that is continually shaped by communal discussion about what goods constitute the tradition. She argues that the second understanding is true of the feminist tradition but not the first. See Susan Moller Okin, *Justice, Gender, and the Family* (New York: Basic Books, 1989), 60–61. My own view of the Reformed tradition encompasses both understandings. As a tradition that seeks always to be in the process of reform, the Reformed tradition nonetheless also recognizes the authority and guidance of Scripture as a binding constraint on that process. I was first introduced to Okin's interpretation of MacIntyre through Jeffrey Stout, *Democracy and Tradition* (Princeton, NJ: Princeton University Press, 2004), 135–36.

37. Aquinas, *ST* 2-2, q.47, a.14, ad 1. I am indebted to Jennifer Herdt for her treatment of Thomas's account of infused prudence. See Herdt, *Putting on Virtue*, 88–89.

38. Aquinas, *ST* 2-2, q.47, a.14, ad 3.

39. Ibid., 2-2, q.24, a.7 as quoted in Herdt, 88.

40. *CD* IV/2, 572.

41. Barth writes, "The doctrine of Calvin obviously suffers from a curious over-emphasising of *mortificatio* at the expense of *vivificatio.*" *CD* IV/2, 575. Barth can attest to the contrary that our being enlivened by the Spirit of God is the telling note in the event of salvation because of his objective soteriology. Since de jure we are saved by God's electing choice, the "yes" of God has already won the day.

42. Ibid., 560ff.

43. Ibid., 527.

44. Ibid., 533–53.

45. Dietrich Bonhoeffer, *Nachfolge* ([n.p.]), 35, as quoted in *CD* IV/2, 541–42.

46. Werpehowski, "Command and History," 307.

47. See *CD* II/2, 200.

48. Werpehowski, "Command and History," 305.

4. THE SHAPE OF REFORMED VIRTUE AFTER BARTH

1. See Bruce McCormack, "What's at Stake?" in *Justification: What's at Stake in the Current Debates*, ed. Mark Husbands and Daniel J. Treier (Downers Grove, IL: InterVarsity Press, 2004), 81–117.

2. Ibid., 109.

3. Barth, *CD* IV/2, 560ff.

4. For Thomas Aquinas, however, sin remains a problem, though perfection in the moral virtues in this life is theoretically possible (but highly improbable).

5. Barth, *CD* IV/2, 547.

6. *CD* IV/3.2, 888–89. Barth's analysis of the twelve forms of ministry is found in *CD* IV/3.2, §72.4, "The Holy Spirit and the Sending of the Community." Each of these twelve forms of ministry serves as a witness to Christ both to the community of faith and to those outside that community. Barth discerns the basic forms of the church's witness by turning to the Gospels and to the letters of Paul to discern forms of ministry and witness articulated there that have persisted into the present. He hopes in this endeavor to come up with a "general law of the differentiation of the Church's ministry." *CD* IV/3.2, 860. He concludes there is a twofold form in all Christian witness: speech and action. Barth's treatment starts with the six forms having to do predominantly with speech, followed by the six having to do with action. The list of twelve is as follows: praise, proclamation of the gospel in the assembly of the community, instruction of the community, evangelization, mission to the nations, the ministry of theology, prayer, cure of souls, the production and existence of definite personal examples of Christian life and action, diaconate, prophetic action, and establishing fellowship.

7. *CD* IV/3.2, 888–89.

8. I am tempted to include a section on Barth's response to Bonhoeffer's decision to participate in an assassination attempt on Hitler's life. In his *Ethics*, Bonhoeffer alludes to this difficult decision in which he struggled to hear the command of God. Ostensibly, he never did receive confirmation that he heard God's command rightly, but he nonetheless went through with the act and died as a result. Later Barth was asked whether Bonhoeffer made the right decision. One of Barth's objections to Bonhoeffer's decision was that Bonhoeffer did not clearly hear the command of God. On such a matter, unless we hear the command of

God clearly, we ought not to act. See Karl Barth and John Drew Godsey, *Table Talk* (Richmond, VA: John Knox Press, 1963).

9. Aquinas, *ST* 1-2, q.61, a.3.

10. Ibid., 1-2, q.63, a.4. Here Thomas is quoting 1 Cor. 9:27.

11. See ibid. and 2-2, q.47, a.6.

12. Ibid., 2-2, q.47, a.13.

13. Ibid., 2-2, q.23.

14. Ibid., 1-2, q.62.

15. Ibid., 1-2, q.24.

16. Ibid., 2-2, q.24, a.11.

17. Ibid., a.12.

18. Interestingly, the other theological virtues are not cast out by one act of mortal sin; rather, they remain but in a formless state (dormant until infused with charity). It would seem to follow that charity also can remain in this formless state even when a mortal sin has been committed. Aquinas responds to this objection by differentiating between charity and the other theological virtues. Charity denotes union with God whereas faith and hope do not. Since every mortal sin marks a turning away from God, it is necessarily contrary to charity. This is not the case with faith and hope. Only those mortal sins that destroy the habit of faith and hope are contrary to them. See ibid.

19. Anders Nygren, *Agape and Eros* (Philadelphia: Westminster Press, 1953). Barth mentions Nygren in his own treatment of Christian love in *CD* IV/2.

20. Martin Luther, *Lectures on Galatians* (1535) in Martin Luther, vol. 26 of *Luther's Works*, American ed. (St. Louis: Concordia, 1955), 279. Gal. 3:13 reads as follows, "Christ redeemed us from the curse of the law by becoming a curse for us—for it is written, 'Cursed is everyone who hangs on a tree.'" Luther repeatedly employs the image of Christ wrapped in our sins in his discussions of justification. It is not surprising that one of his favorite verses was Col. 3:3: "For you have died, and your life is hidden with Christ in God."

21. Nygren, *Agape and Eros*, 205. Nygren provides a table of differences between eros and agape on 210.

22. Ibid., 499.

23. Ibid., 530–31.

24. Ibid., 684.

25. Ibid., 718.

26. Barth, *CD* IV/2, 737. Barth's position, then, is different from Nygren's in this respect. Nygren's view of *caritas* tends to collapse the tension so that the meaning of the term is synonymous with *eros*.

27. See, for example, David Clough, "Eros and Agape in Karl Barth's Church Dogmatics," *International Journal of Systematic Theology* 2, no. 2 (2000): 189–203.

28. Regarding the Septuagint translation of the Old Testament, this was of course a matter of interpretation, since Hebrew does not use different words to distinguish types of love.

29. Barth, *CD* IV/2, 738.

30. Ibid., IV/2, 743–44.

31. See Amy Laura Hall, "Complicating the Command: Agape in Scriptural Context," *Annual of the Society of Christian Ethics* 19 (1999): 97. Hall bases her thesis on texts from the Pentateuch, Hosea, the Gospel of Luke, and the Gospel of John.

See also the *Journal of Religious Ethics*, 24, no. 1, published in 1996. In this issue, Colin Grant defends Nygren while Gene Outka presents another view of agape.

32. Amy Laura Hall, "Complicating the Command," 101.

33. Ibid., 106.

34. See Barth, *CD* IV/2, 744.

35. Ibid., IV/3.2, 843.

36. Ibid.

37. Ibid., 860.

38. Ibid., 865–901.

39. Ibid., 889.

40. With the notable exception of the Confessing Church.

41. Hauerwas, *With the Grain of the Universe: The Church's Witness and Natural Theology: Gifford Lectures Delivered at the University of St. Andrews in 2001* (Grand Rapids: Brazos Press, 2001), 193. The Barth quote comes from *CD* IV/3.2, 826.

42. Barth, *CD* IV/3.2, 826.

43. Barth has been charged with having an abstract ecclesiology because of his emphasis on God's action in the church rather than on our human response. But which truly defines the church: the human response to God's grace or God's grace? Surely it is God's grace. As Nicholas Healy explains, the charge made against Barth may easily be turned on its head: "For to omit or deemphasize the primary constitutive elements of the church—God's action in Word and Spirit— is, Barth would say, to construct an abstract ecclesiology." Nicholas Healy, "Karl Barth's Ecclesiology Reconsidered," *Scottish Journal of Theology* 57, no. 2 (2004): 296.

44. In defense of Hauerwas, his position has changed somewhat since he wrote *With the Grain of the Universe*. In a later book, written in collaboration with Romand Coles, *Christianity, Democracy, and the Radical Ordinary*, he considers the possibility that civic groups may also be seedbeds of virtue. But even here he is concerned that there is no reliable mechanism for passing down these virtues from generation to generation in these groups like there is in the church. See Stanley Hauerwas and Romand Coles, *Christianity, Democracy, and the Radical Ordinary: Conversations between a Radical Democrat and a Christian*, Theopolitical Visions (Eugene, OR: Cascade Books, 2008), 345.

45. Karl Barth, "The Christian Community and Civil Community," in Karl Barth, *Community, State, and Church: Three Essays* (Gloucester, MA: Peter Smith, 1968), 158.

46. Ibid., 166.

47. Ibid., 169.

48. Ibid., 158.

49. Ibid., 154.

50. Ibid., 165.

51. Ibid.

52. Ibid., 173. Barth goes on to say that churchgoers ought to choose those social movements that ensure the greatest measure of justice.

53. Commenting on the ingenuity of God's revelation, Barth famously wrote, "God may speak to us through Russian Communism or a flute concerto, a blossoming shrub, or a dead dog. We shall do well to listen to Him if He really does so." While Barth was reflecting on the church's responsibility to hear the Word of

God, in whatever form it takes, the quote may easily be extended to apply to those outside the church as well. *CD* 1/1, 60.

54. Barth, "Christian Community," 164.

5. LIVING OUT THE REFORMED VIRTUES

1. John Calvin, *Institutes of the Christian Religion* 2.7.12, vol. 20, Library of Christian Classics, ed. John Thomas McNeill, trans. Ford Lewis Battles (Philadelphia: Westminster Press, 1960).

2. Ibid., 2.11.6.

3. See Max Weber, *The Protestant Ethic and the Spirit of Capitalism* (London: Routlege Classics, 1930). For an in-depth evaluation of Max Weber's work, see David Little, *Religion, Order, and Law: A Study in Pre-Revolutionary England* (Chicago: University of Chicago Press, 1969).

4. Weber notes that the Reformed church's conception of how God works in us was critical to its understanding of vocation: "A real penetration of the human soul by the divine was made impossible by the absolute transcendentality of God compared to the flesh: *finitum non est capax infiniti*. The community of the elect with their God could only take place and be perceptible to them in that God worked (*operatur*) through them and that they were conscious of it. That is, their action originated from the faith caused by God's grace, and this faith in turn justified itself by the quality of that action." *Protestant Ethic*, 68.

5. Jagdish Bhagwati, *In Defense of Globalization* (Oxford: Oxford University Press, 2004), 3.

6. See Amartya Sen, *Development as Freedom* (New York: Anchor Books, 1999). The public debate between Bhagwati and Sen continues to this day. In a letter to *The Economist*, Bhagwati claims that Sen's recent book, *An Uncertain Glory*, rather belatedly supports growth through globalization. Sen's response identifies several of his writings over the last fifty years that have pointedly demonstrated the need for such growth. The difference between them remains, for Sen, that such growth needs to be supplemented by government programs to address illiteracy and malnutrition. See Jean Drèze and Amartya Sen, *An Uncertain Glory: India and Its Contradictions* (Princeton, NJ: Princeton University Press, 2013). See also Jagdish Bhagwati and Arvind Panagariya, *The Economist*, July 13, 2013, 16; and Amartya Sen, *The Economist*, July 20, 2013, 14.

7. Hereafter referred to as *Hope* and ACSWP, respectively.

8. See James A. Nash, "Toward the Revival and Reform of the Subversive Virtue: Frugality," *Annual of the Society of Christian Ethics* (1995): 139. My analysis of frugality in Calvin is indebted to this article.

9. Committee on Social Witness Policy, Presbyterian Church (U.S.A.), *Restoring Creation for Ecology and Justice: A Report Adopted by the 202nd General Assembly of Presbyterian Church (U.S.A.)* (Louisville, KY: Office of the General Assembly of the Presbyterian Church (U.S.A.), 1990), 26.

10. *Hope*, 85.

11. Ibid.

12. Nash, "Toward Revival and Reform."

13. According to the 2006 Manual of the General Assembly, a policy statement "establishes the fundamental principles that guide the denomination's social

witness. From this policy base a strategy is developed, a program is defined, and personal social witness is empowered." A resolution, on the other hand, "applies existing policy statements to new circumstances." "The Resolution on Just Globalization: Justice, Ownership, and Accountability" was approved by the 217th General Assembly in 2006. Presbyterian Church (U.S.A.), *Manual of the General Assembly of the Presbyterian Church (U.S.A.): 197th General Assembly, Birmingham, Alabama, June 15–22, 2006* (New York: Office of the General Assembly, 2006). Hereafter the resolution is referred to as *2006 Resolution*.

14. As reported by the Energy Information Administration, U.S. Department of Energy, www.eia.doe.gov. This figure was determined by measuring per capita BTU use in 2003.

15. James B. Martin-Schramm, "Power to Change: U.S. Energy Policy and Global Warming," in *Annual Meeting of the Society of Christian Ethics* (January 2009), presentation handout. The social policy by the same name was adopted by the 219th General Assembly of the PC(USA) in June 2008.

16. *The Constitution of the Presbyterian Church (U.S.A.): Part II, Book of Order* (Annotated) (New York: Offices of the General Assembly, Presbyterian Church (U.S.A.), 1992). Recently a task force was assembled to modify the form of government put forward in the *Book of Order*. Proposed changes were approved by the 2010 General Assembly. These changes have led to a renewed emphasis on the foundations for church governance by placing these foundations in a separate section at the beginning of the book. In addition, there was minor rewording of the denomination's principles of governance, but no substantive changes have been made. Changes made to other areas of the *Book of Order*, however, may change the way such principles are applied in the future.

17. Speaking of "the Presbyterian Church" is like speaking of Theseus's ship whose planks were replaced one by one, raising the question of whether it was the same ship before and after repairs. What in fact constitutes the church as the church? Several denominations in the United States profess to be Presbyterian. The PC(USA) is itself a product of division and reunification. The church, which divided along geographical lines primarily over the issue of slavery, was reunified in 1983. In the interim, the northern United Presbyterian Church in the United States of America (UPCUSA) had embraced the *Book of Confessions*, while the southern PCUS church had not. One of the terms of union required the southern church to adopt the *Book of Confessions*, thus recognizing that the confession of the church is broader than what is captured in the Westminster Confession.

18. See James D. Hudnut-Beumler, "The Rights and Dignity of Persons," *Church and Society* 81, no. 2 (1990): 11–20. I use Hudnut-Beumler's analysis of the "Preliminary Principles of Church Order" and their impact on social witness policy as a springboard for my own examination here. These principles are provided at the beginning of the *Book of Order* of the Presbyterian Church (U.S.A.). See *Book of Order*, G-1.0000.

19. The quote is taken from the Westminster Confession of Faith, 6.109, in the *Book of Confessions*, the other book that forms the constitution of the PC(USA). The full quote reads: "God alone is Lord of the conscience, and hath left it free from the doctrines and commandments of men which are in anything contrary to his Word, or beside it, in matters of faith or worship. So that to believe such doctrines, or to obey such commandments out of conscience, is to betray true liberty of conscience; and the requiring an implicit faith, and an absolute and

blind obedience, is to destroy liberty of conscience, and reason also." *Book of Confessions*, 195.

20. *Book of Order* G-1.0301. Strong traces of Calvin's thought are present here. For example, Calvin speaks of freedom of conscience from all human law by which he is specifically referring to papal pronouncements rather than civil law. See *Inst.* 3.19.14. Calvin makes the distinction between political and spiritual governance. The latter has to do with the life of the soul; the former, with practical matters of living. Christians are commanded to obey laws set forth by magistrates because of God's general command to recognize the authority of political leaders (Rom. 13:1), but it is not the civil law itself that has any power to bind the conscience of a Christian. See *Inst.* 4.20.5. Regarding the issue of whether the church may lawfully bind consciences by its laws, Calvin has the following to say: He defines *conscience* as an awareness of our guilt or innocence before God that constitutes a special relationship between that individual and God. Unless dictated by Scripture, laws that prescribe new ways to worship God lay undue claim to our conscience. Here Calvin is attacking the practice of certain bishops of the Catholic Church of his time. In effect, then, the church has no power to bind consciences by its laws, for the power of binding ultimately rests on God's word, not the church. See *Inst.* 4.10.3.

21. Archie Crouch, "Racial-Ethnic Ministry Policies—An Historical Overview," *Journal of Presbyterian History* 57, no. 3 (1979): 281.

22. Ernest Trice Thompson, *Presbyterians in the South* (Richmond, VA: John Knox Press, 1963), 564–65.

23. Hudnut-Beumler, "Rights and Dignity," 13.

24. See George M. Marsden, "Reformed and American," in *Reformed Theology in America: A History of Its Modern Development*, ed. David F. Wells and Roger R. Nicole (Grand Rapids: Wm. B. Eerdmans Publishing Co., 1985), 6.

25. Italics found in the original. Christian Iosso, intro. to *Church & Society* 74, no. 4 (1984): 5.

26. *Book of Confessions*, 316.

27. The Westminster Confession of Faith, 6.009, *Book of Confessions*, 175–76. The next article is equally instructive (10). "The Supreme Judge, by which all controversies of religion are to be determined, and all decrees of councils, opinions of ancient writers, doctrines of men, and private spirits, are to be examined, and in whose sentence we are to rest, can be no other but the Holy Spirit speaking in the Scripture."

28. The Confession of 1967, 9.27, *Book of Confessions*, 325.

29. This is not to say that there is *no* emphasis on reconciliation in the Westminster Confession of Faith. See for instance chap. 8, "Of Christ the Mediator." It is only to say that C67 makes reconciliation its primary focus.

30. The Confession of 1967, 9.27, *Book of Confessions*, 326.

31. See Calvin, *Inst.* 4.10.4.

32. *Book of Order*, G-1.0303.

33. See, for example, Matt. 10:16 and Rom. 16:9.

34. *Hope*, 76. See also World Commission on Environment and Development, *Our Common Future* (New York: Oxford University Press, 1987). In addition, see United Nations Conference on Environment and Development, *Agenda 21: Programme of Action for Sustainable Development* (Herndon, VA: United Nations Publications, 1992).

35. Ibid., 77.

36. Dennis Goulet, "Development: Creator and Destroyer of Values," *World Development* 20, no. 3 (1992): 467–75.

37. *Hope*, 89.

38. Ibid., 59.

39. Ibid., 65.

40. Ibid., 67.

41. Ibid., 70–71.

42. Nicholas Wolterstorff, *Justice: Rights and Wrongs* (Princeton, NJ: Princeton University Press, 2008).

43. Ibid., 38–42, 176–79.

44. Ibid., 152–53.

45. Ibid., 176.

46. Ibid., 177.

47. Wolterstorff, too, believes that worth is bestowed on us by God, not based on some capacities that human beings uniquely possess. See Wolterstorff, *Justice*, 352–60.

48. Aristotle, *The Politics*, 1324a, Cambridge Texts in the History of Political Thought (New York: Cambridge University Press, 1988), 24–25.

49. See Iosso, intro. to *Church and Society*, 5.

CONCLUSION

1. Alasdair MacIntyre, *After Virtue*, 2nd ed. (Notre Dame, IN: University of Notre Dame Press, 1984).

2. Jeffrey Stout, *Democracy and Tradition* (Princeton, NJ: Princeton University Press, 2004), 118–35.

3. Jeffrey Stout, *Blessed Are the Organized: Grassroots Democracy in America* (Princeton, NJ: Princeton University Press, 2010), 4–5.

4. See Alasdair MacIntyre, *Whose Justice? Which Rationality?* (Notre Dame, IN: University of Notre Dame Press, 1988), 260–80.

5. Ibid., 276–80.

6. MacIntyre notes, "And if in our society we find it difficult to imagine ourselves back into the state of mind for which evidentness is an important epistemological property, it is not only because of the relative paucity of such beliefs in our own time and place . . . but also because we are well aware how different and incompatible sets of beliefs have had the same property of evidentness ascribed to them in different cultures." Ibid., 223.

7. Jonathan Edwards's notion of a new spiritual sense, which comes upon the believer at conversion, has certain affinities to Hutcheson's concept of the common moral sense. Unlike Hutcheson's concept, Edwards's notion distinguishes between believers and nonbelievers, making true virtue possible only for Christians. For a helpful overview of the influence Hutcheson's concept of the moral sense had on Edwards's spiritual sense, see Cochran, *Receptive Human Virtues*, chapter 5.

8. Gerald McKenny, *The Analogy of Grace: Barth's Moral Theology* (Oxford: Oxford University Press, 2010), 266–69.

9. This quote is the motto of the Jeremiah Group, whose work is highlighted by Stout's book, *Blessed Are the Organized*. Tellingly, the group is faith based but works with non-faith-based organizations as well. The NRSV translation of Jer. 29:7 reads, "But seek the welfare of the city where I've sent you into exile, and pray to the LORD on its behalf, for in its welfare you will find your welfare."

10. Stout's argument opposes that of Richard Rorty, as expressed in his essay "Religion as a Conversation Stopper." Rorty subsequently revised his position, but was still wary of faith-based organizations. For a fuller explanation of their disagreements over religion and politics, see Jeffrey Stout, "Rorty on Religion and Politics" and "Reply to Jeffrey Stout," in *The Philosophy of Richard Rorty*, ed. Randall E. Auxier and Lewis Edwin Hahn, The Library of Living Philosophers 32 (Chicago and La Salle, IL: Open Court, 2010), 523–45, 546–49.

11. *Millenials: A Portrait of Generation Next*, Pew Research Center Report (Washington DC, February 2010), 86.

12. According to the report, approximately 20 percent of this group grew up in a religiously observant household. Ibid., 88.

13. *Millenials*, 5–6.

14. Aristotle, *Nicomachean Ethics*, 1103a, trans. and ed. Roger Crisp (New York: Cambridge University Press, 2000), 14–18.

15. C. S. Lewis, *The Screwtape Letters*, rev. ed. (New York: McMillan Publishing, 1982), 12.

16. Speaking of the bias of digital media, Rushkoff notes, "This bias toward non-local thinking can be threatening to parochial interests, and explains much of the origins of resentment for the Judeo-Christian tradition and its text-inspired emphasis on a universal deity and ethics over the local gods and laws of particular regions." Douglas Rushkoff, *Program or Be Programmed* (New York: O/R Books, 2010), 38–39.

17. Lynn White Jr., "The Historical Roots of Our Ecologic Crisis," *Science*, March 10, 1967, 1203–7.

18. In the NRSV translation the passage reads, "Be fruitful and multiply, and fill the earth and subdue it; and have dominion over the fish of the sea and over the birds of the air and over every living thing that moves upon the earth."

19. Lamin Sanneh, *Translating the Message*, 2nd ed. (Maryknoll, NY: Orbis Books, 2009), 232.

BIBLIOGRAPHY

Anderson, Raymond. *Love and Order: The Life-Structuring Dynamics of Grace and Virtue in Calvin's Ethical Thought*. Chambersburg, PA: Wilson College, 1973.

Aquinas, Thomas. *Summa Theologiae: Latin Text and English Translation, Introductions, Notes, Appendices and Glossaries*. 60 vols. New York: McGraw-Hill, 1964.

———. *Commentary on Saint Paul's Epistle to the Ephesians*. Translated by Matthew L. Lamb. Vol. 2, Aquinas Scripture Series. Albany, NY: Magi Books, 1966.

———. *De Malo*. Translated by Richard J. Regan. New York: Oxford University Press, 2001.

———. *Questions on the Soul [Quaestiones de Anima]*. Translated by James H. Robb. Milwaukee: Marquette University Press, 1984.

Aristotle. *Aristotle's Poetics*. New York: Hill & Wang, 1998.

———. *Nicomachean Ethics*. Cambridge Texts in the History of Philosophy. Translated by Roger Crisp. New York: Cambridge University Press, 2000.

———. *The Politics*. Cambridge Texts in the History of Political Thought. Translated by Stephen Everson. New York: Cambridge University Press, 1988.

Augustine. *The City of God against the Pagans*. Edited by R. W. Dyson. Cambridge: Cambridge University Press, 1998.

———. *Confessions*. Penguin Classics Deluxe ed. New York: Penguin Books, 2006.

———. *De Gratia et Libero Arbitrio*. Edited by J. P. Migne. Vol. 22, *Patrologiae cursus completus, series latina*. Paris, 1844–55.

Barth, Karl. *Church Dogmatics*. Edited by G.W. Bromiley and T .F. Torrance. 4 volumes. Edinburgh: T. & T. Clark, 1936–1975.

———. *Community, State, and Church: Three Essays*. Gloucester, MA: Peter Smith, 1968.

———. *The Epistle to the Romans*. Translated by Edwyn Hoskyns. 6th ed. Oxford: Oxford University Press, 1933.

———. *The Holy Spirit and the Christian Life: The Theological Basis of Ethics*. 1st ed., Library of Theological Ethics. Translated by R. Birch Hoyle. Louisville, KY: Westminster/John Knox Press, 1993.

———. *The Humanity of God*. Richmond, VA: John Knox Press, 1960.

———. *Table Talk*. Edited by John Drew Godsey. Richmond, VA: John Knox Press, 1963.

———. *The Theology of the Reformed Confessions*. Translated and annotated by Darrell L. Guder and Judith J. Guder. Louisville, KY: Westminster John Knox Press, 2002.

Barth, Karl, and Christoph Blumhardt. *Action in Waiting*. Translated by the Society of Brothers. Rifton, NY: Plough Publishing House, 1969.

Bass, Dorothy C., and Craig Dykstra, eds. *Practicing Our Faith*. San Francisco: Jossey-Bass Publishers, 1998.

Bhagwati, Jagdish. *In Defense of Globalization.* Oxford: Oxford University Press, 2004.

Bhagwati, Jagdish, and Arvind Panagariya. "Go for Growth in India." *The Economist.* July 13, 2013, 16. Letter.

Biggar, Nigel. *The Hastening That Waits: Karl Barth's Ethics.* Oxford Studies in Theological Ethics. Oxford: Clarendon Press, 1993.

Billings, J. Todd. *Calvin, Participation, and the Gift.* Oxford: Oxford University Press, 2007.

Bonhoeffer, Dietrich. *Nachfolge.* One copy in the Special Collections department of the Princeton Theological Seminary library. Princeton, NJ, n.p., 195–.

Bouwsma, William James. *John Calvin: A Sixteenth-Century Portrait.* New York: Oxford University Press, 1988.

Bowlin, John. "Barth and Aquinas on Election, Relationship, and Requirement." In *Thomas Aquinas and Karl Barth: An Unofficial Catholic-Protestant Dialogue,* edited by Bruce McCormack and Thomas Joseph White, 237–61. Grand Rapids: Wm. B. Eerdmans Publishing Co., 2013.

Brunner, Emil, and Karl Barth. *Natural Theology: Comprising "Nature and Grace" by Emil Brunner and the Reply "No!" by Karl Barth.* Eugene, OR: Wipf & Stock, 2002.

Calvin, John. *The Bondage and Liberation of the Will: A Defence of the Orthodox Doctrine of Human Choice against Pighius.* Edited by A. N. S. Lane. Translated by Graham I. Davies. Grand Rapids: Baker Books, 1996.

———. *The Epistles of Paul to the Romans and the Thessalonians.* Edited by David W. Torrance and Thomas F. Torrance. Translated by Ross MacKenzie. Grand Rapids: Wm. B. Eerdmans Publishing Co., 1980.

———. *The First Epistle of Paul the Apostle to the Corinthians.* Edited by David W. Torrance and Thomas F. Torrance. Translated by John W. Fraser. Grand Rapids: Wm. B. Eerdmans Publishing Co., 1989.

———. *Institutes of the Christian Religion.* Vols. 20, 21. Library of Christian Classics. Edited by John Thomas McNeill. Translated by Ford Lewis Battles. Philadelphia: Westminster Press, 1960.

"Chalcedonian Formula." http://anglicansonline.org/basics/chalcedon.html.

Cicero. *De Natura Deorum.* Translated by H. Rackham. Cambridge, MA: Harvard University Press, 1979.

Clough, David. "Eros and Agape in Karl Barth's *Church Dogmatics.*" *International Journal of Systematic Theology* 2, no. 2 (2000): 189–203.

Cochran, Elizabeth Agnew. "Consent, Conversion, and Moral Formation: Stoic Elements in Jonathan Edwards's Ethics." *Journal of Religious Ethics* 39, no. 4 (2011): 623–50.

———. *Receptive Human Virtues.* University Park: Pennsylvania State University Press, 2011.

Crouch, Archie. "Racial-Ethnic Ministry Policies—An Historical Overview." *Journal of Presbyterian History* 57, no. 3 (1979): 272–312.

Davaney, Sheila Greeve. *Divine Power: A Study of Karl Barth and Charles Hartshorne.* Harvard Dissertations in Religion. Philadelphia: Fortress Press, 1986.

Delattre, Roland A. *Beauty and Sensibility in the Thought of Jonathan Edwards: An Essay in Aesthetics and Theological Ethics.* Eugene, OR: Wipf & Stock, 2006 [1968].

Drèze, Jean, and Amartya Sen, *An Uncertain Glory: India and Its Contradictions* (Princeton, NJ: Princeton University Press, 2013).

Duhigg, Charles. "Warning: Habits May Be Good for You." *New York Times*, July 13, 2008.

Dykstra, Craig. *Growing in the Life of Faith*. 2nd ed. Louisville, KY: Westminster John Knox Press, 2005.

Edwards, Jonathan. *Concerning the End for Which God Created the World*. Edited by Paul Ramsey. Vol. 8, *The Works of Jonathan Edwards*. Edited by John E. Smith. New Haven, CT: Yale University Press, 1989.

———. *The Nature of True Virtue*. Edited by Paul Ramsey. Vol. 8, *The Works of Jonathan Edwards*. Edited by John E. Smith. New Haven, CT: Yale University Press, 1989.

———. *Religious Affections*. Edited by John E. Smith. Vol. 2, *The Works of Jonathan Edwards*. Edited by Perry Miller. New Haven, CT: Yale University Press, 1959.

Finnis, John. *Natural Law and Natural Rights*. Reprinted with corrections. Clarendon Law Series. New York: Oxford University Press, 1980.

Gallagher, David M. *Thomas Aquinas and His Legacy*. Studies in Philosophy and the History of Philosophy. Washington, DC: Catholic University of America Press, 1994.

Geest, Paul van, J. M. J. Harm, Carlo Leget Goris, and Mishtooni Bose. *Aquinas as Authority: A Collection of Studies Presented at the Second Conference of the Thomas Instituut te Utrecht, December 14–16, 2000*. Publications of the Thomas Instituut te Utrecht. Leuven: Peeters, 2002.

Gilson, Etienne. *Being and Some Philosophers*. 2nd ed. Toronto: Pontifical Institute of Medieval Studies, 1952.

Goulet, Dennis. "Development: Creator and Destroyer of Values." *World Development* 20, no. 3 (1992): 467–75.

Grabill, Stephen John. *Rediscovering the Natural Law in Reformed Theological Ethics*. Emory University Studies in Law and Religion. Grand Rapids: Wm. B. Eerdmans Publishing Co., 2006.

Green, Clifford. *Karl Barth: Theologian of Freedom*. San Francisco: Collins, 1989.

Gregory, Eric. *Politics and the Order of Love: An Augustinian Ethic of Democratic Citizenship*. Chicago: University of Chicago Press, 2008.

Gustafson, James M. *Protestant and Roman Catholic Ethics: Prospects for Rapprochement*. Chicago: University of Chicago Press, 1978.

Hall, Amy Laura. "Complicating the Command: Agape in Scriptural Context." *Annual of the Society of Christian Ethics* 19 (1999): 97–113.

Hartwell, Herbert, and Karl Barth. *The Theology of Karl Barth: An Introduction*. London: G. Duckworth, 1964.

Hauerwas, Stanley. *Character and the Christian Life: A Study in Theological Ethics*. San Antonio: Trinity University Press, 1985.

———. *The Peaceable Kingdom: A Primer in Christian Ethics*. 2nd ed. London: SCM Press, 2003.

———. *With the Grain of the Universe: The Church's Witness and Natural Theology: Gifford Lectures Delivered at the University of St. Andrews in 2001*. Grand Rapids: Brazos Press, 2001.

Hauerwas, Stanley, and Romand Coles. *Christianity, Democracy, and the Radical Ordinary: Conversations between a Radical Democrat and a Christian.* Theopolitical Visions. Eugene, OR: Cascade Books, 2008.

Healy, Nicholas. "Karl Barth's Ecclesiology Reconsidered." *Scottish Journal of Theology* 57, no. 2 (2004): 13.

Helm, Paul. "John Locke and Jonathan Edwards: A Reconsideration." *Journal of the History of Philosophy* 7 (1969): 51–61.

Heppe, Heinrich. *Die Dogmatik der evangelisch-reformirten Kirche: Dargestellt und aus den Quellen belegt.* Elberfeld: R. L. Friedrichs, 1861.

Herdt, Jennifer A. *Putting on Virtue: The Legacy of the Splendid Vices.* Chicago: University of Chicago Press, 2008.

Hittinger, Russell. *A Critique of the New Natural Law Theory.* Rev. ed. Notre Dame, IN: University of Notre Dame Press, 1987.

Hodge, Charles. *Systematic Theology,* 3 vols. Grand Rapids: Wm. B. Eerdmans Publishing Co., 1986.

Horton, John, and Susan Mendus. *After Macintyre: Critical Perspectives on the Work of Alasdair Macintyre.* 1st University of Notre Dame Press ed. Notre Dame, IN: University of Notre Dame Press, 1994.

Hudnut-Beumler, James D. "The Rights and Dignity of Persons." *Church and Society* 81, no. 2 (1990): 11–20.

Hunsinger, George. *Disruptive Grace: Studies in the Theology of Karl Barth.* Grand Rapids: Wm. B. Eerdmans Publishing Co., 2000.

———. *How to Read Karl Barth: The Shape of His Theology.* New York: Oxford University Press, 1991.

———. "A Response to William Werpehowski." *Theology Today* 43, no. 3 (1986): 354–60.

Husbands, Mark, and Daniel J. Treier. *Justification: What's at Stake in the Current Debates.* Downers Grove, IL: InterVarsity Press, 2004.

Iosso, Christian. Introduction to *Church & Society* 74, no. 4 (1984): 4–6.

Johnson, Keith L. "*Analogia Entis*: A Reconsideration of the Debate between Karl Barth and Roman Catholicism, 1914–1964." PhD diss., Princeton, NJ, Princeton Theological Seminary, 2008.

Jones, Serene. *Calvin and the Rhetoric of Piety.* Louisville, KY: Westminster John Knox Press, 1995.

Jordan, Mark D. "Aquinas's Construction of a Moral Account of the Passions." *Freiburger Zeitschrift für Philosophie und Theologie* 33 (1986): 71–97.

Kerr, Fergus. *After Aquinas: Versions of Thomism.* Malden, MA: Blackwell Publishers, 2002.

Lewis, Clive Staples. *The Screwtape Letters.* Rev. ed. New York: McMillan Publishing, 1982.

Lewis, Paul. "The Springs of Motion: Jonathan Edwards on Emotions, Character, and Agency." *Journal of Religious Ethics* 22, no. 2 (1994): 275–97.

Little, David. *Religion, Order, and Law: A Study in Pre-Revolutionary England.* Chicago: University of Chicago Press, 1969.

Lonergan, Bernard J. F., and J. Patout Burns. *Grace and Freedom: Operative Grace in the Thought of St. Thomas Aquinas.* New York: Herder & Herder, 1971.

Luther, Martin. *Luther's Works.* Amer. ed. Edited by Jaroslav Pelikan and Helmut T. Lehmann. St. Louis: Concordia, 1955.

MacIntyre, Alasdair C. *After Virtue: A Study in Moral Theory*. 2nd ed. Notre Dame, IN: University of Notre Dame Press, 1984.

———. *Whose Justice? Which Rationality?* Notre Dame, IN: University of Notre Dame Press, 1988.

Marga, Amy. "Partners in the Gospel: Karl Barth and Roman Catholicism, 1922–1932." PhD diss. Princeton, NJ, Princeton Theological Seminary, 2006.

Marsden, George. *Jonathan Edwards*. New Haven, CT: Yale University Press, 2003.

Martin-Schramm, James B. "Power to Change: U.S. Energy Policy and Global Warming." Paper presentation, annual meeting of the Society of Christian Ethics, Chicago, IL, January 8–11, 2009.

McClymond, Michael J., and Gerald R. McDermott. *The Theology of Jonathan Edwards*. Oxford: Oxford University Press, 2012).

McCormack, Bruce L. *Justification in Perspective: Historical Developments and Contemporary Challenges*. Grand Rapids: Baker Academic, 2006.

———. *Karl Barth's Critically Realistic Dialectical Theology: Its Genesis and Development, 1909–1936*. New York: Oxford University Press, 1995.

McCormack, Bruce L., and Thomas Joseph White, eds. *Thomas Aquinas and Karl Barth: An Unofficial Catholic-Protestant Dialogue*. Grand Rapids: Wm. B. Eerdmans Publishing Co., 2013.

McKenny, Gerald. *The Analogy of Grace: Barth's Moral Theology*. Oxford: Oxford University Press, 2010.

Migliore, Daniel L. *Faith Seeking Understanding: An Introduction to Christian Theology*. 2nd ed. Grand Rapids: Wm. B. Eerdmans Publishing Co., 2004.

Millenials: A Portrait of Generation Next. Pew Research Center Report. Washington DC, February 2010, 86.

Miller, Perry. *Jonathan Edwards*. New York: Meridian Books, 1949.

———. "Jonathan Edwards and the Sense of the Heart." *Harvard Theological Review* 41 (1948): 123–45.

Miner, Robert C. *Thomas Aquinas on the Passions: A Study of Summa Theologiae: 1a2ae 22–48*. Cambridge: Cambridge University Press, 2009.

Muller, Richard. *After Calvin*. Oxford: Oxford University Press, 2003.

———. *Post-Reformation Reformed Dogmatics: The Rise and Development of Reformed Orthodoxy, ca. 1520 to ca. 1725*. Vol. 1, *Prolegomena to Theology*. 2nd ed. Grand Rapids: Baker Academic, 2003.

Nash, James A. "Toward the Revival and Reform of the Subversive Virtue: Frugality." *Annual of the Society of Christian Ethics* (1995): 137–60.

Neder, Adam. "'A Differentiated Fellowship of Action': Participation in Christ in Karl Barth's Church Dogmatics." PhD diss., Princeton, NJ, Princeton Theological Seminary, 2005.

———. "Review of *Being in Action: The Theological Shape of Barth's Ethical Vision*." *International Journal of Systematic Theology* 10, no. 2 (2008): 4.

Niebuhr, H. Richard. "Religious Realism in the Twentieth Century." In *Religious Realism*. Edited by D. C. Macintosh. New York: MacMillan Co., 1931.

Niebuhr, Richard R. *Streams of Grace: Studies of Jonathan Edwards, Samuel Taylor Coleridge, and William James*. Kyoto: Doshisha University Press, 1983.

Nimmo, Paul T. *Being in Action: The Theological Shape of Barth's Ethical Vision*. London: T. & T. Clark, 2007.

Nolan, Kirk J. "Developing Reformed Moral Virtue Ethics within the Reformed
    Theological Tradition," PhD diss., Princeton, NJ, Princeton Theological
    Seminary, 2010.
Noll, Mark. *America's God: From Jonathan Edwards to Abraham Lincoln.* Oxford:
    Oxford University Press, 2002.
Nygren, Anders. *Agape and Eros.* Philadelphia: Westminster Press, 1953.
O'Meara, Thomas. "Virtues in the Theology of Thomas Aquinas." *Theological
    Studies* 58 (1997): 254–85.
Okin, Susan Moller. *Justice, Gender, and the Family.* New York: Basic Books, 1989.
Oliver, Simon. "The Sweet Delight of Virtue and Grace in Aquinas's Ethics."
    International Journal of Systematic Theology 7, no. 1 (2005).
Pauw, Amy Plantinga. "The Future of Reformed Theology: Some Lessons
    from Jonathan Edwards." In *Toward the Future of Reformed Theology.* Edited
    by David Willis and Michael Welker. Grand Rapids: Wm. B. Eerdmans
    Publishing Co., 1999.
Peter, Lombard, Giulio Silano, and Pontifical Institute of Mediaeval Studies. *The
    Sentences.* Mediaeval Sources in Translation. Toronto: Pontifical Institute of
    Mediaeval Studies, 2007.
Presbyterian Church (U.S.A.). *The Constitution of the Presbyterian Church (U.S.A.),
    Part I, Book of Confessions: Study Edition.* Louisville, KY: Geneva Press, 1999.
———. *The Constitution of the Presbyterian Church (U.S.A.), Part II, Book of Order.*
    New York: Offices of the General Assembly, 1992.
———. *Manual of the General Assembly of the Presbyterian Church (U.S.A.): 197th
    General Assembly, Birmingham, Alabama, June 15–22, 2006.* New York: Office of
    the General Assembly, 2006.
Presbyterian Church (U.S.A.). Advisory Committee on Social Witness Policy.
    Hope for a Global Future: Toward Just and Sustainable Human Development. A
    Report Adopted by the 208th General Assembly (1996), Presbyterian Church
    (U.S.A.). Louisville, KY: Office of the General Assembly, 1996.
Presbyterian Church (U.S.A.). Committee on Social Witness Policy. *Restoring
    Creation for Ecology and Justice.* A Report Adopted by the 202nd General
    Assembly (1990), Presbyterian Church (U.S.A.). Louisville, KY: Office of the
    General Assembly, 1990.
Przywara, Erich. *Ringen der Gegenwart: Gesammelte Aufsätze 1922–1927.* 2 vols.
    Augsburg: B. Filser-Verlag, 1929.
Przywara, Erich, and Alan Coates Bouquet. *Polarity: A German Catholic's
    Interpretation of Religion.* London: Oxford University Press, 1935.
Quelquejeu, Bernard. "Naturalia manent integra." *Revue des Sciences Philosophiques
    et Théologiques* 94 (1965): 640–55.
Rorty, Richard. "Reply to Jeffrey Stout," in *The Philosophy of Richard Rorty.* Edited
    by Randall E. Auxier and Lewis Edwin Hahn. Vol. 32, *The Library of Living
    Philosophers.* Chicago: Open Court, 2010.
Rushkoff, Douglas. *Program or Be Programmed.* New York: O/R Books, 2010.
Sen, Amartya. "Amartya Sen Responds." *The Economist,* July 20, 2013, 14. Letter.
———. *Development as Freedom.* New York: Anchor Books, 1999.
Shanley, Brian. "Aquinas on Pagan Virtue." *The Thomist* 63 (1999): 553–77.
Sherman, Nancy. *Aristotle's Ethics: Critical Essays.* Critical Essays on the Classics.
    Lanham, MD: Rowman & Littlefield, 1999.

Söhngen, Gottlieb. "*Analogia Fidei: Gottänhlichkeit allein aus Glauben?*" *Catholica* 3, no. 3 (1934): 113–36.

Spohn, William C. "Union and Consent with the Great Whole: Jonathan Edwards on True Virtue." *Annual of the Society of Christian Ethics* 5 (1985): 19–32.

Stotts, Jack L. "Reflections and Forecast of the Work of the Committee on Mission Responsibility through Investment, 1970–1980 and Beyond." *Church and Society* 74, no. 4 (1984): 110–17.

Stout, Jeffrey. *Blessed Are the Organized: Grassroots Democracy in America.* Princeton, NJ: Princeton University Press, 2010.

———. *Democracy and Tradition.* New Forum Books. Princeton, NJ: Princeton University Press, 2004.

———. "Rorty on Religion and Politics." In *The Philosophy of Richard Rorty.* Edited by Randall E. Auxier and Lewis Edwin Hahn. Vol. 32, *The Library of Living Philosophers.* Chicago: Open Court, 2010.

Stump, Eleonore. *Aquinas.* New York: Routledge, 2003.

Thompson, Bard, Hendrikus Berkhof, Eduard Schweizer, and Howard G. Hageman. *Essays on the Heidelberg Catechism.* Philadelphia: United Church Press, 1963.

Thompson, Ernest Trice. *Presbyterians in the South.* Richmond, VA: John Knox Press, 1963.

Torrance, T. F. *The Scottish Theology.* Edinburgh: T. & T. Clark, 1996.

United Nations Conference on Environment and Development. *Agenda 21: Programme of Action for Sustainable Development.* Herndon, VA: United Nations Publications, 1992.

VanDrunen, David. *Natural Law and the Two Kingdoms.* Grand Rapids: Wm. B. Eerdmans Publishing Co., 2010.

Vlastuin, W. van. "Personal Renewal between Heidelberg and Westminster." *Journal of Reformed Theology* 5 (2011): 49–67.

Wawrykow, Joseph Peter. *God's Grace and Human Action: "Merit" in the Theology of Thomas Aquinas.* Notre Dame, IN: University of Notre Dame Press, 1995.

Weber, Max. *The Protestant Ethic and the Spirit of Capitalism.* London: Routlege Classics, 1930.

Webster, John. *Barth's Ethics of Reconciliation.* New York: Cambridge University Press, 1995.

———. *Barth's Moral Theology.* Grand Rapids: Wm. B. Eerdmans Publishing Co., 1998.

Wells, David F., and Roger R. Nicole. *Reformed Theology in America: A History of Its Modern Development.* Grand Rapids: Wm. B. Eerdmans Publishing Co., 1985.

Werpehowski, William. "Command and History in the Ethics of Karl Barth." *Journal of Religious Ethics* 9, no. 2 (1981): 298–320.

———. "Narrative and Ethics in Barth." *Theology Today* 43, no. 3 (1986): 334–53.

———. "Practical Wisdom and the Integrity of Christian Life." *Journal of the Society of Christian Ethics* 27, no. 2 (2007): 55–72.

White, Lynn, Jr. "The Historical Roots of Our Ecologic Crisis." *Science,* March 10, 1967, 1203–7.

Wilson, Stephen A. "Jonathan Edwards's Virtue: Diverse Sources, Multiple Meanings, and the Lessons of History for Ethics." *Journal of Religious Ethics* 31, no. 2 (2003): 201–28.

———. *Virtue Reformed: Rereading Jonathan Edwards.* Boston, Brill, 2005.

Wilson, Stephen A., and Jean Porter, "Taking the Measure of Jonathan Edwards for Contemporary Religious Ethics." *Journal of Religious Ethics* 31, no. 2 (2003): 183–99.

Wolterstorff, Nicholas. *Justice: Rights and Wrongs*. Princeton, NJ: Princeton University Press, 2008.

World Commission on Environment and Development. *Our Common Future*. New York: Oxford University Press, 1987.

INDEX

access to God, via God's revelation, 88
Advisory Committee on Social
　　　Witness Policy (ACSWP),
　　　111, 132
Adopting Act of 1729, 19
aesthetic experience of God, 26
affections, intellectual dimension of, 31
After Virtue (MacIntyre), 73, 135–37
agape (love), 95–101, 126, 129, 137,
　　　143–44, 158–59n31
Agape and Eros (Nygren), 96
agency, divine and human, 4
ἀκολούθησις (discipleship), 78
ἀκολουθεῖν (following), 78
America, no establishment of religion,
　　　115–16
American Protestantism, 33
analogia entis (analogy of being,
　　　Creator and humans), 68
　　affirmed by Catholics, 6, 45–54,
　　　153–54n40
　　rejected by Barth, 6, 23, 37–38,
　　　45–54, 153–54n40
　　used by some Reformers, 6
Analogy of Grace (McKenny), 6
ancient Near Eastern religions, local
　　　deities, 143
Anderson, Raymond K., on Calvin and
　　　virtue, 146n5
Anglican polity, 19
anhypostatic/enhypostatic, 56–58, 121,
　　　144, 154n43
Anknüpfungspunkt (point of contact),
　　　God's initiative, 53
anthropocentric focus, 143
Aquinas. *See* Thomas Aquinas
Aristotle, 3, 5, 11, 15, 134
　　acquired habit lacks struggle, 85, 91
　　on acquired virtues, 88

"act best and live happily," 131
　　and Aquinas, virtue as a mean, 4, 91
　　choosing, practical reasoning, 73
　　community for moral exemplars, 141
　　equal rights for citizens, 131
　　framework for virtue, 131
　　on intellect knowing good, 30
　　intellectual virtue from birth, 72
　　love of the virtue itself, 73
　　merit reward system, 137–38
　　metaphysical biology, 135
　　mimēsis (imitation), 73
　　moral virtues from habit (*ethikē*,
　　　ethos), 71–72
　　nature of being, tied to substance, 51
　　neglects slaves and women, 131
　　perfectionist ethics, 4
　　on practical wisdom, 72, 137–38
　　on true happiness, 130
　　on virtue, 27
　　prudence, giving what is due, 93
　　stability of character, 73
　　tradition of virtue, 135
　　training in moral virtue, 72–74, 78
　　transformed passions and reason, 73
　　virtue ethics, unity of character, 86
　　virtue from habit formation, 27, 141
　　virtues acquired differently, 141
　　virtues personal and political, 112
　　virtuous actions chosen, from char-
　　　acter, 72
atheist, agnostic, nothing, 140–41
atonement, 12
　　damnation for rejecting, 34
　　substitutionary, 21
Augsburg Confession, 18
Augustine , 13–17, 48
　　a basis for *analogia entis*. *See also*
　　　analogia entis

Augustine (*continued*)
    on grace, 4
    caritas (charity) as acquisitive,
        desire for God, 96
    Confessions, 153n34
    on grace, 96
    Grace and Free Will, 14
    on inability to do good, sans grace,
        30
    influenced by Neoplatonism, 96
    kinds of virtue, 149–50n66
    and medieval conceptions of grace,
        146n6
    on pagan virtue as glittering vice,
        30
    on reaching toward God, 153n34
    on sin, 137–38
Austen, Jane, 11

baptism, of infants, 31–32
Barmen Declaration, 102, 145n2
Barth, Karl, 6, 8–9, 12, 23–24, 33–36,
        110, 144
    on a unique community, 87
    accepts *analogia fidei*, 53, 153–54n40
    on active participation in Christ, 78
    on actualism in covenantal ontol-
        ogy, 47, 51, 151–52n17,
        153n34
    analogia entis (substance theology)
        rejected, 23, 37–38, 45–54,
        153n34, 153–54n40. *See also*
        analogia entis
    on Aquinas's grace-nature axiom,
        151n16
    on agape and *eros* (love as desire),
        97–98
    on anhypostatic/enhypostatic dis-
        tinction, 154n43
    begins with God's revelation in
        Christ, 49
    on biblical narrative, on, 64–66
    on Blumhardt, 41
    bottom-up communities of virtue,
        35
    bound by Christ alone, 86
    breaks from liberalism, 41–42,
        150n3
    calls to discipleship, 78

on Chalcedonian patterns, 1, 8, 26,
        28, 33, 55, 57, 60–62, 70, 83,
        89, 103, 108, 121–22, 144
on character development via
        God's revelation, 71
on Christ/Christ's
    attested in Scripture, 33
    choosing the church to witness,
        103
    christocentric anthropology,
        38–54
    christological, relentlessly, 33
    confirming our election, 84
    focus on, 41
    freedom from us and for us, 65, 70
    human and divine natures,
        55–56, 38. *See also*
        anhypostatic/enhypostatic
    human essence in tune with
        God, 59
    incarnation, 48–50, 54–58, 68,
        141–44, 152n28
    kingdom (John 18:36), 105
    Lord over history, 33, 52, 91
    the Son of Man, 55
    at the state's center, 35
Christians acknowledge sin, 77
christocentric anthropology, 37–46,
        54
Christology from God's decision,
        54–61, 69
Christology, anhypostatic/enhypo-
        static, 56–58, 121, 144, 154–43
church
    defined by God's grace, 159n43
    ecclesiology, 35, 102
    indolent, confronted, 105–6
    key witness, 35, 135
    not necessary for world's salva-
        tion, 103–4
    points to God's coming, 105
    political significance of, 105
    post-Constantinian church, 35–36
    proclaims rule of Christ, 105
    provides some order, 104
    ministry to the poor, 105
    roles of church and state, 104–8
    for social justice, 105
    and state, 35, 102, 104–8, 135

vital role of, 103
witness to the state, 103, 105
Church Dogmatics, 39, 43, 54, 63, 67,
    76, 97, 100, 102
  circle as root metaphor of, 60
commentary on Romans, 32–33, 42,
    45–48
common morality as God reveals
    self, 34–35
continuity of character, 7, 62–64,
    145–46n13
conversion as response, 84, 155n10
covenantal ontology, 84
critiques divinization of human-
    ity, 55
critiques domesticating God, 33
critiques Protestant liberalism, 32
critiques virtue based on *imago Dei*
    (image of God), 46
decision required, 80
divinization of human nature
    rejected, 58–59
early Barth, less on human action, 39
ecclesiology. *See* Barth, church
Edwards's doctrine of creation, 34
election, 34
    as ontological, 85
    prior to creation, 69
enlivened by the Spirit, 157n41
epistemological effect, 83
eros as moving upward, 97
eschatological regeneration of all, 36
essence and existential state, 84
eternal life, 86
ethics
    Barth's ethics neglected, 150n1
    disobedience ingrained, 86
    divestment of possessions, 91
    of divine command, 64, 80, 89,
        100, 138–39, 157–58n8
    eating/drinking (Matt. 6:31), 87
    eschatological view, 148n40
    habitual grace rejected, 37–38,
        45, 54–61
    inner ethical struggle, 86
    via God's presence, revelation,
        action, 35, 41–42
    "halt" to the totally sinful, 77
    and history, 63

implications of his theology, 33
love God and neighbor, 98
moral exemplars via the church,
    88
natural morality, overly optimis-
    tic, 108
obedience to Christ first, 104
obedience to God's commands, 71
of reconciliation (*CD* IV/4), 44
not utilitarian or deontological, 64
openness to God's command,
    64, 80
possessions not sovereign, 87
"proceed" to the new person, 77
provoked by command, 80
recognizing pagan virtue, 102,
    104–5
relationship with God, 64
repetition and renewal, 64
response to God's commands,
    52, 79, 87
the Ten Commandments, 65
theological ethics, 7
training via interaction, 81
virtue ethics, 62, 129
virtues via divine-human coop-
    eration, 81
virtues via participation in
    Christ, 76
willing to act aright, 85
exemplars for the world, 88
exemplary individuals, 101
god of natural theology an idol, 35
God/God's
    arouses moral sensibility, 80
    calls to responsibility, 43
    commands and our response,
        65, 81
    complete in Godself, 39
    deals with humankind, 33
    electing decision, 83
    humanity of God, 34
    humbling and sovereignty, 43
    initiates contact with humanity,
        44, 46
    initiative in Christ, 37–38
    mediated commands, 106
    mentoring, 141
    patience outlasting resistance, 34

Barth, Karl (*continued*)
  God/God's (*continued*)
    power constrained by love, 40
    presence with us, 44
    self-revelation each moment, 53
    sovereignty, 34
    speaks via varied sources,
        159–60n53
    thundering presence of God, 39
    theocentrism of Barth, 39, 42, 46
    transcendence, 33
    unique command, 91
    works via the state, 106
  grace of God
    bound to Christ, 43
    a disruptive force, 47
    changes actions, not our being, 47
    determines Christ's human
        nature, 59
    disruptive nature, 54
    via divine command, 83
    divine giving, human receiving,
        56
    enables hearing God, 53
    free response to, 70
    gift of grace via the state, 106
    God's condescension, 43
    habitual grace as pernicious
        idea, 56
    helps postfall humanity, 43
    nature and grace, 54
    not a human possession, 56
    ongoing reality, not inborn, 50
    pursues us, 35
    raises awareness of God's pres-
        ence, 46
    transforms, 71
  Holy Spirit enlivens God's Word, 35
  Holy Spirit, lectures on (1929), 50
  human/s
    agency, 38–39, 43–44, 56
    essence chosen by God, 84
    existence via our actions, 84
    freedom and responsibility, 39
    freedom as God's gift, 44
    hubris of human knowing, 39
    nature receives grace, 38
    reasoning, 71
    stranded, incapacitated, 71

hyper-Augustinian, as, 151–52n17
identification with Christ renewed,
    53
imago Dei, views on, 50, 70,
    152–53n31
individualistic and idealistic theol-
    ogy rejected, 40
influence of Barth, 32
justification
    continual, 76
    epistemological, 85
    by grace through faith alone, 52
    completed in eschaton, 53
    justified and sinner, each and
        communities, 106–8
    See also simul iustus . . .
Karl Barth Society, 37
lectures on Reformed confessions
    (1923), 22
ministry, twelve forms, 100, 157n6
movement to righteousness, 153n39
narrative, from particular to gen-
    eral, 155n17
natural theology rejected, 6, 24,
    34–35, 46
necessary repetition and renewal,
    155–56n22
ongoing repentance, renewal, per-
    severance, 67
ontological commitments via cov-
    enant, 83
original sin, 46
our history and Christ's history, 63
pagan virtue. *See under* Barth, ethics
participation in Christ, 77–78
pastor, as, 41
practical wisdom, 66–68, 86–87
preserves distinction between God
    and us
presuppositions of, 39
progress as deepening relation to
    Christ, 77
radical claims of Scripture, 155n17
reasoning rightly, 85
synergism rejected, 60, 70
resources for moral virtue, 135
revelation from/about God, 141, 144
    contexts for, 102
    Word of God, sole source of, 33

occurs moment by moment, 51
and reason opposed, 50
response to God's commands,
52, 79, 87
Roman Catholicism, on, 154n45
saints in eschatological sense,
155n16
sanctification, 54, 76
as awareness of relation to
Christ, 54
involving excellence, on, 61
not a change in our nature, 52
and vocation, 60
saying no to sin, 77
sexual relationships, 91
sin as decisive break, 48, 50, 69
sin impedes, 52, 85
social justice, 151n11, 159n52
on socialism, 41–42
soteriology objective, 42, 103–4
state, the. *See also* Barth, church
as parable of the kingdom, 104–6
to provide safety, 104
roles of, 104, 106
subject to Christ, 104
theocratic state, 105
status corruptionis (state of misery),
52
the redeemed depend on Christ, 89
theology, 8, 37, 90, 119, 140
transforming the world for Christ,
35
unaware reception of God's will,
106
unequal partnership, God and us,
79
universal salvation implied, 34, 77
webs of relationships, 105
WWI, on, 40
Barth's Ethics of Reconciliation
(Webster), 7, 44
Bass, Dorothy, 2
beatific vision, 30
beauty, in moral behavior, 29
beauty, primarily in God, 29
Benedict, Saint
applied in secular realm, 136
life of virtue, 135–36
order for community life, 135

prayer and work, 135–36
Rule of, 135–36
Bhagwati, Jagdish, 110
Bhagwati and Sen debate globaliza-
tion, 160n6
Biggar, Nigel, 6
Biggar, on neglect of Barth's ethics,
150n1
Blessed Are the Organized (Stout) , 136
Blumhardt, Christoph, 41–42
body of Christ, Eucharist, 144
Bondage and Liberation of the Will
(Calvin), 13
Bonhoeffer
Christ's lordship, 79
on God's command, 157–58n8
Nachfolge (discipleship), 78
simple obedience, 78
Bowlin, John, 37, 151–52n17
Brunner, Emil, 46

Calvin, John (on), 5, 8, 11–19, 34
challenges economic presumptions,
112
church fathers and the fall, 147n12
christocentric, 34
church and state, 162n20
church government, 19
conscience and our status, 121
Constantinianism residual in, 35
doctrine of vocation broadened,
109
each has a calling, 109
freedom of Christians, 45
God's grace stressed, 134
God's judgment stressed, 77
God's reign, present and future, 41
sans grace, bondage to sin, 45
human freedom only in relation to
God, 45
natural images clarify Lord's
Supper, 33
influence of, 19
justification, 45
justification ≠ regeneration, 16
law as enlivening, 21
law used as guide, 109
limited atonement, 77
moral virtue ethics, 34

Calvin, John (on) (*continued*)
    mortificatio (mortification) reduces
        vivificatio (vivification), 157n41
    ordo salutis (order of salvation), 21
    participation, 146n8
    personal frugality, 112
    political and spiritual governance,
        162n20
    priority of God's love, 21
    priority of union with Christ, 21
    progress in the Christian life, 77
    regeneration, 21
    sanctification, 77
    stewardship, 112
    union with Christ, 21
    worshiping God, 112
Calvinist/s, 19, 24, 137–38
    and frugality, 109
care for the earth (Gen. 1:28), 143
caritas (charity), 96–97, 158n26
catechisms, 19
Chalcedon, 1, 8, 55, 70. *See also* Barth,
        on Chalcedonian patterns
    asymmetry, intimacy, integrity, 60,
        89, 121
    divine and human natures of
        Christ, 28, 33
    divine-human interaction, 62
    grace engaging human faculties, 26
    on relationships, 57, 83, 144
charity, grounds social justice, 123
Cherry, Conrad, on Edwards, 24
Christ, Jesus Christ (as), 9
    assuages God's wrath, 21
    atonement, 16
    displays the virtues, 34
    exemplar, 25
    firstborn of creation (Col. 1), 69, 71
    "Follow me," 141
    found in real people, 142
    fullness of human agency, 40
    his command internalized, 79
    his divine and human natures, 8, 56
    his humanity divinized, 57–58
    human and divine natures of,
        26–27, 57
    hypostatic union of, 144
    judges structural and personal sin, 70
    lives in relationship with God, 34

Lord and head, 122
Lord of all creation, 122
    mediator, 59
    obedience to God, 59
    reconciliation, via the Holy Spirit, 122
    reconciling the world to God, 118
    recruits church members, 33
    reveals human obedience to God, 34
    on the Sabbath, 43, 65
    shows who God is for us, 117
    virtue of, 25
Christian life, 2, 8, 13, 18
Christian prudence, 93. *See also* practi-
        cal wisdom
Christianity, universal message, 143
Christians, embodied agents of grace,
        144
Christians, face-to-face relationships,
        144
christocentric thinking, 34, 38–54, 61, 70
church and state, 9, 19, 35, 115, 123,
        134–35. *See also* state
church changing society, 109
church
    as body of Christ, 102, 122
    appeals to consciences, 123
    appeals to USA and UN, 123
    basis of appeals, 123
    Corinthians, spiritual milk, 78
    culturally relevant, 33
    defending its own interests, 116
    fathers, 16
    forming virtue, 99–102
    giving glory to God, 122
    governance, 115
    independent churches, 19
    as institution and as body of Christ,
        102
    membership, declining, 33
    officers, authority, 122
    online, 142
    power of persuasion, 123
    practices, for virtue, 100
    practices and Holy Spirit, 100
    preserving human freedom, 123
    promoting reconciliation, 122
    reconciling body, 118
    and salvation of the world, 102
    as seedbed of virtue, 102

virtual alternative, 143
as visible and invisible, 102
witness via word and act, 100
witnesses to God known in Christ, 33
See also Constantinianism
Churches' Center for Theology and
Public Policy, 112
Cicero, 15
circumstances, changing current, 113
civil authority, 102
for security, 115
not to constitute religion, 115
Cochran, Elizabeth, 5, 27
collective welfare, 139
communal life, 99, 117, 122
communicatio idiomatum, 57–58
communio naturarum, 57
communion by intinction, 142
communities of character, 1
communities, physical or virtual,
140–41
Concord, Formula of, 109
confessions. *See also* Concord;
creeds; Heidelberg; Nicene;
Westminster
and catechisms, pedagogy, 18
during conflict, 18
earlier and later, respected, 119
ecumenical spirit, 18
practical, 18
provisional and local, 18
Reformed confessions, 22
Confessions (Augustine), 153n34
Confucianism, 143
congregants/congregation, 9, 32, 35,
111, 116, 120, 123, 133–34,
142–43
body of Christ together, 142–43
examine their consumption, 120
motley assortment, 142
practical wisdom, 120
conscience
freedom of, 120–21
and human commandments, 116,
161n19
Constantinianism, 35–36
residual in Calvin, 35
Dutch Reformed Church in South
Africa, 35

consumers
American, 112
Ethiopian, 112
examine consumption, 120
German, 113
Indian, 112
use of oil, 113–14
consumption, 111–14, 120, 124, 126
contemplation, 3–4
conversion, spiritual sense, taste, sight,
27
Corinthians, spiritual milk, 78
courage for obedience, 11, 113, 136,
140–44
covenant/s of God, 9
with all of creation, 143
with Christians, 65
as constitution, 21
context of, 83–85
with Israelites, 65
as lively dialogue, 99
as partnership, 43–44
in Scripture, 128
theology of, law is central, 22
with us, integrity and intimacy, 70
of works, 21
creation, 10, 112
out of nothing, 48
Creator, 13, 23, 45, 47–51, 56, 67, 79, 81,
107, 125–28
creature, 43, 45, 47–50, 56, 69, 79, 81,
84, 96, 130, 132, 151n14
creeds, 18, 119, 126
Critique of Pure Reason (Kant), 40
Cromwell, Oliver, 19

Damascus experience, 139
Davaney, Sheila, 39, 45, 60
critique of Barth, 42
decently and in order, 118
defense spending, 114
deists and atheists, 137
Delattre, Roland, on Edwards, 24
Democracy and Tradition (Stout) , 136
Dewey, John, 137
"A Differentiated Fellowship of
Action" (Adam Neder),
153n35
digital media, nonlocality, 143

discernment, in Christian community, 2, 32, 80, 82, 93, 123, 141
distribution inequality, 111
divine command, 7–8, 43, 60–67, 71, 79–89, 99, 131, 135, 138–40, 151n17
divinization, 15, 55–58, 70
dogma, eschatologically driven, 121
dogmaticians. *See* scholasticism
dying well, 2
Dykstra, Craig, 2–3

early church fathers, 13, 15, 147n12
eco-justice, 9, 111
economic globalization. *See* globalization
Edwards, Jonathan, 5, 8, 11–12, 24–32, 34
  on aesthetics, 25
  on atonement, 25, 34
  captured by God's beauty, 28
  christocentric, 34
  Christology of, 25
  on Christology and creation, 34
  on common morality, 29, 145n9
  on conscience, 29
  Constantinianism of, 35
  on conversion, 148n46
  on creation, 29
  on discerning the Spirit's work, 32
  disciplines youths, 31
  dismissed as pastor, 32
  dissertations on, 149n53
  on doctrine of creation, 34
  on God's grace, 134
    creating new spiritual sense, 28
  on goodwill, 25
  on habitual love, 26
  on Holy Spirit
    gifting virtue, 27
    transforming, 27–28
    instilling new spiritual sense, 31
    working in saints and others, 28–29
  on human receptivity, 27
  images from nature, 33
  on inward perception, 149n67
  on justification now, 27
  on limited love, 25
  linking theology, aesthetics, ethics, 24–25
  on love for God and neighbor, 25–26
  metaphor of a spring, 28
  on moral virtue ethics, 34
  on new spiritual sense at conversion, 31, 138, 163n7
  on pagan virtue as false, 29, 145n9
  on pity and familial love, 29
  on postfall morality, 30
  Reformed moral virtue ethic, 24
  religious affections key to Christian life, 31
  salvation via Christ's redemptive work, 28
  on sanctification in process, 27
  on self-love, 25
  on settled dispositions of character, 32
  on true religion, 25
  on true virtue only in Christians, 25, 27, 163n7
  on virtue from spiritual regeneration, 31
election, 6, 44
Emerson, Ralph Waldo, 137
ends, divinely revealed, 20
ends, via human reason, 20
energy policy, U.S., 113
engaging the world, 122
England, mixed political and religious powers, 115
English Puritans, seventeenth-century, 109
English Reformation, 19
enhypostatic. *See* anhypostatic/enhypostatic
entrepreneurial interests, 109
environmental concerns, 110–14, 144
Episcopalian, 19
Erastian, 19
  civil authorities and the church, 147n24
eschatological virtue/sanctification, 6, 22, 34, 36, 41, 52–53, 76, 84–85, 97, 107, 121, 148n40, 155n16
essence, as Greek philosophical concept, 58

ethicists. *See* theologians
ethics. *See also* Reformed, moral virtue
    ethics; virtue ethics
    in context, 23, 30, 33, 35, 64–65,
        71–75, 83, 87, 91–93, 110–112,
        119, 128, 131–32, 136, 144
    of frugality, 9, 109–14, 126, 133, 144.
        See also frugality
    and Scripture, 18, 64, 91, 120–23, 144
    needing human self-determination,
        63
    of Protestants, divine command
        and grace, 66
    relational, 8, 45, 76, 128
    of Roman Catholics, natural law
        and virtue, 66
Eucharist. *See* Lord's Supper
eudaimonists, Stoic and Peripatetic,
    128–31
exemplars, moral, 3–4, 11, 25, 34, 65,
    75, 87–88, 99–101, 107, 116,
    141
existence as gift, 48

faith, 13, 16, 18. *See also sola fide*
    benefits believer, 16
    in Christ, required for works, 20
    essential virtue, 16–17
    with hope and love, 16, 93–94
    nurtured by Holy Spirit, 17
    practical application of, 19
fall, the, 3, 15, 43, 47, 51, 53
    postfall common morality, 30
fasting, 2
federalist theology, 21
Feuerbach, Ludwig, God as human
    construction, 150–51n5
fides caritate formata (faith formed by
    love), 95–97
finitum non est capax infiniti, 160n4
Finney, Charles, embraced religious
    revival, 24
First Great Awakening, 24
forgiveness, 2
Frederick III, 19
    supervised review of Heidelberg
        Confession, 147n26
free will, 13
freedom for witness, 17

frugality
    and agape, 126
    benefits of, 112
    for each and all, 111–14
    individual and systemic, 114
    in global marketplace, 112
    as good stewardship, 144
    personal and social, 112
    in response to the covenant, 144
    and social justice, 111–14
    and sustainability, 112
fruit of repentance, 14–15
fruits of the Spirit, 20, 35

General Assembly, upholds federal
    government (1861), 116
genus majestaticum (a glorifying of
    Christ's human nature), 59
genus tapeinoticum (a humbling of
    Christ's divine nature), 59
German nationalism, 32
German theologians, supporting WWI,
    39
Gifford Lectures (2001), 102
gifts for each (1 Cor. 12), 142
globalization, 108, 110–17, 120, 123–25,
    128, 132, 160n6, 161n13
    and developing countries, 110–32
    environmental impact of, 110–13,
        120, 125, 134, 143–44
    statements on, 120
    unjust and unsustainable, 108, 124
    See also Hope for a Global Future
God
    and absolute commitment, 142
    to be glorified, 18
    as the Being of beings, 25
    and the church, 115
    coaxes us, 70
    commands of, 7–10, 122
        via agencies, 91–92
        continuous character, 100
        and human freedom, 62
        in social context, 99–100
        like Thomas's infused virtues, 91
        trump our claims about God, 121
    covenant of, 7–8, 123
    dealings with humankind, 33
    deliverance, 17

God (*continued*)
    dependence on, 14
    drawing of, 16
    election of humankind, 8–9
    embodiment of, 142
    glory of, 25
    "Gott in uns oder über uns?"
        (Przywara), 47
    grace of, 17–18
    involved in creation, 143
    knowledge of, 40
    love from, 3, 124
    loves being in general, 25
    and money, 91
    moral goodness of, 25
    as power for life, 14
    as primary cause for grace/virtue,
        27
    reconciling love of, 9
    regenerative power of, 14
    relationship with , 6
    revelation of, 9, 24
    righteousness of, 13
    sovereignty of, 27, 37
    speaks today, 120–21
    truth of, 119
    for us, 83
    will of, 18
    word of, binds conscience, 121. *See
        also* Word of God
    working in the will, 14
godly prudence, involves prodigal-
    ity, 93
goods, 22, 30, 69, 74, 91, 130, 136
    given by God, 113
    by merit, 137–38
    in moderation, 92, 113, 126–27
    for needs and joy, 113
    proximate and long-range, 113
gospel
    as local and universal, 144
    message in context, 144
    tells of grace and truth, 144
Gospels, 1, 78, 100, 141, 157n6
Goulet, Dennis, 125
Grace and Free Will (Augustine), 14
grace of God, 2, 14
    in Christian community, 99
    christological form of, 89, 122–23

continuous and disruptive, 99
cooperative, 14
embodied, 142
as gift, 59–60
given in revelation, 83
from the God known in Christ, 83
infused, 14
justifying, 18
medieval conception of, 21
primary in acquisition of virtue, 27
received by faith, 16
reflects relations in the Trinity, 122
Reformers' conception of, 21
gratia habitualis, 56. *See also* habits;
    habitual grace
Great Awakening, the, 31
Great Banquet (Luke 14:12–14), 93
Greco-Roman, erotic love, 97
group decision making, protocols for,
    119
Growing in the Life of Faith (Dykstra), 2–3
Gustafson, James
    critiques Barth's ethics of com-
        mand, 52, 62–64
    docile response to command, 80

habits, 9, 15, 18, 26–27, 38, 47, 56, 72,
    75, 82, 90–91, 94, 109, 111,
    113, 124, 141, 153n35, 154n56,
    158n18. *See also* habitual
    grace; practices
habitual grace, 7, 37–38, 45, 53–62, 69,
    70, 153n35. *See also* habits
Hall, Amy Laura
    on covenantal love, 98–99
    on love in Hosea, 98
handling difficult situations, 119
Hastening That Waits (Biggar), 6
Hauerwas, Stanley, 1, 102
    on Barth's ethics of command,
        62–64, 102–3
    character as moral history, 155n3
    on church giving witness, 102
    on church for world's salvation,
        103–4
    on church practices for character
        formation, 103
    on church needed to pass down
        virtues, 159n44

on civic groups as seedbeds of virtue, 159n44
healing of divisions, 118
heart, 15, 17, 26, 28, 34, 60, 85, 109, 121
Heidelberg
    Catechism, 19
    Confession, mortification of sinful self, 20–21
Herdt, Jennifer, 75
Herrmann, Wilhelm, 40, 54
    Christ event = human experience, 41
    Christology of, 40–41
    God as Idea, 41
    on historical facts and natural facts, 40
    idealistic, 41
    minimizes church's witness to Christ event, 41
    miraculous knowledge of God, 40
    Spirit makes Christ real, 41
Hinduism, 143
historical-critical research, in Germany, 41
Hitler, Adolf, as spiritual leader, 102
Hodge, Charles
    constitutional protest (1861), 116
    on Edwards's stressing conversion, 148n46
holiness. *See* sanctification
Holy Spirit, 5, 7, 16
    agent of regeneration, 18
    ally of the church, 33
    brings new life, 21
    cooperating with, 18
    fruits, 20
    indwelling, 17
    interprets Scripture, 144
    nurtures faith, 17
    reveals God's action in history, 40
    in Scripture as supreme judge, 162n27
    working, 4, 110
Homer, 11
Hope for a Global Future, 110, 120, 123
    on acquiring and consuming, 127
    biotic rights, 128
    blueprint for development, 124
    calls for legislative change, 124
    change of habits needed, 124

charity added, 124–29
Christ as God's image, 127
church as sign of God's reign, 127
conflicting ideas of justice, 124
and covenants, 126–28
for creation, 124–28
critique of economic system, 124
describes the just and sustainable, 124
distributive justice, 125
divine providence, 126
divine sovereignty, 126
dominion of humans, 127
early creeds, 126
ecological degradation, 127
economic development, 125
global poverty enriches the elite, 124
globalization unjust, unsustainable, 124
God's image, 126–27
God's justice and love, 127
on hope, 128
human development, 125
human responsibility, 126
humanistic grounds, 126
illusion of self-sufficiency, 127
individual charity, 126
just relations, 127
justice for all life-forms, 123, 125, 127, 132
justice rooted in covenant, 126–127
legal remedies, 126
liberal democratic framework, 126
love and justice, 127
on nations exploiting resources, 125
on need for virtue, 125
overconsumption, overpopulation, 124
plundering, 127
political and economic life, 126
problematic prescriptions, 124
proper development, 128
reign of God, 127
relationships, 127
resurrection of Christ, 128
self-centeredness, 127
self-sacrificing love, 126
shared agreements, 125–26, 128
sin as injustice, 127

Hope for a Global Future (*continued*)
　sin and repentance, 127
　on sovereign right of nations, 128
　status of human beings, 126
　stewardship of nature, 127
　sustainability, justice, humanity, 125
　universal human rights, 126
hope, 2, 16–17, 37, 54, 67–68, 93–94,
　　105, 110, 126, 128, 142. *See*
　　also Hope for a Global Future
hospitality, 2
Hudnut-Beumler, James D., 116
human/humanity, 58
　action/agency, 2–4, 7, 27, 38–45, 53,
　　56, 60, 62, 67–70
　and animals at risk, 123
　depravity, 13
　flourishing as goal, 11, 71, 78, 104–
　　5, 119, 122–23, 128–33, 138
　freedom, 7, 17, 38–39, 44–45, 52,
　　60–65, 70–71, 76, 79–81, 86,
　　104, 114, 116, 120–23, 136
　pride, 13, 15–16, 30, 134
　sinfulness, 3, 25, 37, 48, 50, 53, 67,
　　77, 85, 98, 107, 134
　willing, 11, 14–18, 27, 30–34, 45, 64,
　　91–92, 114
humility, 18
　epistemological, 120
　essential virtue, 17
　a key virtue, 134
　in seeking God's guidance, 7
　virtue or vice, 11
Hunsinger, George, 60
　on asymmetry, intimacy, integrity, 89
　on Barth and virtue ethics, 154n56
　on Barth as true to Chalcedon, 60
　on Barth valuing prayer, 154n56
Hutcheson, Frances, 137
　on common moral sense, 29, 138
　similar to Aristotle, 137

Iliad (Homer), 11
image of God, the, 20, 50, 127, 143,
　　153n31
images from nature, deficient, 33–34
imitatio Christi (imitation of Christ), 78
incarnation, 54–56, 144. *See also under*
　　Christ

　basis for community, 141–42
　dynamic in biblical narrative, 55
　scholastic, static views, 55
　upward movement affects human-
　　ity, 55
information age, 140
Institutes (Calvin, 1559), 12–13, 15, 17, 19
intellect, function of, 30

Jeremiah Group/programs, 136
　churches involved, 136
　community organizers, 136
　faith based, works with others,
　　164n9
　promoting moral virtue, 136
　seeking peace/welfare (Jer. 29:7), 139
　speaking for the poor, 136
　thinking strategically, 136
Jesus. *See* Christ
John the Baptist, prophetic, 136
Johnson, Keith, 153–54n40
justice, social, 8–9, 12, 29, 35, 93, 105,
　　108, 110–44. *See also Hope for*
　　a Global Future
justice of God, of humans, 12, 126–27
justification, 13–14, 20–21, 26–27, 45, 47,
　　50, 52–53, 67, 76, 84–85, 93–98,
　　134. *See also simul iustus . . .*
　choice not to sin, 16
　via Christ, 20
　by faith alone, 16–17
　forgiveness of sin, 16
　infusion of grace, 16, 37
　and legal fiction, 84
　receive Christ's righteousness, 16
　work of Holy Spirit, 16

Kant, Immanuel, idealism, 40, 150n4
　Critique of Pure Reason, 40
Keckermann, Bartholomäus, 6
kingdom of Christ, breaking in, 106–7
kingdom/reign of God, 41–42, 102–6,
　　127. *See also* sovereignty of
　　God
knowledge of God, 6, 12, 41, 50, 54,
　　120, 150n5
knowledge of ourselves, 12, 49–50, 54,
　　119
Kutter, Herrmann, 42

law, 2, 7, 21–23, 41–45, 63–66, 73,
96, 98, 100, 104–5, 106, 109,
116, 123, 126, 131–32, 135,
140, 145n9, 155n22, 157n6,
158n20, 162n20, 164n16. *See
also* Westminster Confession;
Calvin
leaders, church, 15, 31–32, 118, 123, 133
legalism, 32, 148n35
legislation to conserve resources, 114,
116, 124–25
Letters, NT, 100, 140, 157n6
Lewis, Bernard, 1
Lewis, C. S., on recent convert, 142
life, new, 20–21
limits on freedom, 44, 112, 115–16
Lincoln, declares war (1861), 116
lives to emulate, 65
local environment, neglect of, 143
Logos, eternally existing, 56
Lord's Supper, 33, 56, 57, 59
love, self-giving. *See also* agape
via God's revelation, 99
models of, 88, 101, 140. *See also*
exemplars
for neighbor, 8, 16, 25, 67, 93, 98–99,
101, 112–13, 126, 130
ours and God's, 27
as speech and act, 101
Luther, 13
as hyper-Augustinian, 151–52n17
charity via works of love, 96
Christ wrapped in our sins, 158n20
eros and agape coexist, 97
on the Eucharist, 57–58
justification, 47, 53, 76. *See also simul
iustus . . .*
completed in eschaton, 53
on Gal. 3:13, 95–96
from God's agape, 97
as God's descent, 96–97
sola fide, 95, 97
on salvation, assurance of, 95
on works righteousness, 95, 109
Lutheran churches, 18
Lutheran theologians, 18, 20, 55–59, 109
on Chalcedon, 57
on Christology, 59
Formula of Concord, 109

MacIntyre, Alasdair, 1–2, 73–74, 135–
40, 163n6
After Virtue, 73, 135–37
Benedictine monasticism, 135
binding constraints, evolving narrative, 156n36
on evidentness, 163n6
fracturing of society, 135
framework from Aristotle via
Aquinas, 137
impending Dark Ages, 135
living tradition, across generations,
74, 135
narrative interprets acts, 73–74, 135
on philosophical and theological,
135
response to outside challenges, 137
and Roman Catholic faith, 135
and Thomistic natural law, 140
Mahican (Mohican) Indians, 25
Marburg, 40
Marga, Amy, 46
Marga Institute in Sri Lanka, 125
marriage, 11
Martin-Schramm, James B., 113
Mason-Dixon line, 116
McCormack, Bruce, 41, 84–85
McKenny, Gerald, 6, 138–39,
151–52n17
medieval. *See* scholasticism
Melanchthon, Philipp, 12
Metaphysics (Aristotle), 51
Middle Ages, 13, 55, 97, 109, 135. *See
also* scholasticism
vocations of the religious, 109
military, U.S., oil use, 113. *See also*
warfare
millennials, religion, community,
141–42
Miller, Perry, bio of Edwards, 24,
149n67
ministry forms, 88, 100, 103, 122, 157n6
monastery vs. multicultural milieu,
135–36
moral
laxity, 32
sense from creation, 29
standards, minimal, 31–32
virtue ethics, 5–12, and throughout

mortal sin, 16, 27, 52–53, 94, 158n18.
        See also original sin; sin
Moses and Israelites, 65, 127, 141–42
motivation, 16, 25, 31, 73, 75, 116, 126
Muller, Richard A., 5–6, 146n1
Münster, 48
mutual agreement, 123, 128, 137, 140

narrative, biblical, religious, 1–3, 35,
        41, 55, 62, 64–67, 70, 73–74,
        98, 135–36, 143, 155n17,
        156n36
Nash, James A., 112
nations, 11, 123, 125, 128, 136, 157n6
natural law, 2, 23, 66, 106, 135, 140,
        145n9
natural resources, 111, 114, 127, 143
natural theology, 6, 9, 24, 34–35, 46,
        62, 138
Nature of True Virtue (Edwards), 25, 29
nature, sacred or not, 143
Nazi Germany, 102
neo-orthodoxy, 33
Neoplatonism, 33, 81, 96
New England Puritans, 31
New Orleans after Katrina, 136, 139
New School Presbyterians (north),
        116
Nicene Creed, 119
Nicomachean Ethics (Aristotle), 131
Niebuhr brothers (Reinhold and H.
        Richard), 148n48
Niebuhr, H. Richard, 24, 148n48
Niebuhr, Richard R., 24
Nietzsche, will to power, 135
Noah, covenant witness, 127, 143
norms, 11, 18, 100, 112–13, 125
Northampton, MA, 31–32
Nygren, Anders, *Agape and Eros*,
        95–99, 158n26
    caritas (charity) = eros, 96, 158n26

obedience, 34, 59, 65, 71, 73, 76, 78–81,
        84, 86, 93, 99, 104, 107, 122,
        131, 161–62n19
offices of the church, 27, 35, 49, 53
Okin, Susan Moller, 156n36
olive-tree image, 14, 26, 28
online community, 140, 142, 144

oppression, 110, 118, 127, 131, 139–40.
        See also poor
optimism, nineteenth century, 24
ordering of loves/desires, 16, 89
ordo salutis (order of salvation), 21
original sin, 3–6, 24, 30, 46, 138

pagan prudence/virtue, 5–6, 13, 15, 16,
        23, 29–31, 34, 88, 91–93, 102–
        6, 145n9, 147n14, 149–50n76
patience, 17, 32, 34, 136, 142
Paul, apostle, 11, 14, 33, 100, 139
    1 Cor. 12, model of, 76, 142
    1 Cor. 13, love, 16
Pax Romana, 140
Peaceable Kingdom (Hauerwas), 1–2
peacekeeping, 2
Pelagians, 14, 26
people, animals, plants, 110
performing God's work, 142
perseverance, 14, 16–17, 63, 67, 155n22
personal charisma, 123
personal liberty, 114
Pharisees, on the Sabbath, 43, 65
philosophers, pagan, 13, 15, 17, 129
phronēsis (practical wisdom), 137
Pighius, Albert, 13–14
polis (society), 11, 105
politically correct or not, 122
Politics (Aristotle), 131
Pollock, Jackson, 26
poor, poverty, 87–88, 91, 93, 105, 110–
        11, 117–18, 124, 139. *See also*
        oppression
postdissertation stress disorder, 37
practical wisdom, 2, 8, 29, 30, 62,
        66–69, 72–75, 78–82, 85–93,
        110, 113–23, 123, 133, 137–38,
        141, 144
    Chalcedonian character of, 89
    and social justice, 114–23
practices, 1–3, 9, 17, 22, 27, 31, 53, 63,
        65, 67, 73–75, 82, 87, 91–95,
        100–103, 107, 109, 111, 114,
        116, 119, 135–37, 155n22,
        162n20. *See also* habits
Practicing Our Faith (Bass and
        Dykstra), 2
praise, 4, 15, 20, 100–101, 142, 157n6

prayer, 2–3, 135, 154n56, 157n6, 164n9
preaching, 35, 104, 121–23, 144
Presbyterian Church (U.S.A.), 9, 108, 110
  Book of Discipline, 116
  Book of Order, 114–18, 121–22,
    161nn16, 18; 162n20
  communal life, 122
  communication, 133
  confessional statements, 114–18, 132
  congregants, 111, 116, 120, 123,
    133–34, 142–43
  divestiture, 133
  General Assembly, 110–16, 160–
    61n13, 161n15
  on globalization (1996–2006), 110–
    15on individual behavior, 133
  ministry of reconciliation, 122
  policy, strategy, program, 160–61n13
  political structures, 132–33
  "Resolution on Just Globalization,"
    112
  "Restoring Creation," 111
  against social injustices, 132
  practical wisdom, frugality, charity,
    110, 112, 133
  principles of order, 123
  shift on social issues, 132
  Resolution of 2006, 120
  for social justice, 110–14, 116–18,
    120, 123–34
  social witness policies, 110–33, 137,
    160–61n13
  systemic change promoted, 110
Presbyterian churches, 19
  American, 12
  in England, 19
  on globalization, 117. See also
    globalization
  motivated by Barth, 117
  others' well-being trumps free con-
    science, 116, 121
  proclamations rarely enforced, 116
  reunion, the confessions (1983),
    161n17
  against slavery (1818), 116
  social concerns/witness, 115–17
  split, north and south (1850s), 116
  on transnational corporations, 117
  on unjust policies, 117
  in USA, 19
  on use of political means, 116
Pride and Prejudice (Austen), 11
pride, 11, 13, 15–16, 30, 134
Princeton school/theology
  on bondage of the will, 24
  for doctrinal orthodoxy, 24
  on sovereignty of God, 24
  used Edwards, 24
Princeton Theological Seminary, 7, 24,
    116
private virtue, 111
Protestant thinking, 1–8, 32–33, 66, 84,
    102, 109, 134, 146n1
prudence. See practical wisdom
Przywara, Erich, 46–50
  for analogia entis (analogy of being),
    46–50. See also analogia entis
  God as transcendent and imma-
    nent, 48
  on revelation, 49
  on sin as disease, 48–49, 69
  supernatural and incarnation,
    152n28

Ragaz, Leonhard, 42
Ramsey, Paul, 29–30
reality, 6, 34, 40–41, 44, 50, 66–69,
    84–85, 101, 106, 139, 142–43
reason, "Because God told me to," 139
Receptive Human Virtues (Cochran), 27
reconciliation, 7, 44, 54, 69, 117–18,
    122, 127, 162n29
redemption, 20, 25, 45, 52, 67, 69, 76,
    89, 107, 121, 128
reform. See repentance
Reformation, 5–6, 16, 18–19, 47, 52–53,
    63, 109, 120
Reformed (on)
  Christian vocation, 109
  christocentric, 34, 37–38, 42, 54, 61, 70
  churches, 11, 18–19, 32, 134, 137, 144
  concerns, 5, 9, 75
  confessions/polity, 18–19, 22, 110
  consequences of sin, 47
  course correction, 113
  democracy in ecclesial polity, 137
  God's commands, 93
  God's sovereignty, 39

Reformed (on) (*continued*)
  grounds for moral virtue, 25
  human freedom, 44–45
  human sinfulness, 134
  interpreting Chalcedon. *See* Barth,
    on Chalcedonian patterns;
    Chalcedon
  mending relationships, 122
  moral virtue ethics, 4–36, 38, 45–47,
    52–53, 61–62, 71, 76–82, 85,
    91, 110–11, 113–14, 124, 132–
    33, 135, 140–43
  new habits and virtues of, 109
  ordered by confessions, 117
  practical wisdom, 82, 122–23
  priesthood of all believers, 88
  salvation by grace alone, 26, 88,
    148n35
  sanctification, 134
  spiritual discernment, 82
  stress on sanctification, 109
  temperance, 29–30, 86, 90–92, 112,
    137
  theologians, 18, 39, 52, 56–57
  Thomistic virtues compared, 90–99
  tradition, 1–37, 42, 44, 49, 52, 68–69,
    83, 112–13, 117, 119, 122, 134,
    137–38, 144, 158n36
  virtues
    as activity, 101, 130
    charity, 95–99, 124, 128
    in church and state, 134–35
    contextual approach, 119
    covenantal and historical charac-
      ter, 119–20
    developed, 88
    God's blessing, 131
    God's polyphonic agapic love,
      129–32
    infused in believers, 108
    lived eccentrically, 129
    neglected, reclaimed, 134
    in natural law, 134–35
    relationality, 128
    renewal aspect, 101
    true identity and relationship, 130
    worshiping God, 131
    shaped by grace, 108
  vocation, 109

Reformers, 18, 21, 26, 33, 35, 51, 58,
    95, 109
regeneration, 5, 13–23, 26, 31–36, 84, 134
reign of God, 42. *See also* kingdom of
    God
relationship, God and us, 3–7, 15, 21,
    26, 34–75, 79, 83–90, 98–99,
    106, 115, 119, 121–22, 124,
    127–31, 139, 141, 144
*Religionsphilosophie katholischer
    Theologie* (Przywara), 48
Religious Affections (Edwards), 24–25,
    28, 31–32, 148n46
repentance, 8, 15, 20, 22, 27, 67–68, 89,
    101, 122, 127
responsiblity, 39, 43, 79–80, 104, 121–
    22, 126–27, 133, 159n53
revelation, 6, 9, 20, 23–24, 29, 31–35,
    42, 49–55, 58, 67, 71, 80–83,
    88, 90, 99–108, 118, 120–21,
    135, 138, 141–44, 151n17,
    152n28, 155n10, 159n53
  unidirectionality of, 51, 83, 88, 108,
    120–21
Revival of Religion (Edwards), 24
Revivals of Religion (Finney), 24
rich benefit more, 105, 110. *See also*
    wealth
rich young ruler, 91
rights, 31, 115–16, 123–32, 139–40, 144,
    161n18
  rooted in God's love, 124
Roman Catholic(s), 6. *See also* habit-
    ual grace; scholasticism,
    medieval
  on cooperative grace, 26
  dogma, 13
  ethics, 2, 7, 45, 89
  on sin as disease, 69. *See also* sin
  theologians, 1–8, 13, 26, 32, 45–48,
    56, 66, 69, 82, 89, 95, 97, 135,
    152n28, 153n35, 153–54n40,
    154n45, 162n20
  tradition, 4, 45, 47, 153n35, 154n45
Roman centurion, 107
Rorty, Richard, wary of faith-based,
    164nn10, 16
Rushkoff, Douglas, on nonlocal, 143,
    164n16

Sabbath keeping, 2, 23, 35, 43, 65, 116
sacrifice, 25–26, 126, 129
salvation, 5–6, 23–28, 33–34, 58, 75,
 84–89, 92, 95–109, 151n14,
 157n41
sanctification, holiness, 14, 20–23,
 26–27, 52–54, 58–61, 70, 76–78,
 90, 96–97, 101, 109, 134
 basic for virtues, 76
 continuing, via Holy Spirit, 20–22
 depends on Christ, 90
 and eschatology, 22
 growth in, 23
 and human framework, 22
Sanneh, Lamin, 144
Schleiermacher, Friedrich, 23
scholasticism
 Lutheran, 55, 59
 medieval, 14, 56–57
 Protestant, 5–6, 56–57, 146n1
 Reformed, 55, 57
Scottish moral philosophy, 137–38
Scottish state church, 19
Screwtape Letters (C. S. Lewis), 142
Scripture, 13, 18–19, 28, 33, 51, 58, 64,
 91, 107, 117–23, 128, 137, 144
 as guide, 120, 123
 high status of, 18
 infallibility of, 117–18
 interpreted via Holy Spirit, 118–23,
 144
 wooden application of, 123
 word of God written, 118
self-interests, 29, 128, 137–38
self-justification, 67
self-love, trained to extend, 25, 29
self-reflection re motives, 120
semi-Pelagian, 26
semper reformanda (always to be
 reformed), 117, 119, 127
Sen, Amartya, 110
Septuagint, words for love, 158n28
sexuality, 90–91, 97, 118
Shanley, Brian, kinds of virtue,
 149–50n66
sharing goods, 67, 111, 125
Shrewd Manager (Luke 16:1–8), 92
simul iustus (totus) et peccator (totus)
 (totally righteous and at the

same time totally sinner), 47,
 52–53, 66–67, 70, 76–77, 83–88,
 97, 108, 120, 155n16
sin, 122. *See also* mortal sin; original sin
 as decisive break, 48–50, 69
 as disease, 48–49, 69
 effects of, 2, 4, 6, 16–17, 30, 32, 34,
 42, 47, 52, 77, 108, 118, 147n12
slavery issue, 116, 121, 123, 131,
 161n17
social
 affairs, 4
 ills from broken relationships, 122
 justice, 8–9, 105, 111–44, 151n11
 media, 140, 143
 witness, 9, 108, 110, 114–22, 132–34,
 137, 160–61n13, 161n18
socialist movement, religious, 42
societies, 2, 11, 35, 100, 109–12, 117–18,
 132–38
Society of Christian Ethics, 7, 66
Söhngen, Gottlieb, 153–54n40
sola fide (by faith alone), 26, 97
sola gratia (by grace alone), Reformed,
 26, 138n45
sola gratia (by grace alone), Roman
 Catholic, 26
sola scriptura (Scripture alone), 18
Sombarth, Werner, 41
Son of God, 48, 55–59, 76, 121
Son of Man, 55, 59, 76–77, 153–54n40
soul, the, 17, 21, 25, 28, 31, 33, 51, 94,
 96, 100, 157n6, 160n4, 162n20
sovereignty of God, 3, 24, 26–27, 34,
 37–39, 42–45, 53, 57, 61–64,
 68–69, 76, 79, 86–87, 94–95,
 98, 126, 134. *See also* kingdom
 of God
Sozialismus Bewegung (Sombarth), 41
Spirit. *See* Holy Spirit
state, the, 91–92, 101–8, 136. *See also*
 church and state
 and care for creation, 106
 and civic virtue, 92, 102, 107
 defense, 106
 God's revelation, 102
 and reign of God, 102
 role in forming virtue, 101–6
 as a secular parable, 102

stewardship, 112, 127, 144
still, small voice, 139
Stimmen der Zeit, 47
Stoddard, Solomon, 31
stone tablets, 121
stories of God, 1. *See also* narrative
Stout, Jeffrey, 136–40
substance and accident, 15
sustainability, 9, 111–13, 124–5. *See also* eco-justice
synergism, 14–15, 60, 70
systemic synergy/changes, 110, 114, 120, 124

technology, 110, 141, 143
temperance, 29, 30, 86, 90–91, 112, 137
theologians/ethicists, 1, 13, 18, 29, 39, 46, 48, 52, 57, 62, 75, 84, 153n40. *See also* scholasticism
Thomas Aquinas (on), 2, 4–7, 14, 16, 38, 134, 108
    affirms *analogia entis* (analogy of being), 6, 45–54. *See* also *analogia entis*
    characteristics of the species, 48
    church's offices for justification, 53
    civic virtue, 30
    continuity, souls, 51, 89
    cooperative grace, 16, 27, 81
    created order as contingent, 51
    critiqued by Luther and Reformers, 95
    divine light, 94
    either justified or in mortal sin, 52
    God as creation's first cause, 51, 152n26
    human nature, 27, 47,
    justification, 52–53, 153n38
    love, of Father and Son, 94
    love for God produces faith, 95
    mortal sin and theological virtues, 158n18
    natural law, 145n9. *See also* natural law
    necessary being of God, 48
    need exemplars and practice, 75
    Neoplatonism, Aristotelianism, 81
    perfecting our nature, 4, 83
    postfall morality, 30

regeneration = justification, 16
repentance, restoration, 27
sin corrupts, 30, 94, 157n4
soul and Holy Spirit, 94
substance ontology, 47, 51, 83
willing, 30, 150n78
Thomas Aquinas Institute (Washington, DC), 37
Thomas Aquinas–Karl Barth conference (2011), 37
virtues, 54
    Aristotle's adapted, 4, 74, 81
    acquired, 75, 94, 141. *See also* habits
    charity, 93–95
    grace, 30, 43, 46, 49, 71, 83, 99, 147n15
    grace-nature axiom, 151n14
    "imperfect virtue," 20
    kinds of, 90, 149–50n66
    infused, 2, 4, 9, 71, 74–76, 81–83, 87, 90–96, 108, 156n37, 158n18
    natural vs. infused virtues, 74
    perfect prudence, 92
    perseverance, 16
    personal and political, 112
    prudence, 74–75, 92–93
    temperance, acquired and infused, 90–91
    true but imperfect virtue, 30
Torrance, T. F., 21, 148n35
tradition, Reformed. *See* Reformed, tradition
tradition, Roman Catholic. *See* Roman Catholic, tradition
traditionalism, 9, 113
transformation
    of group, 109, 120, 132
    of person, 22, 27, 32, 43, 60, 67, 95, 152–53n31
translatability of Bible, 97, 129, 144, 158n28, 164nn9, 18
triune God, 6, 84, 107, 130
Turretin, Francis, 5

U.N. papers, 125–26
unicorn, 48
unio hypostatica (hypostatic union), 57

union with Christ, 21, 33, 54–55, 59–60, 121, 158n18
universal reason, 140
universal salvation, 6, 34
United Presbyterian Church USA (north)
  Book of Confessions, 115, 117, 119, 121
  Confession of 1967, 117–18, 122
  lobbying efforts, 117
  on race, poverty, hunger, 117
  reshaped social witness policy, 117

Vermigli, Peter Martyr, 5–6
virtue
  as active, 27
  Christian, 1–7, 12–18, 46, 58, 62, 100–101, 106–7
  from God in Christ, 88
  human, 12, 15, 27, 53
  pagan. *See* pagan prudence
  progress in, 2, 17, 22, 32, 66, 77, 94, 96, 151–52n17
  true, 5, 16, 25, 27–30, 34, 85–86, 134, 163n7
virtue ethics, 1–10
  command and response, 61
  focused on God in Christ, 61
  follows Chalcedonian pattern, 61
  and globalization, 113
  and habit formation, 113
  Aristotelian/Thomistic, 37
  Barthian, 37. *See under* Barth
  communal dimension, 87
  consistent character, 87
  criticisms of, 128
  exemplary mentors, 87
  focus on practices/habits, 53
  for communities and individuals, 87
  help for obedience, 87
  involves choice, 22
  of Edwards, 24. *See also* Edwards
  without natural morality, 71–72
  Reformed, 37. *See also* Reformed, virtues
  renouncing possessions, 87
  Roman Catholic, 45. *See also* Roman Catholic, ethics
  two-tier system, 2
  via participating in Christ, 87

Virtue Reformed (Wilson), 5
virtues. *See also* virtue; virtue ethics
  goal of faithful witness, 88
  virtues, lists, 90, 146n1
  virtues, unity of = practical wisdom, 113
vision of God, 4
visiting absentees, 143
Vlastuin, Willem van, 20–21

warfare, 11, 20, 22, 33, 38–40, 102, 116, 118, 135
wealth, 91, 120
Weber, Max, on roots of capitalism, 109, 160n4
Webster, John, 7, 43–44, 68
Werpehowski, William, 7–9, 45, 61–71, 79–81, 92–93, 107, 155n11
Westminster Assembly, 19
Westminster Standards (Confession, Catechism), 5, 8, 12, 18–24, 34, 114–18, 134, 137
  authoritative for Presbyterians in USA, 19, 114–19, 132, 134, 137
  Constantinianism of, 35
  on existence of God, 23
  on God's salvation, 23
  on grace as slow process, 22
  on law as threat, 21
  legal view of justification, 21
  legalism of, 148n35
  on natural law, 23
  neglects God's initiating action, 22
  on pollutions of the soul, 21
  on primary and secondary causes, 23
  on regeneration, 21–22
  Sabbath restrictions of, 23
  on union with Christ, 21
White, Lynn, 143
Whose Justice? Which Rationality? (MacIntyre), 137
will, the, 14–18, 30
  bad, good, free, unfree, 14–15
  "a moved mover," 30
  postfall, ruled by passions, 30
  turned by God, 15
willpower, 3, 135
Wilson, Stephen A., 5
Wilson, Stephen L., on Edwards, 24

wisdom
    of God, of humans, 12
    practical. *See* practical wisdom
    wisdom of the church, 113, 118
    wisdom, via leadership, 118
With the Grain of the Universe
        (Hauerwas), 102
witness
    as body of Christ, 122
    continuity of, 115
    as individuals, 122
    in the public square, 137
    social. *See* social witness
Wolterstorff, Nicholas, 128–30
    on calculations, 130
    on eudaimonism, 128–30

    on instrumental goods, 130
    neglects politics, 131
    on passivities, 130
    on rights and worth, 128–32, 163n47
    on Thomistic virtue theory, 129
word of God, 26, 33, 35, 55, 58, 100,
        118, 121, 144, 151n11
works, good, 17, 20–22, 50, 94–96, 109,
        136
world religions, 134, 143
World War I and II. *See* warfare

young adults and the church, 140–41

Zanchi, Girolamo, 6
Zwingli, Huldrych, 33